How Could This Happen?

Jan U. Hagen
Editor

How Could This Happen?

Managing Errors in Organizations

Editor
Jan U. Hagen
ESMT Berlin
Berlin, Germany

ISBN 978-3-319-76402-3   ISBN 978-3-319-76403-0   (eBook)
https://doi.org/10.1007/978-3-319-76403-0

Library of Congress Control Number: 2018946610

Cover illustration: Anja Schaefer / Alamy Stock Photo

Printed on acid-free paper

This Palgrave Macmillan imprint is published by the registered company Springer Nature Switzerland AG
The registered company address is: Gewerbestrasse 11, 6330 Cham, Switzerland

Preface: A New Field

Editing this book was a privilege. It meant being able to work with experts from a variety of professions who are at the forefront of research on error and error management. Their contributions cover a wide range of topics; their backgrounds comprise academic institutions and high-reliability organizations. Readers of this book will be able to relate to their own past experiences with error, recognize the problems with which they have dealt, and discover the solutions that these experts have to offer. Hopefully, this book will awaken the readers' interest in error management, to the extent that they will transfer its contents to their own organizations, and start assessing why they do not have discussions regarding the management of errors. They may also wonder why they themselves feel reluctant to talk about their mistakes, or why, for example, hardly anyone posts their mistakes on Facebook.

We err, and that is a fact. More interesting, though, is the way we deal with our errors. It is actually twofold. On the one hand, mistakes add to our sense of orientation. When we scan our environment and interpret what we see, the correction of errors is a natural and helpful part of the process. If we enter a dead-end road that we thought was a shortcut, we will not enter it again. If we have lost some time, it will not bother us much. Maybe we will call ourselves stupid, but even that will hardly do us any harm. We have learned something and proceed from there. End of story.

On the other hand, there are mistakes that can make us profoundly unhappy. They can lead to resentment toward the person who has alerted us to them, and the last thing we want is to learn from them. Instead, we want to forget them, together with the embarrassment, grief, blame, shame, and guilt involved.

For organizations, these emotionally charged errors are of concern. These are the ones that people deny having committed, lie about, and sweep under the carpet—all actions that prevent organizational learning. It is a behavior that is oftentimes so engrained into a culture that it is considered normal. It is not normal, not if we want to increase an organization's knowledge.

So where should organizations begin when they plan to manage errors constructively? First of all, they should start with the emotional turmoil that errors can produce. This means no blame and no sanctions for the one who makes the mistake. It also means dealing rationally with cover-ups and recognizing them as expressions of fear—the fear of losing status, reputation, job, and self-esteem. Depending on the size of the mistake, it can require great courage to say "Yes, I did that, it was my mistake" and to live with the consequences. This should be honored. After that, one has to begin exploring the reasons or chain of events that led to the mistake. In the case of cover-ups, it may also become necessary to put the organizational culture under the microscope and find out which conditions led its members to behave that way. There should always be one guiding rule, namely, to learn from what went wrong. Punishing the one who made the mistake—or even firing them—would be the next mistake. It would signal to everybody in the organization that they should bury a mistake as deeply as possible. In turn, this would just increase people's fears about making one.

The insights that this book provides are inroads into an area of organizational behavior that, so far, has received little attention. Therefore, I cannot adequately express how grateful I am to the contributors, who have dedicated their time and knowledge, both to this book and to the new field of error management. They have diagnosed the root causes of mistakes in organizations, analyzed the cultures that prevent both error management and learning from errors, and identified the cultural and practical requirements that will make it possible to openly discuss as well as learn from errors. Their results are the guideposts for further research, and because of their inputs, error management has begun to receive the attention it deserves.

Berlin   Jan U. Hagen
April 2018

Acknowledgments

The realization of this book would have been impossible without the support of the following individuals. I thank Melanie Seyffert for her help in preparing the graphs, Robert Furlong for his meticulous proofreading, and Sebastian Niemann for the design of all tables and figures. I especially owe, once more, a great deal of gratitude to my colleague Gabriele Weber-Jarić, who, from the beginning, pushed for this project. She supported me through all of the stages and was a highly valued partner when discussing the content and structure of the book. Furthermore, she kept a sharp eye on the text to see to its readability and consistency.

Contents

Notes on Contributors

Immanuel Barshi is a senior principal investigator in the Human Systems Integration Division at NASA Ames Research Center in California. His research addresses cognitive issues involved in the skilled performance of astronauts and pilots, mission controllers, and air traffic controllers. His research has been published in books and papers on basic and applied psychology, linguistics, and aviation.

René Bernard is a senior scientist, quality management specialist, and open science trainer at the Department of Experimental Neurology of Charité Universitätsmedizin Berlin.

Nadine Bienefeld gained her PhD in work and organizational psychology from ETH Zurich before she became head of the Centre for Human Resources, Development, and Sports Psychology at Zurich University of Applied Sciences. She is now a postdoctoral researcher and lecturer at ETH Zurich.

Jan Brommundt is a medical doctor in anesthesiology as well as international, humanitarian, and disaster medicine. He works and teaches at the University of Groningen and University Medical Center Groningen, the Netherlands.

John S. Carroll is the Gordon Kaufman Professor of Management and Professor of Work and Organization Studies at the MIT Sloan School of Management. His recent work focuses on organizational learning, change, and culture in industries that manage significant hazards, such as nuclear power, petrochemicals, and healthcare.

Nicolas Dechy is a specialist in human and organizational factors at *Institut de radioprotection et de sûreté nucléaire* (IRSN), which provides expertise to the French nuclear safety authority. His expertise and research areas focus on investigating and learning from events and accidents (e.g., Fukushima, Toulouse), emergency response, risk analysis, safety, and subcontracting management in maintenance in the nuclear and petrochemical industrial sectors.

Yves Dien has a social sciences background and is a researcher at Association CHAOS—*Collectif Heuristique pour l'Analyse Organisationnelle de la Sécurité* (Heuristic Association for Organisational Analysis of Safety). He has led research dealing with the organizational causes of industrial accidents at the EDF Research & Development Center for more than 15 years.

Ulrich Dirnagl is the director of the Department of Experimental Neurology at Charité Universitätsmedizin Berlin. Since 2017, he has also been the founding director of the QUEST Center for Transforming Biomedical Research at the Berlin Institute of Health. Through meta-research, he is trying to identify opportunities for improving research practice and to obtain evidence for the impact of targeted interventions.

Amy C. Edmondson is the Novartis Professor of Leadership and Management at Harvard Business School and the author of numerous articles. In her books—*Teaming: How Organizations Learn, Innovate, and Compete in the Knowledge Economy*; *Teaming to Innovate*; and *In Building the Future: Big Teaming for Audacious Innovation*—she examines the challenges and opportunities of teaming across industries. Edmondson received her PhD in organizational behavior from Harvard University.

Vincent Giolito is a senior researcher with the Baillet Latour chair on error management at Solvay Brussels School of Economics and Management. He was a leadership coach in Paris for the past six years. Previously, he was a business reporter and editor in the French media for more than 15 years. He was the business pages editor of the French newspaper *Le Figaro*.

Gudela Grote is Professor of Work and Organizational Psychology at the Department of Management, Technology, and Economics at ETH Zurich. She has published widely on topics in organizational behavior, human factors, human resource management, and safety management.

Jan U. Hagen is an associate professor at ESMT Berlin and the author of *Confronting Mistakes—Lessons from the Aviation Industry When Dealing with Mistakes*. His recent work focuses on error management, team interaction, and leadership in high-reliability organizations such as aviation, healthcare, and the military.

Mallory Johnson is a researcher, evaluator, and administrator with the University of California Davis School of Medicine and the Betty Irene Moore School of Nursing. She is a Presidential Management Fellowship alumna with extensive experience in quality improvement data analysis. She holds a master of public administration degree from George Washington University and a BA from the University of Alabama, where she graduated summa cum laude and is a Phi Beta Kappa.

Tony Kern is the CEO of Convergent Performance and the author of eight books, including *Blue Threat: Why to Err Is Inhuman* and *Going Pro: The Deliberate Practice* *of Professionalism.* He is a former command pilot in the B-1B bomber and Chair of the US Air Force Human Factors Steering Group.

Peter Klement is Director of Aviation Safety of the German Federal Armed Forces in the rank of Brigadier General. During his career, he flew 3000 hours in fighter aircraft and has held numerous leadership and staff positions, during which he actively promoted aviation safety and flight training programs. In his current position, he is responsible for Accident and Incident Investigation, Accident Prevention, and Aviation Safety Training programs of the German Armed Forces.

Helmut Kunz is the head of training at the Air Berlin flight school. He used to be the deputy fleet chief of LTU's Airbus A330 and A320 fleets. Apart from his responsibilities as a training and check captain, he was involved in fleet administration and management and was part of the "Fleet 21" analysis team.

Zhike Lei is an associate professor at the Pepperdine Graziadio Business School in California. Previously, she was a faculty member at Georgetown University, ESMT Berlin, and George Mason University. Her research on organizational errors, psychological safety, and crisis management has been published in numerous leading management journals.

L. David Marquet is a former nuclear submarine commander of the US Navy and author of *Turn the Ship Around!: A True Story of Turning Followers into Leaders.*

Eric Marsden manages research projects at FonCSI (Foundation for an Industrial Safety Culture), a French public interest research foundation. He works on organizational aspects of safety in high-hazard industries, including experience feedback procedures, benefit-cost analysis for risk-related decision making, and risk regulation.

Julianne Morath is the president and CEO of the Hospital Quality Institute (HQI), a collaboration of the California Hospital Association and three regional associations. She is a founding and current member of the NPSF Lucian Leape Institute. As the author of two books, *The Quality Advantage* and *To Do No Harm*, she has published widely on the topics of quality, patient safety, leadership, and patient/family engagement.

Jean-Marie Rousseau is a cognitive psychologist. He spent 16 years as a consultant in private French companies before joining the *Institut de radioprotection et de sûreté nucléaire* (IRSN) in 2003. Specialized in decision making and safety management, he manages a unit dealing with Operating Experience Feedback (OPEX). He leads a transversal project for renewing the IRSN OPEX system regarding methods, organization, and tools.

Robert Schroeder is a check and training captain with Lufthansa German Airlines, flying Airbus A330s/350s and 340s. He has also been working as a flight safety manager for almost 20 years. In 1997, he received training as an accident investigator at the University of Southern California. He participated in major accident investigations and has conducted a large number of confidential reviews with flight crews following safety-relevant incidents.

Avner Shahal is a human factors specialist. He has worked on the development of avionics for commercial aviation. His research focuses on human factors, both in aviation and in the design of man–machine interfaces for rehabilitation purposes and for the elderly.

Paul J. Verdin is the director of the Baillet Latour Chair on Error Management at Solvay Brussels School of Economics and Management, where he also holds the Chair in Strategy and Organization. He is a visiting professor at the Berlin School of Creative Leadership and Deusto Business School and was a former full-time faculty member at IESE, INSEAD, KU Leuven, and Tilburg University.

Abbreviations

AECL	Atomic Energy Canada Limited
ATC	Air Traffic Control
ATSB	Australian Transport Safety Bureau
CIRS	Critical Incident Error Reporting System
CRM	Crew Resource Management
CSB	US Chemical Safety and Hazard Investigation Board
ECAM	Electronic Centralized Aircraft Monitor System
FAA	Federal Aviation Administration
FENOC	FirstEnergy Nuclear Operating Company
HRO	High-Reliability Organization
HSE	UK Health and Safety Executive
IAF	Israeli Air Force
ISOM	Isomerization Unit
NRC	Nuclear Regulatory Commission
PIC	Pilot in Command
SMS	Safety Management Systems
SOP	Standard Operating Procedure
STAMP	System-Theoretic Accident Model and Processes
TCAS	Traffic Alert and Collision Avoidance System
UAI	Uncertainty Avoidance Index

List of Figures

List of Tables

1

Fast, Slow, and Pause: Understanding Error Management via a Temporal Lens

Zhike Lei

When an error occurs, in the race to act, people may decide to quickly handle things on their own. However, although thesquick fixes seem to work well, and even create a sense of gratification for having swiftly solved a problem, they can preclude performance improvement over time by impeding operational and structural changes that would prevent the same errors and failures from happening again.

Still, fast action should not necessarily be discouraged. Rather, we should be alerted to the side effects of emphasizing speed over analysis. In the heat of the moment, it is hard to know the proper way to make sense of information and regain control. In fact, when hyperdynamic interactions of error signs and interruptions create an interlude, people may experience a blank, a freezing moment that calls into question the orderliness of a structure, a task, or a protocol. As a result, understanding and sensemaking collapse, and fast actions can be ill-conceived. When it comes to high-reliability organizations, we may even see paradoxes: Actions and responses happen at a rapid pace, yet people need to pause, reflect, explore various concerns, and come up with analyses and solutions.

Understanding error management via a temporal lens raises quantitative and methodological questions, and it promotes dialogues concerning behavioral options in organizational practice. Although the element of time has always been in the background of the theory and research on errors and error reporting, it has yet to be—and should be—brought to the foreground of observation.

Z. Lei
Malibu, USA

© The Author(s) 2018
J. U. Hagen (ed.), *How Could This Happen?*, https://doi.org/10.1007/978-3-319-76403-0_1

1

Preface Many people believe that to prevent catastrophe, the sooner an error is reported and declared, the higher the chances for organizational entities to detect and correct it, and vice versa. Yet, for the decision of error reporting, is it always true the faster the better? When is acting quickly an asset? When is it a liability? Is there a clear rule for timely reporting across cultures? These questions heighten why a temporal lens is needed to better understand error management and error reporting. As such, we begin to think not just about whether or not errors are reported, but also about how fast (or slowly) errors are reported, and when and why error reporting starts and stops. Moreover, we should be alerted to potential side effects of emphasizing speed over analysis. When it comes to high-reliability organizations, we may even see paradoxes: Actions and responses happen at a rapid pace, yet people need to pause, reflect, and explore various concerns, and come up with analyses and solutions. Understanding error management and error reporting via a temporal lens raises quantitative and methodological questions, and it promotes dialogues concerning behavioral options in organizational practice and across cultures. Although the element of time has always been in the background of the theory and research on errors and error reporting, it has yet to be—and should be—brought to the foreground of observation.

Errors are a recurring fact of organizational life and can have either adverse or positive organizational consequences. In organizational research, errors are defined as unintended—and potentially avoidable—deviations from organizationally specified goals and standards (Frese and Keith 2015; Hofmann and Frese 2011; Lei et al. 2016a). Consider the manufacturing errors that led to massive Samsung Galaxy Note 7 recalls, medical errors that are responsible for thousands of deaths in US hospitals each year, and positive mistakes that have led to product innovation at the 3M company. The wisdom of managing and learning from errors is incontrovertible.

Managing errors in real time requires errors to be reported in a timely manner so that remedies can be taken before harm occurs (Hagen 2013; Zhao and Olivera 2006). Yet, reporting errors or openly discussing them is not as easy as it sounds; it is a more natural tendency in organizations for people to be silent or cover errors up (Morrison and Milliken 2000; Nembhard and Edmondson 2006). I have attempted to use different lenses—psychological, structural, and system—to understand why and how errors are, or are not, reported. Although each of these lenses leads us to focus on certain variables and relationships, an overlooked and understudied perspective is the temporal lens. Putting the time and timing of error reporting front and center is important because the temporal lens offers its own view of the error-reporting phenomenon, its own set of variables and relationships, and its own set of parameters to guide organizational practice (Ancona et al. 2001a, b). The goal of this chapter is, thus, to sharpen the temporal lens so that we can use it to conduct error research and suggest managerial interventions.

Joining colleagues who have called for more temporal research (Ancona et al. 2001a; Goodman et al. 2011; Lei et al. 2016a), I suggest we begin to think not just about whether or not errors are reported but also about how fast (or slow) errors are reported and the trajectories and cycles they align with: when and why error reporting starts and stops. We should begin to examine the cultures of time and how tight versus loose and high versus low power-distance cultures affect the very nature of error-reporting behavior and what happens as we move across temporal cultures. Overall, it is time to rethink and reframe error reporting via a new temporal lens and examine some new variables and issues (e.g., timing, pace, cycles, rhythms, and temporal differences) in this direction.

Rationale: Why Take on a Temporal Lens?

To better understand the rationale behind adopting a temporal lens, let us start with a real-life example: the 89th Academy Awards ceremony that took place on the night of February 26, 2017 (Buckley 2017). The night ended with a dramatic finish when Warren Beatty and Faye Dunaway awarded the Best Picture award to the makers of the film *La La Land* instead of the rightful winner, *Moonlight*. The extraordinary mix-up occurred live on stage after Brian Cullinan, a partner at the accounting firm PwC, handed Beatty the incorrect envelope moments before the actor went onstage with Dunaway to present the Oscar. PwC, the accounting firm based in London and formerly known as PricewaterhouseCoopers, has been tabulating the votes for the Academy Awards for 83 years.

Reaction to the mistake was swift and harsh. Some criticisms were directed at Beatty. Standing before some 33 million television viewers, he appeared confused by the contents of the envelope. The actor explained that he read the card in the envelope: "I thought, 'This is very strange because it says best actress on the card.' And I felt that maybe there was some sort of misprint." Beatty did not stop the show and say so. As for PwC, the company admitted that "protocols for correcting it (the error) were not followed through quickly enough by Mr. Cullinan or his partner [Ruiz]."

This spectacular Oscars mishap highlights some key temporal dimensions in error situations. First, error disclosing or reporting can manifest as a tipping point for some hidden problem, issue, or mistake that crosses a threshold *over time*. Although the act of error reporting may be a one-time event, Perrow (1984) has noted that error occurrence or potentially adverse consequences are often the end products of long strings of seemingly inconsequential issues and conditions that accumulate and are chained together. Many questioned why the two PwC partners were serving as "balloting leader" to the Oscars team, why there were no rehearsals, and why electronic gadgets were even allowed (which seemed to be the reason that Mr. Cullinan was distracted moments before he handed out the wrong envelope).

Second, an outsized share of accidents happen near the end of projects or missions. So it was with the Oscars mishap, which occurred during the presentation of the biggest, and final, award of the night. As such, time and timing are deeply embedded in our discussion on error detection and reporting.

Third, error situations are sometimes characterized by feedback loops and unexpected interruptions. What is hard—in the heat of the moment—is knowing the proper way to make sense of the shock and regain control (Weick 1993). When hyperdynamic interactions of error signs and interruptions create an interlude, one experiences a blank, a freezing moment that calls into question the orderliness of a structure, a task, or a protocol; understanding and sensemaking collapse together. As such, the seemingly lackadaisical reactions of Beatty, Cullinan, and Ruiz are surprisingly common in the midst of trouble and disasters.

The Oscars story helps explain why we should utilize a temporal lens: It provides an important framework for explaining and understanding the error phenomena as *emergent, dynamic* constructs, rather than discrete, static ones. For this, the temporal view not only broadens the meaning and accounting of error reporting, but it also connects psychological, structural, and/or system perspectives—time is implicitly embedded in all of these aspects. Moreover, applying a temporal lens sharpens our empirical approaches to studying error reporting. The timing of the reporting and the duration before—or time lags in—noticing and reporting errors are fundamental issues, despite the challenges of including the variables of duration, pacing, and shocks in most field studies and experiments of organizational research (although it has been done; see Gersick 1988; Lei et al. 2016b).

In the remainder of the chapter, I take a closer look at three key temporal issues of error reporting in organizations: (1) timing, pace, and rhythms; (2) feedback loops and latent errors; and (3) temporal differences in cross-cultural settings. I explicitly discuss some counterintuitive, paradoxical issues embedded in the act of reporting errors in organizations. I then propose recommendations for future research and for organizational practice in the domain of disclosing, reporting, and discussing errors. I hope to add to organizational scholars' efforts to make inroads into embracing the complexity and flux in management thinking and enable managers to operate effectively when a substantive error situation emerges and evolves.

Tempo of Acts: Timing, Pace, and Rhythms of Error Reporting

The pace of organizational life is the flow or movement of time that people experience (Levine 1997). Consider how goods are produced and services delivered, or how employees are trained, socialized, and engage with one another. Organizational life is characterized by rhythms (What is the pattern of work time to downtime? Is there a regularity to meetings or social events?), by sequences (Is it one particular procedure before another one or the other way around?), and by synchronization (To what extent are employees and their activities attuned to one another?). First and foremost, the pace of organizational life is a matter of tempo, like the tempo of a music piece: We may play the same notes in the same sequence, but there is always that question of tempo (Levine 1997). Similarly, error reporting has much to do with tempo, which refers to the speed, pace, and timing at which an error is disclosed and reported, and it has dramatic effects on organizational performance and outcomes.

Many people believe that to prevent a catastrophe, the sooner an error is reported and declared, the higher the chances for organizational entities to detect and correct it, and vice versa (Hagen 2013; Reason 1990). This seems to make perfect sense because only when an error situation is reported and declared can organizational entities and actors then readily formulate interpretations and choices for corrections and mobilize resources. Also, an early declaration of errors or threats means a prolonged recovery window, defined as the period between a threat and a major accident—or prevented accident—in which collective action is possible (Edmondson et al. 2005). A narrow recovery window may mean there is little that can be done to stop the looming catastrophe.

Consider the case of Dr. Harrison Alter working in the emergency room of a hospital in Tuba City, Arizona, when he saw dozens of patients in a three-week period suffering from viral pneumonia (Groopman 2007). One day, Blanche Begaye (a pseudonym), a Navajo woman, arrived at the emergency room complaining of having trouble breathing. Alter diagnosed her condition as "subclinical pneumonia," even though Begaye did not have several characteristics of that disease (e.g., the white streaks, the harsh sounds—called "rhonchi"—or elevated white blood cell count). Alter ordered the patient to be admitted to the hospital and given intravenous fluids and medicine to bring her fever down. He referred Begaye to the care of an internist on duty and began to examine another patient. A few minutes later, the internist approached Alter and argued (correctly) that Begaye had aspirin toxicity, which occurs when patients overdose on the drug.

Doctors do not make correct diagnoses as often as we think. The diagnostic failure rate is estimated to be 10–15 percent, according to a 2013 article published in the *New England Journal of Medicine* (Croskerry 2013). Alter's misdiagnosis of subclinical pneumonia resulted from the use of a heuristic called "availability," because he had recently seen so many cases of the infection. Despite all imperatives to avoid troublesome misdiagnoses, "debiasing" does not happen easily; to make things worse, many clinicians are unaware of their biases. In Alter's case, if the internist had not spoken up and pointed out Alter's misdiagnosis, and if she had not reported it immediately—within the critical recovery window—Begaye's health or life could have been at great risk. Even though people may always feel uncomfortable pointing out mistakes, in some areas, such as medicine and aviation, failing to do so could cost lives. One of the ways airlines and hospitals are trying to reduce potentially fatal errors from occurring is to use psychological techniques to embrace what is known as a safety culture (Edmondson 1999; Hofmann and Mark 2006; Katz-Navon et al. 2005; Naveh and Katz-Navon 2014; Singer and Vogus 2013). In a safety culture, people at all levels are encouraged to speak up if something is about to go wrong.

It is known that doing nothing, holding an erroneous diagnosis, or acting slowly clearly makes the error situation deteriorate over time. When deciding to report errors or not, is it always true that faster is better? When is acting quickly an asset? When is it a liability? Although there is no one answer to such questions, in a recent simulation study, Rudolph et al. (2009) illustrate patterns concerning how generating problem-solving alternatives too quickly—just as acting too slowly—can make it difficult to collect enough supporting information to resolve a medical crisis.

Rudolph and colleagues found that the doctors fell into four modes of problem-solving as they attempted to address a simulated ventilation problem: stalled, fixated, vagabonding, and adaptive (Rudolph et al. 2009; see also Rudolph and Raemer 2004). The stalled doctors were those who had difficulty generating any diagnoses. In contrast, those in the fixated mode quickly established a plausible but erroneous diagnosis, despite countervailing cues. Rather than advancing through multiple steps of a treatment algorithm to rule out diagnoses, fixated doctors repeated the same step or became stuck. For the third type of doctors, who generated a wide range of plausible diagnoses, Rudolph and colleagues found that broadening the possibilities could incur a problem of "diagnostic vagabonds." These doctors jumped from one action to another without utilizing multiple steps of the treatment algorithms. Doctors in the adaptive sensemaking mode, who are characterized by the generation of one or more plausible diagnoses, and by the exploitation of multiple steps of known treatment algorithms, tended to rule out some diagnoses, take effective action, and—unlike those in any other problem-solving mode—resolve the patient's ventilation problem.

In examining the different pacing involving problem-solving and acting, Rudolph et al. (2009) discovered some important, counterintuitive study results. First, different rates of taking action generate qualitatively different dynamics. A bias for action (i.e., taking action faster) can produce the information needed to improve the diagnosis and protects the problem solver from incorrectly rejecting the correct diagnosis. However, small differences in the speed of acting and cultivating solutions can result in people remaining between desirable adaptive problem-solving, on the one hand, and undesirable fixation or vagabonding, on the other.

When acting fast entails the consideration of multiple alternatives, seeking outside or additional counsel, and potentially integrating multiple decisions in the heat of the moment, people can fall into some dysfunctional modes, including the "paradox of choice" (Schwartz 2004) and the "switching" trap. According to Schwartz (2004), exposure to more information and additional choices may greatly increase levels of anxiety and stress for decision-makers. Fast action also suggests switching between different task domains and modes, which often engenders cognitive dissonance. Psychological evidence has proven that individuals are not good at switching tasks (Cooper 2007).

When an error occurs, in the race to act, people may not naturally choose to report errors. Instead, they might decide to handle things on their own. Tucker and Edmondson (2003) found that nurses often implement short-term fixes for the overwhelming majority of medical errors and failures, without recording or reporting these errors. Ironically, although these quick fixes seem to work well and even create the sense of gratification of having overcome problems without outside help, they can preclude performance improvement over time by impeding operational and structural changes that would prevent the same errors and failures from happening again.

The interpretation of the findings mentioned above is not that fast action or rapid error reporting should be discouraged. Rather, we should be alerted to the side effects of emphasizing speed over content, which can leave little time for error reporting, the analysis of root causes, and learning. Observations based on "high-reliability organizations" (HROs) such as nuclear power plants and airlines reveal some paradoxes of the system in these organizations.

Actions and responses during critical events (e.g., device malfunctions, deteriorating conditions of patients) in HROs happen at a rapid pace. Yet, at the same time, these organizations must pause, reflect, and explore various observations, concerns, and questions (Weick et al. 1999). In essence, it is imperative to take advantage of effective error reporting and create a recovery window when signs of potential threats and problems surface. This principle is also one of the core elements of the quality control method, for example, the "Andon" system pioneered by Toyota (Spear and Bowen 1999). It empowers workers to stop production when a defect or error is found and immediately call for assistance. The work is stopped until a solution has been found. Moreover, alerts may be logged to a database so that they can be studied as part of a continuous improvement program. The real difference of acting fast in an Andon system is that, although employees take almost no time to identify errors when in doubt, they take all the time necessary to analyze, improve, and learn. When Toyota failed to apply the principles of its manufacturing process—known as the "Toyota Way"—and operated around the concept of quickly detecting, reporting, and responding to problems, there were devastating consequences: The recall crisis in 2010 cost Toyota hundreds of millions of dollars and public trust, among other negative outcomes (Bunkley 2011).

Time Lags and Feedback Loops: Latent Errors and Error Reporting

In 1852, Massachusetts General Hospital was featured in a *New York Times* article detailing a series of events that led to the death of a young patient. The patient had received chloroform instead of the usual chloric ether anesthesia under the care of the surgeon. More than 150 years later, a 65-year-old woman was admitted to the day surgery unit at this hospital to cure a case of trigger finger in her left ring finger. Instead, the surgeon, Dr. David C. Ring, performed a completely different procedure—for carpal tunnel syndrome. How could this have happened?

The question is more complex than it initially appears. In Dr. Ring's wrong-site surgery case, according to his own reflections, published in a *New England Journal of Medicine* article (Ring et al. 2010), multiple distractions—including personnel changes, an inpatient consult, and a previous patient's needs—interfered with the surgeon's performance of routine tasks. There was deviation from universal protocol for a full time-out (i.e., performing a check to make sure that the correct patient is about to undergo the correct procedure, on the correct site). There was also a language barrier, such that Dr. Ring was speaking Spanish to the patient, whereas other team members were unable to do so. Since the replacement staff members were unable to verify communication between the physician and the patient, the nurse thought that a conversation between the patient and the surgeon represented a full time-out.

The medical industry, as well as many others, has traditionally treated errors as being due to failings on the part of individuals or inadequate knowledge or skill (Carroll 1998). The system approach, by contrast, takes the view that errors are caused by interdependent actions and multiple interacting elements that become chained together and are extremely vulnerable to "normal accidents," which are virtually inevitable (Perrow 1984). As such, more complex and tighter coupling systems, such as in medicine or in oil drilling, are likely to have a higher rate of errors because the potential interactions between interdependent actions and elements in such systems cannot be thoroughly planned, understood, anticipated, and guarded against. J. Reason, one of the most influential psychologists in error research, echoes a similar view, namely that catastrophic safety failures are almost never caused by isolated errors committed by individuals (Reason 1990). Instead, most accidents result from multiple smaller errors in environments with serious underlying system flaws. In his "Swiss cheese" model, Reason notes that hazards will result in harm when each individual defensive barrier is incomplete and contains random holes, like the holes in slices of Swiss cheese; occasionally, these holes line up, allowing those hazards to create harm.

Reason further uses the terms "active errors" and "latent errors" to distinguish individual errors from system ones. Active errors almost always involve frontline personnel and occur at the point of contact between a human and some aspect of a larger system (e.g., a human-machine interface). By contrast, latent errors are events, activities, or conditions "whose adverse consequences may lie dormant within the system for a long time, only becoming evident when they combine with other factors to breach the system's defenses" (Reason 1990). In Dr. Ring's case, the active errors included the failure to complete a full universal protocol and the marking of the site but not the actual operative site. The latent errors included problems in the scheduling and deployment of personnel, which delayed and then interrupted the procedure and distracted the surgeon; the use of the surgeon as an interpreter instead of the use of a professional interpreter during the procedure; the poor placement of computer monitors; and a culture that allowed nurses who were not directly involved in the procedure to perform tasks such as marking the surgical site.

Latent errors are relevant to the key temporal aspect of error reporting—time lags. Ramanujam and Goodman (2003, 2011) use the collapse of Barings

Investment Bank to illuminate latent errors. Barings was the oldest investment bank in Britain, listing among its clients the Queen herself. In order to survive in the late twentieth century, Barings called on young go-getters who knew how to work the new instruments of global finance such as derivatives. In 1992, Nick Leeson, an ambitious, young back-office banker, was put in charge of Barings Futures Singapore. He was a star: At one point, his speculations accounted for 10 percent of Barings' profits. However, Leeson also knew how to manipulate the internal system and created a secret Barings account, whose losses the bank automatically covered. He started risking huge amounts of money on the Nikkei, betting that the Japanese stock market would go up. Instead, the market crashed down following a gigantic earthquake in Kobe on January 17, 1995. In just a few weeks, Leeson racked up hundreds of millions of pounds in losses. The bank collapsed that March and was bought by the Dutch financial company ING for one British pound. Barings' collapse highlighted a basic premise concerning latent errors: Whereas they seldom produce adverse consequences by themselves, *over time* they steeply accelerate the creation of new latent errors and create conditions that make such consequences more likely.

Powerful stories like Barings' prompt us to consider some critical issues in dealing with latent errors and error reporting. Here I focus on two issues: normalization of deviance (Vaughan 1996) and feedback loops (Lei et al. 2016a; Ramanujam and Goodman 2003). Sociologist D. Vaughan defines the social normalization of deviance as a process in which people within the organization become so accustomed to a deviant behavior that they do not consider it to be deviant, despite far exceeding their own rules for elementary safety and reliability (1996). Similarly, as latent errors (i.e., deviations with no immediate consequences) persist over time, organizational members incorrectly learn to accept such deviations as normal and fail to see the need for remaining vigilant. The likelihood of error detection and reporting—and, therefore, corrective action—can be significantly reduced. This dangerous process of the normalization of deviance was demonstrated at Barings: As trading volumes increased over time and no losses were recognized, the underlying deviations were understood (or learned) to be a normal feature of trading operations.

Normalized deviance was also evident in the Challenger and Columbia Space Shuttle tragedies. Vaughan has written extensively about *Challenger* (1996) and served on the commission that investigated the Columbia tragedy. On Challenger, an O-ring seal failed on a rocket booster, causing a breach that let loose a stream of hot gas, which ignited an external fuel tank; 73 seconds after the launch, the shuttle broke apart over the Atlantic on January 28,

1986. The O-ring erosion problem had already been discovered in 1981, and the erosion had been evident on earlier launchings, but flying with them became routine. Gradually, NASA redefined evidence that deviated from an acceptable standard so that it *became* the standard (Vaughan 1996). With Columbia in 2003, a piece of insulating foam broke off from an external tank during the launch and struck the left wing. When the space shuttle reentered the Earth's atmosphere after a two-week mission in space, hot atmospheric gases penetrated the wing structure. The shuttle broke apart over Texas and Louisiana. NASA had fallen prey to the normalization of deviance for a second time. Shuttles returning with damaged foam strikes had become the norm. As Vaughan commented in a *New York Times* article (Haberman 2014), both "Challenger and Columbia had a long incubation period with early warning signs that something was seriously wrong, but those signals were either missed, misinterpreted or ignored."

Organizational failures and disasters rarely have a single cause. Rather, an overaccumulation of interruptions and latent errors can shift an organizational system from being a resilient, self-regulating regime that offsets the effects of this accumulation into a fragile, self-escalating regime that amplifies them (Rudolph and Repenning 2002). What makes things worse is that the deviance of early warning signs or error signals has been normalized as acceptable over time. Then the question is: How to signal and amplify early warning signs so that it becomes critical to intervene and break the pattern of the normalization of deviance?

To answer this question, this chapter draws attention to the role of feedback loops in latent errors and error reporting. In system dynamics language (Rudolph et al. 2009; Rudolph and Repenning 2002), a feedback loop occurs when outputs of a system are routed back as inputs as part of a chain of cause-and-effect that forms a circuit or loop. Feedback loops can be either error-amplifying (i.e., positive feedback loops) or error-corrective (i.e., negative feedback loops). Ramanujam and Goodman (2003, 2011) suggest that error-amplifying processes often manifest as deviation-induced behaviors, escalation of commitment, and reduced vigilance, as observed in the collapse of Barings, the space shuttle tragedies, and the Deepwater Horizon oil spill. Ample experiences and evidence from a vast variety of disciplines such as psychology, sociology, management, and system dynamics have suggested that changing and removing error-amplifying processes is difficult (Lei et al. 2016a). Counterintuitively, Rudolph and Repenning (2002) propose that an unquestioned adherence to preexisting routines may be the best way to break the error-amplifying feedback loops and prevent the overaccumulation of pending latent errors. To demonstrate the point, they refer to a turnaround time rule among climbing teams tackling major mountains such as Everest. On the day a climbing team attempts the summit, all members must turn around by a specified time, regardless of whether they have achieved their goal. The rationale behind this is that the capacity to process information and make decisions is severely restricted by low oxygen levels at extreme altitudes; even a few interruptions, such as unplanned delays, can create dire threats. Experiences and accounts of the Everest disaster in 1996 (Roberto 2002) highlight how it is better not to leave the turnaround time up to on-the-spot decision making and how violating such rules resulted in the loss of human lives. Moreover, it also seems paradoxical that rules such as the turnaround time—which, to be effective, must be followed without question—are themselves the product of adaptively reflecting and reframing. In the process of reflection and reframing, feedback loops create an ongoing opportunity for the variation, selection, and retention of new practices and patterns of action within routines and allow routines to generate a wide range of outcomes, including considerable change (Feldman and Pentland 2003).

But what are the rules in organizations that can generate error removing or negative feedback loops? Edmondson's influential work consistently shows that learning organizations—characterized by a psychological safety climate and willingness to identify, report, discuss, and remedy failures—will have fewer latent errors (Edmondson 1999; Edmondson and Lei 2014; Tucker and Edmondson 2003). One notable initiative is that at NASA's Goddard Space Flight Center, E. Rogers, Goddard's Chief Knowledge Officer, instituted a "pause and learn" process, in which teams discuss what they have learned after reaching each project milestone (Tinsley et al. 2011). They not only expressly examine perceived successes but also cover mishaps and the design decisions considered along the way. By critically examining projects while they are under way, teams aim to identify, report, and discuss alarming events and latent errors for what they are. Other NASA centers, including the Jet Propulsion Laboratory, which manages NASA's Mars program, have also begun similar experiments. According to Rogers, most projects that have used the pause-and-learn process have uncovered some latent errors—typically, design flaws that had gone undetected. "Almost every mishap at NASA can be traced to some series of small signals that went unnoticed at the critical moment," he says. Compared to the Andon system in manufacturing, which was designed as a just-in-time but reactive system to detect errors, this "pause and learn" process builds in a proactive, ex ante mechanism to seek feedback and signal alarms just in time (Schmutz et al. 2017). The key is that organizations need to maintain the learning DNA and reinforce monitoring, reporting, established rules, and routines as a way of removing positive, error-amplifying feedback loops and stopping the accumulation of (latent) errors.

Temporal Differences in a Cross-cultural Context

On March 11, 2011, an earthquake and tsunami crippled the Fukushima Daiichi Nuclear Power Station. The Fukushima Daiichi accident, the worst since Chernobyl, triggered fuel meltdowns at three of its six reactors and a huge radiation leak that displaced as many as 100,000 people and brought about a crisis of public confidence in the country's nuclear program. There were many similar patterns observed in the Fukushima Daiichi nuclear crisis as seen in other man-made disasters discussed above (e.g., the space shuttle tragedies, the collapse of Barings Bank), including a false belief in the country's "technological infallibility," a normalization process of deviance that continuously downplayed prior safety concerns, and a lack of preparedness for a crisis (Funabashi and Kitazawa 2012).

What also makes the Fukushima Daiichi disaster unique is that its causes are deeply rooted in Japan's rigid societal and political structure, cultural norms of saving face and punishment, and management culture (Lovins 2011). Scholars in the psychology field, in management, and in operations management have suggested a similar view, emphasizing that cultural factors have become critical in understanding how error strategies unfold in an ever-growing global context (Gelfand et al. 2011a; Lei et al. 2016a). For example, there is more tolerance for error-making and more emphasis on creativity and entrepreneurship in Israel compared to countries such as Germany, where adherence to rules, standards, and procedures is highly valued.

Moreover, much of the existing sociological, anthropological, and psychological work in a cross-cultural context has a temporal emphasis, investigating how people from various cultures differ in their temporal perceptions of time as well as preferences and behaviors toward time. For example, sociologist E. Zerubavel's (1981) work on time concerns the societal changes that took place in various cultures after uniform measures of time were developed. E. Hall, a cultural anthropologist, notes how cultures vary in their focus on monochronic or polychronic time (1983). In monochronic cultures ("one thing at a time"), people (e.g., Americans) tend to emphasize careful planning and scheduling—a familiar Western approach that appears in disciplines such as "time management." By contrast, in polychronic cultures ("many things at one time"), human interaction is valued over time, leading to a lower concern for "getting things done"—thus, a French person may turn up to a meeting late and think nothing of it (much to the annoyance of a German or American coworker). From a psychological perspective, Levine (1997) contrasts the tempo and general pace of life among several cultures. He found that in Western cultures such as the United States, the United Kingdom, Canada, and Germany, people are driven to make productive use of every available moment and are very punctual, whereas in other cultures, such as in Mexico and Latin America, it is common to accept with indifference that what does not get done today will get done tomorrow, and that appointments are mere approximations. Hofstede (1991) found that individualistic cultures put greater emphasis on the use of time and that one's past has relatively little influence on future activities. On the other hand, collectivistic cultures prefer acting in the present by reflecting on and integrating events from the past with the present.

More recently, Gelfand et al. (2011b) suggest how different cultural dimensions (e.g., power distance, uncertainty avoidance, tightness-looseness) affect error prevention and error management. Building on this work, I focus on how these dimensions can affect the pace and rhythm of error reporting. Rather than repeating Gelfand and colleagues' insights (2011a, b) on how error responses vary across different cultures in general, I use tightness-looseness, uncertainty avoidance, and power distance to demonstrate how these cultural dimensions specifically influence error reporting.

Anthropologist P. Pelto (1968) first theorized on tightness-looseness, arguing that societies vary widely in their expressions of and adherence to social norms, tightly or loosely. "Tight" societies refer to those that are rigorously formal and disciplined, have clearly defined norms, and impose severe sanctions on individuals who deviate from norms. "Loose" societies are described as those that have a lack of formality, regimentation, and discipline; have norms expressed through a wide variety of alternative channels; and have a high tolerance for deviant behavior (Gelfand et al. 2006, 2011b). For example, scholars (Pelto 1968; Gelfand et al. 2006) have identified Japan, Singapore, Germany, and India to be examples of tight societies, in which norms are expressed very clearly and unambiguously, and severe sanctions are imposed on those who deviate from norms. By contrast, the examples of loose societies include the United States, Israel, and Brazil, where there is a general lack of formality, order, and discipline, and a high tolerance for deviant behavior.

When errors are discovered, tightness is likely to hinder error-reporting processes. Because violations and errors are viewed to be intolerable and are punished more severely in tight cultures, people in these societies tend to have a negative attitude toward errors (Gelfand et al. 2011b). When an error occurs, individuals in tight cultures are more likely to cover it up and less likely to report it, as compared to those in loose cultures. The emotional burden of being a deviant can further prevent individuals in tight cultures from disclosing or reporting errors or from doing so in a timely manner. This also explains why we observed poor communication and coordination between nuclear regulators, utility officials, and the government in the cascading Fukushima nuclear disaster. The interim report, issued by the Investigation Committee on the Accident at the Fukushima Nuclear Power Stations of the Tokyo Electric Power Company (TEPCO) in 2011, stated that Japan's response to the nuclear disaster was flawed by "poor communication and delays in releasing data on dangerous radiation leaks at the facility." To this point, A. Lovins, a physicist and an environmental scientist, further explains (2011) that "Japan's more rigid bureaucratic structures, reluctance to send bad news upwards, need to save face, weak development of policy alternatives, eagerness to preserve nuclear power's public acceptance (indoctrinated since childhood), and politically fragile government, along with TEPCO's very hierarchical management culture, also contributed to the way the accident unfolded."

Uncertainty avoidance refers to the extent to which members of a society can tolerate uncertainty and ambiguity (Hofstede 1980). The fundamental issue is how people deal with the unknown future. Countries ranking high on the uncertainty avoidance index (UAI) maintain rigid codes of belief and behavior and are less likely to tolerate deviant behavior and ideas. Societies ranking lower on the UAI maintain more relaxed attitudes in which practice counts more than principles. Similar to the tight societies, those cultures high on the UAI are expected to be poorer at error management for several reasons (Gelfand et al. 2011b). First, individuals in cultures high on the UAI tend to have a negative attitude toward errors, given that errors are unexpected and are seen as dangerous and stress-laden deviations. More blaming and less error reporting may emerge as a defensive mechanism. Second, organizational members in cultures high on the UAI often adhere to routines and standardized procedures and become less able to respond flexibly and adapt to unexpected events such as errors. Third, formalized communication associated with cultures high on the UAI may delay error reporting. Such cultures often restrict the exchange of information between people, especially those who are not directly involved in the situation. For example, Merkin (2006) found that in embarrassing situations, such as mistakes, people from cultures high on the UAI used more ritualistic, face-saving, and aggressive communication strategies than people from cultures low on the UAI. The stiff, negative manner of communication may hinder error reporting. Therefore, a lack of—or a delay in—error reporting may increase the likelihood of adverse outcomes from an error.

Finally, power distance also profoundly impacts patterns of error response and error-reporting behavior. Power distance refers to the extent to which individuals in a society accept and expect inequalities of power distribution (Hofstede 1980). In high power-distance cultures, such as Malaysia and Nigeria, people are more likely to conform to a social hierarchy. In contrast, people in lower power-distance cultures, such as Denmark and Israel, are less likely to accept such power differentials. On error management, Gelfand et al. (2011b) explain that higher-status people in high power-distance cultures are particularly concerned about losing face when they cause an error, since they assume greater responsibility in error prevention. As such, they are reluctant to report or delay communication about errors. Accordingly, lower-status subordinates in these cultures often avoid monitoring and pointing out their leaders' errors, thus having a negative impact on error reporting. For example, the award-wining product design firm IDEO, headquartered in Palo Alto in the United States, understood the principle of removing status inequalities. Ask people there about the organizational culture and, invariably, they mention how team members are unafraid to challenge the status quo—which often means the leadership, which is a surefire way to encourage learning and innovation (Edmondson 2011).

In summary, cultural considerations prompt us to not only think of all behaviors, interactions, activities, and events as being embedded within a social context but also to understand these phenomena in a paced, temporal context. Although much is unknown and more needs to be understood, a temporal cultural lens has the potential to significantly contribute to our theoretical underpinnings and organizational practice of error reporting.

Look Forward: Future Research and Organizational Practice

The purpose of writing this chapter is to encourage the reader to think more explicitly about the role of time in error reporting. Choosing a few temporal parameters (e.g., timing, pace, cycles, rhythms, and temporal differences in error reporting) and then applying them to the understanding of error reporting and learning in organizations provide a fresh point of view to inform theorizing and guide practice. Building on previous work (Frese and Keith 2015; Hofmann and Frese 2011; Goodman et al. 2011), in a review article, my colleagues and I (Lei et al. 2016a) began to suggest some general guidelines for pursuing a dynamic, temporal approach to the role of time lags, feedback loops, and reciprocal relationships between different foci or forces in error situations. Here, I hope to take stock of thinking and knowledge to improve the odds that a temporal approach will be more thoroughly infused into the study of error reporting. As such, I highlight four exciting research opportunities and tools that may present error researchers with more help than ever before. I then suggest a few takeaway messages for management when adopting the temporal lens.

Research Challenges and Opportunities

Before exploring the opportunities that the temporal lens provides, it may be informative to consider why a well-articulated temporal approach has not been embedded in organizational research in general (Ancona et al. 2001a; Cronin et al. 2011; Lei and Lehmann-Willenbrock 2015; Waller et al. 2001) and in error research in particular (Goodman et al. 2011; Lei et al. 2016a). First, the unique characteristics associated with errors make them rare events and difficult to observe and study. For example, compared to the amount of successful routine operations and services, the number of errors and mistakes in organizations is, fortunately, much smaller. This is especially true in HROs. Also, because errors can be latent and hidden in the organization for a long time, it is less feasible to study them. Moreover, fundamentally, as many errors are not reported due to a variety of reasons (see insights from other chapters in this book), it makes it difficult to study error reporting.

Concurring with the insights of Ancona et al., another reason for the lack of error research using a temporal lens may be that "it is hard enough to gain organizational access. It is even harder to capture events over time using multiple measures. This not only takes time but additional resources and lots of cooperation" (2001a). Because errors, once publicized, may cost organizations such as hospitals enormous financial resources, generate lawsuits, and result in loss of public trust, gaining access into these organizations to study errors and error reporting becomes particularly hard. Understandably, these concerns preclude the use of a temporal lens.

Finally, another big impediment to using the temporal lens is also related to the current status of knowledge and experiences concerning a temporal perspective. Despite knowledge and technology advancement, we still lack integrative theories and methodologies about time lags, durations, and feedback loops in error research, making it difficult to know when, for how long, and how often to measure key variables, even when we want to adopt a temporal perspective (Ancona et al. 2001a).

In a review article, my colleagues and I (Lei et al. 2016a) began to suggest some general guidelines for pursuing a dynamic, temporal approach to the role of time lags, feedback loops, and reciprocal relationships between different foci or forces in error situations. Here, I hope to take stock of thinking and knowledge in this work and others (Ancona et al. 2001a; Cronin et al. 2011; Waller et al. 2001) to improve the odds that a temporal approach will be more thoroughly infused into the study of error reporting.

First, an explicit consideration of issues relating to the timing, pacing, and feedback loops in error reporting would improve the quality of error research. The field would benefit from pursuing research questions such as: What is the tipping point for reporting latent errors? When is it too late? Is fast reporting always good? To what extent would the acceleration or delay of error reporting prolong or shorten the recovery window when coping with them? When would fast error reporting backfire on learning over time? What are the boundary conditions that allow for both short- and long-term performance benefits? We can develop a better understanding by studying the timing, pacing, and feedback loops in error reporting as well as the range of mechanisms that can accelerate or delay the reporting pace.

Second, researchers should begin to make inroads in combining a temporal lens with other research lenses to complement specific insights based on a specific lens. For example, errors are fundamentally multilevel phenomena and can be attributed to individuals or collective actors, such as a team, a unit, or a system (Goodman et al. 2011; Lei et al. 2016a). Although temporal aspects of error reporting have not been explicitly explored based on the level of analysis (individual vs. collective) in this chapter, a multilevel, temporal approach can provide additional rigor in error research. One set of sample research questions include: When individual goals/priorities and collective goals/priorities (e.g., team, system) are in conflict, what are the implications for individual error reporting as well as for team and system reporting? Similarly, when we take multilevel and cultural lenses to study the pace, duration, and contingencies of error reporting, we may be able to answer questions such as: How do societal timing norms impact teams' and their members' error-reporting patterns? How does the fit between individual and team time urgency impact individual members' error-reporting behaviors? How does the fit impact the team climate on error reporting?

Third, with this chapter providing the opportunity to include different time variables in error research, additional aspects of time can shed light on error-reporting patterns. For example, timing norms (i.e., shared and expected patterns of paced activity that govern many activities in organizational life, Ancona et al. 2001b) can have a profound impact on the timing, duration, and feedback loops of error reporting. As another example, external shocks (e.g., Tsunami, earthquake) and unexpected changes (e.g., change of leadership) often drastically affect organizational decisions and actions. Would these exogenous events make organizational members report errors faster or slow them down? Why so? Moreover, Ancona et al. (2001b) have identified a set of temporal variables that merit study in their own right, such as conceptions of time (e.g., uniform time, cyclical time, subjective time, event time), mapping activities to time (e.g., single-activity vs. repeated- activity mapping), and actors relating to time (e.g., temporal perception and personality).

Finally, in light of the theoretical and practical challenges in examining the dynamics of error reporting in organizations, recent technological and methodological advancements present error researchers with more help than ever before. In the blossoming field of technology advances and data computing, researchers from a range of disciplines—including computer science and engineering, machine learning, biology, and psychology—are collaborating to design and implement novel methods for measuring and modeling individuals' behaviors over time. For example, simulation-based studies with organizational members such as airline pilots and medical professionals provide a psychologically safe environment to observe error-reporting behavior and collect error data (see Lei et al. 2016b; Waller et al. 2014). Also, wireless, unobtrusive sensors that measure activation of the sympathetic nervous system may help unpack individual decision-making processes about whether and when to report errors in a new way (Lei and Lehmann-Willenbrock 2015).

"Big data" is another promising frontier that can shed light on error research. Big data refers to large volumes of high-velocity, complex, and variable data that require advanced techniques and technologies to enable the capture, storage, distribution, management, and analysis of the information (Schneeweiss 2014). The large-scale integration of big data—which comes from sensors, devices, video/audio, networks, log files, transactional applications, web, and social media, much of it generated in real time and on a very large scale—can boost the generation of high-quality evidence on error reporting that was previously inaccessible or unusable (Schneeweiss 2014). Moreover, by using advanced analytics techniques—such as text analytics, machine learning, predictive analytics, data mining, and statistics—researchers can potentially uncover hidden patterns; perform more advanced analyses such as stochastic shocks, recursive and cyclical relationships, and path dependence; and gain new insights, resulting in significantly more accurate and faster predictions.

Practical Implications

One of the most fundamental challenges organizations face is how to infuse positive outcomes of errors as opportunities for learning and innovation while mitigating the negative ones. Using a temporal lens can help researchers to move a step closer toward this goal.

Most organizations and their members face the fundamental tradeoffs between achieving long-term goals and yielding short-term gains. Similarly, employees and their managers are often confronted with competing demands for dealing with errors when they do occur: One demand is for short-term, quick fixes, and therefore leads to little or no error reporting or simply covering up errors; the other demand is for long-term, sometimes painstaking, learning goals that can be achieved through honest and timely error reporting. Many error or disaster examples cited in this chapter imply that this temporal dilemma is embedded in organizational life. Consider the NASA managers in the Challenger and Columbia Space Shuttle missions: They were being heavily pressured by mission deadlines and budget concerns, when in fact safety should have always been the priority and learning should have been the ultimate goal.

To resolve simultaneous conflicting priorities of this kind—short-term versus long-term goals, exploitation versus exploration—organizations may need to utilize ambidextrous designs that differentiate between "their new, exploratory units from their traditional, exploitative ones, allowing for different processes, structures, and cultures; at the same time, they maintain tight links across units at the senior executive level" (O'Reilly and Tushman 2004). Moreover, management scholars also support the idea that the temporal tension of short-term versus long-term goals could be resolved in the organizational context by providing support, trust, autonomy, and psychological safety (Edmondson 1999; Edmondson and Lei 2014; Gibson and Birkinshaw 2004). In the context of error reporting, this means that organizations need to think carefully about how they measure success and on what time horizon, and about how to reward failure as well as success. Moreover, because pointing out what is not working can make individuals unpopular, managers need to encourage and protect employees when they do so.

The second benefit of taking a temporal view is to alert managers to watch for cognitive fallacies that accompany prospective assessments of time. For example, one is the "speed trap" between speed and decision making (Perlow et al. 2002). In the error context, a need for fast action can send organizations on a path to failure because they may need to compromise performance reliability for speed. During his testimony to the US Congress in the midst of the Toyota recall crisis in 2010, A. Toyota, the president and CEO of Toyota, admitted:

> Toyota has, for the past few years, been expanding its business rapidly. Quite frankly, I fear the pace at which we have grown may have been too quick. I would like to point out here that Toyota's priority has traditionally been the following – first: safety; second: quality; and third: volume. These priorities became confused, and we were not able to stop, think, and make improvements as much as we were able to before.

Similarly, part of the problem with the Samsung Galaxy Note 7 phone is that the company's overzealous insistence on speed and internal pressures to outdo rivals had pushed the company to the limit (Mozur 2017). Moreover, a race to succeed can result in a false illusion of efficiency, quality, and liability and create a culture that is just the opposite of a learning one: Concerns and warning signs are discounted or dismissed, and errors are not reported until it may be too late. Becoming alert to the influence of these temporal fallacies and maintaining vigilance and mindfulness of one's own thinking may be a promising first step.

Finally, leaders and managers in a global context may also benefit from cross-cultural knowledge and learn that there are alternative constructions of time, and a new range of options can then be considered when dealing with errors. Consider the dabbawalas in India, who are legendary for their precision and efficiency in delivering home-cooked meals in time for lunch in Mumbai. Their service has attracted worldwide attention, including visits from Prince Charles, R. Branson, and other executives from well-known global companies (Thomke 2012). Timeliness is crucial in the service. "The whole city can be affected by late deliveries," says S. Sangle, coordinator of the Mumbai dabbawalas. Dabbawalas are waved through by members of the public and traffic police alike. "If you see a dabbawala in the street, you will give way," he says.

Beyond the operation and management insights on how the dabbawalas organize (e.g., a flat organizational structure with the local autonomy to manage themselves), manage (with respect to hiring, logistics, customer acquisitions and retention, and conflict resolution), and process (e.g., a simple color-coding system), their shared culture, language, values, work ethic, food, and religious beliefs play a significant role (Thomke 2012). The dabbawalas are devoted to their simple mission: delivering food on time, every time. For the dabbawalas, who are largely uneducated and belong almost exclusively to the Vakari community, which worships the Hindu god Vitthala, their task is akin to delivering medicine to the sick, and serving food is like serving God. Their work environment is characterized by a strong sense of accountability and duty. After an extremely tight morning schedule (as the window of time allotted for a pickup might be less than 60 seconds), the workers often have a much less rigid afternoon schedule, allowing them to interact with customers and build strong, long-term, trusting relationships. I hope that the dabbawalas can offer some lessons that managers from all enterprises around the globe can take to heart.

Conclusion

The goal of this chapter is to advance understanding of error reporting via a temporal lens, which provides a powerful way to view error reporting, raises profound quantitative and methodological questions, and promotes dialogues concerning alternative options in organizational practice. Although the element of time has always been in the background of our theory and research on errors and error reporting, it has yet to be—and should be—brought to the foreground. As much as it has been my goal to offer a rich set of theoretical and methodological tools regarding the role of time and timing in error research, it has also been inherently challenging, as there is relatively little guidance and integration across studies. Therefore, I am not claiming or attempting to provide an all-encompassing framework on the literature on time and error research. Rather, I am attempting to provide a starting point for integrating a temporal approach to error reporting into our understanding and practice. As such, there are tremendous opportunities for examining issues of time in current and future research and experimenting with novel alternatives in practice.

References

Ancona, D.G., P.S. Goodman, B.S. Lawrence, and M.L. Tushman. 2001a. Time: A new research lens. *Academy of Management Review* 26 (4): 645–663.

Ancona, D.G., G.A. Okhuysen, and L.A. Perlow. 2001b. Taking time to integrate temporal research. *Academy of Management Review* 26 (4): 512–529.

Buckley, C. 2017. 2 PwC accountants in Oscars mix-up won't be back, Academy says. *New York Times*.

Bunkley, N. 2011. Recall study finds flaws at Toyota. *New York Times*, B1.

Carroll, J.S. 1998. Organizational learning activities in high-hazard industries: The logics underlying self-analysis. *Journal of Management Studies* 35: 699–717.

Cooper, J. 2007. *Cognitive dissonance: 50 years of a classic theory.* London: Sage.

Cronin, M.A., L.R. Weingart, and G. Todorova. 2011. Dynamics in groups: Are we there yet? *The Academy of Management Annals* 5: 571–612.

Croskerry, P. 2013. From mindless to mindful practice – Cognitive bias and clinical decision making. *New England Journal of Medicine* 368 (26): 2445–2448.

Edmondson, A.C. 1999. Psychological safety and learning behavior in work teams. *Administrative Science Quarterly* 44 (2): 350–383.

———. 2011. Strategies for learning from failure. *Harvard Business Review* 89 (4): 48–55.

Edmondson, A.C., and Z. Lei. 2014. Psychological safety: The history, renaissance, and future of an interpersonal construct. *Annual Review of Organizational Psychology and Organizational Behavior* 1: 23–43.

Edmondson, A.C., M.A. Roberto, R.M. Bohmer, E.M. Ferlins, and L.R. Feldman. 2005. The recovery window: Organizational learning following ambiguous threats. In *Organization at the limit: Lessons from the Columbia disaster*, ed. M. Farjoun and W. Starbuck, 220–245. Malden: Blackwell Publishing.

Feldman, M.S., and B.T. Pentland. 2003. Reconceptualizing organizational routines as a source of flexibility and change. *Administrative Science Quarterly* 48 (1): 94–118.

Frese, M., and N. Keith. 2015. Action errors, error management, and learning in organizations. *Annual Review of Psychology* 66: 661–687.

Funabashi, Y., and K. Kitazawa. 2012. Fukushima in review: A complex disaster, a disastrous response. *Bulletin of the Atomic Scientist* 68 (2): 9–21.

Gelfand, M.J., L.H. Nishii, and J.L. Raver. 2006. On the nature and importance of cultural tightness-looseness. *Journal of Applied Psychology* 91 (6): 1225.

Gelfand, M.J., M. Frese, and E. Salmon. 2011a. Cultural influences on error prevention, detection, and management. In *Errors in organizations*, ed. D.A. Hofmann and M. Frese, 273–315. New York: Routledge.

Gelfand, M.J., et al. 2011b. Differences between tight and loose cultures: A 33-nation study. *Science* 332 (6033): 1100–1104.

Gersick, C.J. 1988. Time and transition in work teams: Toward a new model of group development. *Academy of Management Journal* 31 (1): 9–41.

Gibson, C.B., and J. Birkinshaw. 2004. The antecedents, consequences, and mediating role of organizational ambidexterity. *Academy of Management Journal* 47 (2): 209–226.

Goodman, P.S., R. Ramanujam, J.S. Carroll, A.C. Edmondson, D.A. Hofmann, and K.M. Sutcliffe. 2011. Organizational errors: Directions for future research. *Research in Organizational Behavior* 31: 151–176.

Groopman, J. 2007. What's the trouble? *The New Yorker.*

Haberman, C. 2014. Challenger, Columbia and the nature of calamity. *The New York Times*, June 1.

Hagen, J. 2013. *Confronting mistakes: Lessons from the aviation industry when dealing with error*. Houndmills/Basingstoke/Hampshire: Palgrave Macmillan.

Hall, E. 1983. *The dance of life*. New York: Anchor Books/Doubleday.

Hofmann, D.A., and M. Frese. 2011. Errors, error taxonomies, error prevention, and error management: Laying the groundwork for discussing errors in organizations. In *Errors in organizations*, ed. D.A. Hofmann and M. Frese, 1–44. New York: Routledge.

Hofmann, D.A., and B.A. Mark. 2006. An investigation of the relationship between safety climate and medication errors as well as other nurse and patient outcomes. *Personnel Psychology* 59: 847–869.

Hofstede, G. 1980. Motivation, leadership, and organization: Do American theories apply abroad? *Organizational Dynamics* 9 (1): 42–63.

———. 1991. *Cultures and organizations. intercultural cooperation and its importance for survival. Software of the mind*. London: McGraw-Hill.

Katz-Navon, T., E. Naveh, and Z. Stern. 2005. Safety climate in healthcare organizations: A multidimensional approach. *Academy of Management Journal* 48: 1075–1089.

Lei, Z., and N. Lehmann-Willenbrock. 2015. Affect in meetings: An interpersonal construct in dynamic interaction processes. In *The Cambridge handbook of meeting science*, ed. J.A. Allen, N. Lehmann-Willenbrock, and S.G. Rogelberg, 456–482. New York: Cambridge University Press.

Lei, Z., E. Naveh, and Z. Novikov. 2016a. Errors in organizations: An integrative review via level of analysis, temporal dynamism, and priority lenses. *Journal of Management* 42 (5): 1315–1343.

Lei, Z., M.J. Waller, J. Hagen, and S. Kaplan. 2016b. Team adaptiveness in dynamic contexts: contextualizing the roles of interaction patterns and in-process planning. *Group & Organization Management* 41 (4): 491–525. https://doi.org/10.1177/1059601115615246.

Levine, R.N. 1997. *A geography of time: On tempo, culture, and the pace of life*. New York: Basic Books.

Lovins, A. 2011. *Soft energy paths for the 21st century*. Snowmass: Rocky Mountain Institute (RMI). An abridged version of this article, without notes, was commissioned and published in Japanese by *Gaiko* (Diplomacy) 8: 65–73 (July 2011) as "Nijyuu-isseiki no Soft Energy Path" by Japan's Ministry of Foreign Affairs.

Merkin, R.S. 2006. Uncertainty avoidance and facework: A test of the Hofstede model. *International Journal of Intercultural Relations* 30 (2): 213–228.

Morrison, E.W., and F.J. Milliken. 2000. Organizational silence: A barrier to change and development in a pluralistic world. *Academy of Management Review* 25 (4): 706–725.

Mozur, P. 2017. Political crisis engulfs Samsung, a firm tied to South Korea's success. *New York Times*.

Naveh, E., and T. Katz-Navon. 2014. Antecedents of willingness to report medical treatment errors in health care organizations: A multilevel theoretical framework. *Health Care Management Review* 39: 21–30.

Nembhard, I.M., and A.C. Edmondson. 2006. Making it safe: The effects of lead inclusiveness and professional status on psychological safety and improvement efforts in health care teams. *Journal of Organizational Behavior* 27: 941–966.

O'Reilly, C.A., 3rd, and M.L. Tushman. 2004. The ambidextrous organization. *Harvard Business Review* 82 (4): 74–81.

Pelto, P.J. 1968. The differences between "Tight" and "Loose" societies. *Society* 5 (5): 37–40.

Perlow, L.A., G.A. Okhuysen, and N.P. Repenning. 2002. The speed trap: Exploring the relationship between decision making and temporal context. *Academy of Management Journal* 45 (5): 931–955.

Perrow, C. 1984. *Normal accidents*. New York: Basic Books.

Ramanujam, R., and P.C. Goodman. 2003. Latent errors and adverse organizational consequences: A conceptualization. *Journal of Organizational Behavior* 24: 815–836.

Ramanujam, R., and P.S. Goodman. 2011. The link between organizational errors and adverse consequences: The role of error-correcting and error-amplifying feedback processes. In *Errors in organizations*, ed. D.A. Hofmann and M. Frese, 245–272. New York: Routledge.

Reason, J. 1990. *Human error*. New York: Cambridge University Press.

Ring, D.C., J.H. Herndon, and G.S. Meyer. 2010. Case 34-2010: A 65-year-old woman with an incorrect operation on the left hand. *New England Journal of Medicine* 363 (20): 1950–1957.

Roberto, M.A. 2002. Lessons from Everest: The interaction of cognitive bias, psychological safety, and system complexity. *California Management Review* 45 (1): 136–158.

Rudolph, J.W., and D.B. Raemer. 2004. Diagnostic problem-solving during simulated crises in the OR. *Anesthesia and Analgesia* 98 (5S): S34.

Rudolph, J.W., and N.P. Repenning. 2002. Disaster dynamics: Understanding the role of quantity in organizational collapse. *Administrative Science Quarterly* 47: 1–30.

Rudolph, J.W., J.B. Morrison, and J.S. Carroll. 2009. The dynamics of action-oriented problem solving: linking interpretation and choice. *Academy of Management Review* 34: 733–756.

Schmutz, J.B., Z. Lei, W. Eppich, and T. Manser. 2017. Reflection in the heat of the moment: Temporal approach to team reflexivity in healthcare emergency teams. To be presented at the Interdisciplinary group research (INGroup) conference, St. Louis, MO.

Schneeweiss, S. 2014. Learning from big health care data. *New England Journal of Medicine* 370 (23): 2161–2163.

Schwartz, B. 2004. *The paradox of choice: Why less is more*. New York: HarperCollins.

Singer, S.J., and T.J. Vogus. 2013. Reducing hospital errors: Interventions that build safety culture. *Annual Review of Public Health* 34: 373–396.

Spear, S., and H.K. Bowen. 1999. Decoding the DNA of the Toyota production system. *Harvard Business Review* 77: 96–108.

Thomke, S. 2012. Mumbai's models of service excellence. *Harvard Business Review* 90 (11): 121–126.

Tinsley, C.H., R.L. Dillon, and P.M. Madsen. 2011. How to avoid catastrophe. *Harvard Business Review* 89 (4): 90–97.

Tucker, A.L., and A.C. Edmondson. 2003. Why hospitals don't learn from failures: Organizational and psychological dynamics that inhibit system change. *California Management Review* 45: 55–72.

Vaughan, D. 1996. *The Challenger launch decision*. Chicago: University of Chicago Press.

Waller, M.J., J.M. Conte, C.B. Gibson, and M.A. Carpenter. 2001. The effect of individual perceptions of deadlines on team performance. *Academy of Management Review* 26 (4): 586–600.

Waller, M.J., Z. Lei, and R. Pratten. 2014. Focusing on teams in crisis management education: An integration and simulation-based approach. *Academy of Management Learning & Education* 13: 208–221. https://doi.org/10.5465/amle.2012.0337.

Weick, K.E. 1993. The collapse of sensemaking in organizations: The Mann Gulch disaster. *Administrative Science Quarterly* 38: 628–652.

Weick, K.E., K.M. Sutcliffe, and D. Obstfeld. 1999. Organizing for high reliability: Processes of collective mindfulness. *Research in Organizational Behavior* 21: 81–123.

Zerubavel, E. 1981. *Hidden rhythms. Schedules and calendars in social life*. Chicago: University of Chicago Press.

Zhao, B., and F. Olivera. 2006. Error reporting in organizations. *Academy of Management Review* 31: 1012–1030.

2

Errors and Learning for Safety: Creating Uncertainty As an Underlying Mechanism

Gudela Grote

If learning is to be encouraged, error and the resulting increase in uncertainty need to be permitted, and even actively sought, even though they may collide with an organization's concerns about proving that they are safe.

Hence, when decisions are made on how uncertainty should best be managed for particular work processes, stability and flexibility requirements need to be analyzed in view of the specific necessities for control and adaptation. Uncertainty may be beneficial for safety in situations where there is a danger of the over-routinization of behavior due to highly standardized and repetitive task requirements.

To ensure that uncertainty promotes the intended flexibility rather than create confusion and helplessness, education and training as well as support from supervisors and team members need to be guaranteed to help actors use the flexibility provided. An organizational culture should be established that builds on competence, fairness, and trust.

A crucial part of this culture is speaking up, exactly because it increases uncertainty by opening up new perspectives for decision making and action. To handle this uncertainty, formal trainings aimed at learning are required as well as practice in learning the behaviors needed for constructively speaking up and providing adequate reactions for being spoken up to.

Much of this chapter draws on Grote (2015).

G. Grote
Zürich, Switzerland

© The Author(s) 2018
J. U. Hagen (ed.), *How Could This Happen?*, https://doi.org/10.1007/978-3-319-76403-0_2

As for errors, they should be encouraged in situations where flexibility is sought in responding to high levels of uncertainty. This will often prove particularly challenging, because errors will even increase uncertainty temporarily. Error-management training should thus be aimed at helping individuals and teams to understand error in the context of an overall balance of stability and flexibility in team and organizational processes.

The role of error in promoting safe operations in high-risk organizations has been a long-standing issue in academic and practice-oriented discussions. Whereas originally the aim was to avoid error because it can have detrimental and even devastating effects on safety, a change in understanding error has occurred over the last few decades, pointing to the importance of errors for individual and organizational learning (Frese and Keith 2015; Goodman et al. 2011). Correspondingly, the focus of management and regulatory action has shifted from penalizing errors based on accident and incident analyzes aimed at finding the culprit to seeking learning opportunities through solicitation and broad discussions of reports, also when it concerns minor incidents and recovery in near-miss situations (Dekker 2007; van der Schaaf et al. 1991).

This change in perspective has a number of interesting and even paradoxical consequences that have recently been discussed by Lei et al. (2016). If learning is to be encouraged—as everyone seems to agree on in view of ever more complex and fast-changing organizations and environments these organizations have to survive in—error and the resulting increase in uncertainty need to be permitted, and even actively sought. This collides with organizations' concerns for proving that they are safe, based on the narrowly prescribed and highly predictable behavior of systems and people. In the following, I take up this paradox by discussing the possible benefits of uncertainty for safety more generally, and the organizational conditions that make these positive effects more likely. In a final section, I draw some conclusions on the consequences of this broader approach to uncertainty for error management.

Managing Uncertainty in Organizations

Many accidents have been found to be at least partially caused by the reluctance to challenge authority, encourage divergent thinking, or allow decision latitude (e.g., Air Accident Investigation Branch 1990; NAIIC 2012). These reasons are all related to the unwillingness to deliberately increase uncertainty as part of decision-making processes and adaptive behavior. Concerning the two devastating accidents of NASA space shuttles, Feldman (2004) made the interesting observation that uncertainty could not appropriately enter the discussions because the involved engineers were used to only taking quantifiable uncertainties into account, whereas many of the concerns in these two tragedies were of a qualitative nature: "[The NASA engineers] were not able to quantitatively prove flight was unsafe, so in this culture it became easy for management to claim it was safe.... Under conditions of uncertainty, cultures dominated by the belief in ... objectivity must be silent. This silence makes these cultures vulnerable to power and manipulation" (Feldman 2004, 708). Similarly, Farber (2011) has described the unwillingness of the US Nuclear Regulatory Commission to consider risks that could not be quantified, such as terrorist attacks on nuclear facilities, which led them to ignore those risks in all further decision making.

These examples illustrate the necessity to manage uncertainty in a more explicit and systematic manner and to consider reducing, absorbing, *and* creating uncertainty as options in this process. In the discussions to follow, uncertainty is understood in its most basic form as stemming from a lack of information and/or ambiguous information (Daft and Lengel 1984; Galbraith 1973). With this understanding in mind, it is important to note, however, that more information does not necessarily reduce the amount of uncertainty, but it may open up new perspectives for decision making, for which again further information is required, thereby in fact increasing uncertainty.

The examples also hint at a fundamental difficulty for adequately managing uncertainty in terms of assessing all three options for reducing, absorbing, and creating uncertainty: These three options are founded on fundamentally different conceptions of risk control (see Table 2.1):

Reducing uncertainty to a level of acceptable risk is the main thrust in classic risk mitigation. The overall objective is to create stable systems that allow for a maximum level of central control. Measures such as standardization and automation help to streamline work processes.
Absorbing uncertainty follows from acknowledging the limits to reducing uncertainty in complex systems, which has led to the development of concepts such as "high-reliability organizations" (Weick et al. 1999) and "resil-

Table 2.1 Options for managing uncertainty

	Reducing uncertainty	Absorbing uncertainty	Creating uncertainty
Objective	Stability	Flexibility	Flexibility/innovation
Conceptual approach	Classic risk mitigation	Resilience	Complexity theory
Control paradigm	Central control	Control by delegation to local actors	Shaping contexts for self-organizing agents
Examples of measures	Standardization	Empowerment	Controlled experimentation

Source: Adapted from Grote (2015)

ience engineering" (Hollnagel et al. 2006). Flexibility as a source for resilience—that is, the capability of systems to recover from perturbations—is sought. For this purpose, control capacity needs to be decentralized, for example, by means of empowering local actors.

Creating uncertainty, finally, aims also at flexibility, not only in response to perturbations but also in support of innovation. An important conceptual basis is complexity theory (see, e.g., Anderson 1999) and self-organization as one of the theory's fundamental principles. Self-organizing local agents are assumed to not be directly controllable but can only indirectly be influenced in their adaptive behavior by shaping contexts, for instance, through setting incentives and constraints for experimentation.

Carroll (1998) has pointed out that the different conceptions tend to be prevalent in different professional (sub)cultures in organizations (Schein 1996). Whereas engineers and executives believe in uncertainty reduction through design and planning, operative personnel are very aware of the need for resilience in the face of only partially controllable uncertainties. Finally, social scientists will also argue for openness to learning and innovation, thereby even adding uncertainty.

Building a shared understanding of the legitimacy of all three options for reducing, absorbing, and creating uncertainty across professional boundaries is paramount to developing a more comprehensive approach to managing risk and safety. The predominance of risk control by means of minimizing uncertainty in classic risk mitigation is allied to prescriptive models of rational decision making. Those models, such as maximization of subjective expected utility, are rooted in mathematical conceptions of rationality, implying the consistent and maximum use of information. Hence, in order to stimulate discussion on the potential utility of creating uncertainty, fundamental beliefs about what constitutes rational decision making also have to be reflected upon (Grote 2011).

Empirical evidence has been accumulated to show that the prerequisites for mathematical models of rational choice are often not met in actual decision making. For instance, there should be no a priori preference for (un)certainty, but in fact certainty is often preferred in decisions on gains, whereas uncertainty is preferred when losses are to be decided upon (Kahneman and Tversky 1979). For a long time, instead of revising prescriptive models of decision making according to the research evidence, the main thrust of conclusions drawn has been to point to the fallibility of human decision making and the need to educate and support decision makers in more rational decision making (Mellers et al. 1998). Only in recent years have voices become louder that propose to abandon mathematical models as the gold standard for human decision making and focus on its functionality for adapting to personal and situational requirements instead (Kerr and Tindale 2004; Kahneman and Klein 2009; Shafir and LeBoeuf 2002). Risk-related decisions may be particularly vulnerable to beliefs about the superiority of narrowly defined, mathematically based rationality because these beliefs also promise maximum control. In order to overcome the limitations of current risk assessment and management, which are evident in abundant cases of faulty decision making implicated in recent accidents, crises, and catastrophes (e.g., Farber 2011; Paté-Cornell 2012), these beliefs have to be questioned in very fundamental ways.

Once a common perspective on the management of uncertainty is achieved, options can be chosen in view of establishing an optimal balance between stability and flexibility in team and organizational functioning. Early work in organization theory promoted a contingency perspective, which called for either stability or flexibility, depending on the level of uncertainty with which an organization is faced (see, e.g., Thompson 1967). More recently, consensus has emerged across different management disciplines that organizations need concurrent stability and flexibility because stability and flexibility each offer unique advantages at the organizational, team, and individual levels, which should best be combined (Farjoun 2010; Gebert et al. 2010; Leana and Barry 2000; Manz and Stewart 1997). The high levels of routine, standardization, and formalization, which create stability generally, enhance predictability and control, and reduce the need for ad hoc coordination. The capacity for flexibility and change, on the other hand, allows for learning and ad hoc adaptations in the face of uncertainty and the new and variable demands it creates.

When decisions are made on how uncertainty should be best managed for particular work processes—or more generally in an organization's operations—stability and flexibility requirements need to be analyzed in view of the specific necessities for control and adaptation. Clearly, companies such as Google or Apple, which are geared toward maximum innovation, will look for a different overall balance between stability and flexibility than companies whose operations imply the need to control high levels of risk for human life and the environment. However, for particular processes, even high levels of innovation may require higher levels of control and stability, for instance, when it is crucial to meet a particular release date. On the other hand, a nuclear power plant will have to allow for the uncertainty that comes, for instance, with technical innovations in plant operations—even though, most likely, evolutionary rather than radical innovation will be sought.

In order to determine more specific stability and flexibility requirements, one can take the two classic scenarios discussed in the organization literature—minimizing uncertainty versus coping with uncertainty (Grote 2009)—as a starting point. Whereas the first scenario is oriented toward reducing uncertainty to the utmost through standardization and automation—that is, the Fordist notion of Model-T in black—the second scenario acknowledges the inevitability, and possibly even desirability, of uncertainty. It counts on building resources for local adaptive action, following the socio-technical systems design principle of coping with variances at their source.

Mostly, though neither of these scenarios will be fully applicable to any given organization, appropriate mixes of stability- and flexibility-enhancing mechanisms will have to be found. In this process, stability and flexibility should not be treated as two ends of one dimension but as analytically different dimensions with separate mechanisms operating on them (Grote et al. 2012).

Flexibility is a response to uncertainty, whereas stability is a response to the need for control. Measures that increase flexibility, such as the availability of several responses in a given situation, may in fact also increase stability because control capabilities are increased by making the system more resilient. Measures to increase stability by, for instance, excluding some options for action, and thereby bounding uncertainty, may enhance flexible responses to other uncertainties.

This interconnectedness of stability and flexibility has also been described as the duality of stability and flexibility (Farjoun 2010). Stability and flexibility can interact in positive ways, as in the examples mentioned above. However, there may also be negative effects when, for instance, stabilizing factors such as rules are taken away in an attempt to increase flexibility (but instead actors are disoriented), or when rules are put in place to increase control (but these rules are inadequate so that flexibility is lost without gaining control).

Possible Benefits of Creating Uncertainty for Safety

To further substantiate the claim that error management should be understood and implemented within a broader approach that harnesses uncertainty, possible benefits of higher levels of uncertainty need to be demonstrated. Direct benefits of uncertainty can be seen most easily in contexts where innovation and creativity are sought (Anderson et al. 2014).

Bringing about new ideas requires the willingness to leave existing behavioral routines behind and to engage in exploration and divergent thinking, which implies embracing uncertainty. Consequently, whenever innovation is needed in high-risk settings, uncertainty has to be increased. This is indeed the case in a variety of situations, ranging from responses to changing regulatory, economic, or societal demands to technical performance improvements to handling non-routine operational events. Furthermore, increasing uncertainty can also be beneficial for safety in situations where there is a danger of over-routinization of behavior due to highly standardized and repetitive task requirements. In order to keep levels of attention and motivation high, confronting operators with novel demands can be very useful, even though the learning required may temporarily hamper performance (Gersick and Hackman 1990).

When uncertainty is increased, the levels of stability and control are reduced, which, for high-risk settings, is a particularly uncomfortable situation to be in. Hence, choosing the option of creating uncertainty requires great care and also a good understanding of what it takes to eventually reduce levels of uncertainty and regain control. Premature convergence on inadequate decisions needs to be avoided just as much as unnecessary indulgence in overly complex problem representations. This delicate balance is to be struck in daily operational decision making by operators of high-risk systems but also in strategic decisions by top management, risk managers, or regulators that may even concern the process of risk assessment itself. There is abundant evidence that many tools used in risk assessment are made less than optimal use of because closure in decision making is sought prematurely (Carroll 1998; Nicolini et al. 2011; Schöbel and Manzey 2011). In the following, flexible rules and speaking up are discussed as two examples for possible advantages of creating uncertainty for improving safety.

Designing Flexible Rules

Standards and procedures are prevalent in most high-risk organizations. They permit coordinated action of many different actors without the need for personal coordination (March et al. 2000). As personal coordination is assumed to be error-prone, standards and procedures are also considered a particularly safe way of ensuring coordination (Perrow 1984). However, in view of changing demands and unforeseen situations, actors still need to be able to adapt their behavior by modifying prescribed procedures (e.g., Hale and Borys

Table 2.2 Examples for different rule types

Rule type	Definition (from Hale and Swuste 1998)	Example (taken from flight operations manual of a European airline)
Goal rule	Rule defining goals and priorities	It must be clearly understood that not all combinations of cumulative operational problems (engine failure plus, e.g., terrain, weather, availability of aerodromes, etc.) can be covered by this policy. In such situations, the solution offering the highest degree of safety should be sought
Process rule	Rule providing guidance for deciding on the right course of action	In order to complete a re-planning, any documented cruise systems and all means available may be used, such as flight management systems and data contained in the respective Aircraft Operation Manuals
Action rule	Rule prescribing detailed courses of action	Every evacuation must be carried out as quickly as possible. The passengers must be assisted to leave the airplane without their belongings and directed to a point at a safe distance from the airplane

Source: Adapted from Grote (2015)

2013a; Rasmussen 1997). In order to employ rules—defined in the most general sense as written prescriptions for behavior—in ways that permit the required balancing of stability and flexibility, Grote and colleagues have argued that the notion of flexible rules is important (Grote et al. 2009; Grote 2012). The idea of flexible rules draws on the distinction suggested by Hale and Swuste between goal, process, and action rules (see Table 2.2).

Goal rules only define the goal to be achieved, leaving it open as to how this is accomplished by the actors concerned. Process rules provide guidance for deciding on the right course of action for achieving certain goals. Finally, action rules prescribe detailed courses of action, possibly without even mentioning the goal to be achieved. Goal and process rules and also those action rules that entail some decision latitude constitute flexible rules.

As a rule of thumb on good rule making, action rules should be used when stability of processes is required. Goal and process rules should be used when flexibility is required. The following example from the rulebook of a railway company may serve as an illustration of these distinctions:

The correct functioning of the train control system and the automatic traffic control system is to be monitored by the signaller. If necessary, he/she has to intervene manually. During normal operation, no monitoring is necessary as long as the operational requirements are met. In the case of disturbances or incidents, the notification of the required services and the required alarm procedures must be guaranteed.

When dissecting this set of rules, one can see that the first sentence is an action rule without any decision latitude, and the second sentence is an action rule with some decision latitude, indicated by the expression "if necessary." Together, these two rules aim at creating stability by clearly assigning responsibility for running the highly automated traffic control system to the signaler. The third rule comes as a surprise because it seemingly contradicts the first two rules. It is a process rule, permitting flexibility in executing tasks in response to different operational states, but it also states one definite boundary condition: meeting operational requirements. The last rule is a goal rule, leaving it open as to how the set goal is to be achieved, thereby allowing much flexibility in responding to unforeseen events.

At first sight, this set of rules conveys a rather contradictory message, which, in order to be accepted by the actors involved, needs to be well-grounded in a high level of trust and a shared understanding of the necessity to handle conflicting demands. However, considering the overall task of signalers, which is to ensure smooth operations in a very dense railway network, the rule can be considered as striking the right balance between stability and flexibility. Increasing uncertainty by explicitly acknowledging the conflicting requirements of monitoring an automated system while also relying on its functioning with one's own attention being absorbed elsewhere—one of the hallmarks of the ironies of automation (Bainbridge 1983)—is helpful under those circumstances because the continuous necessity to decide on an appropriate allocation of cognitive resources is highlighted. This benefit can only come to bear, though, if, as in the case of the signalers, the individuals having to follow such rules are well trained and embedded in a trusting and supportive culture, which provides for a good match between accountability and control.

Proposing flexible rules as a form of support for safe operations implies that rules do not necessarily have to reduce levels of uncertainty in order to be good rules, as is generally believed. Goal and process rules partially reduce levels of uncertainty, for example, by setting priorities or defining a certain process to follow in problem-solving. However, much uncertainty is retained by leaving significant decision latitude to the actor in determining the right course of action. Furthermore, uncertainty may even be increased by indicating different options for action from which the actor has to choose, or by—even in action rules—employing modifiers as necessary or in certain circumstances, which again require the actor to decide—possibly without much further guidance as to the necessities and circumstances to be considered. To ensure that this decision latitude promotes the intended flexibility rather than create confusion and helplessness, education and training as well as support by supervisors and team members need to be ensured to help actors adequately use the flexibility provided. An organizational culture should also be established that builds on competence, trust, and fairness.

Speaking Up

Speaking up has been defined as the "discretionary communication of ideas, suggestions, concerns, or opinions about work-related issues with the intent to improve organizational or unit functioning" (Morrison 2011). Benefits of speaking up have been shown in the context of innovation and organizational learning (e.g., Edmondson 2003), and also concerning safety, for instance, in a study by Kolbe et al. (2012), in which the frequency with which nurses spoke up was positively related to handling minor, non-routine events during simulated anesthesia inductions.

One immediate effect of speaking up is that uncertainty is increased because doubts about a particular course of action are raised, new options for actions are suggested, or a new perspective on a situation is opened up. Often, this increased uncertainty is exactly what keeps people from speaking up, as illustrated by the tragic accident of British Midland flight 92 in January 1989 (Air Accident Investigation Branch 1990). Following a fan-blade rupture on the left engine, the captain had mistakenly shut down the right engine. The first officer showed some confusion as to which of the engines was malfunctioning but did not intervene. The cabin crewmembers saw evidence of the fire in the left-side engine, but this information was never conveyed to the cockpit because, as the surviving purser later said, they did not want to undermine the pilots' authority. Flying with one engine shut down and the other engine burning, the aircraft finally crashed on a motorway, killing 47 passengers and seriously injuring 74.

The uncertainty resulting from speaking up will be beneficial in as much as individuals and teams have sufficient cognitive resources for shifting into a mode of divergent thinking during their ongoing activity, but they are also capable of converting back to convergent thinking in order to adapt their course of action in a timely manner, especially in time-critical situations.

For this to happen, three fundamental prerequisites are required. First of all, individuals and teams need to be encouraged to speak up. Research indicates that inclusive leadership—that is, supervisors encouraging and explicitly valuing team member contributions in decision making (Nembhard and

Edmondson 2006)—and psychological safety, defined as team members' belief that they can take interpersonal risks without having to fear punishment, rejection, or embarrassment (Edmondson 1999), are important in this respect. Both of these factors can also counteract low status, which is a significant impeding factor for speaking up (Nembhard and Edmondson 2006; Bienefeld and Grote 2014).

Secondly, speaking up has to happen in a constructive, non-threatening manner. One practical recommendation to that effect is the so-called two-challenge rule (Pian-Smith et al. 2009). This rule states that speaking up should happen from a perspective of curiosity and concern, including an open-ended inquiry that allows the recipient to explain their point of view rather than justify their actions. The rule also proposes, though, that after two attempts at producing a change in the recipient's behavior in this way, the person having spoken up should take the initiative to develop a new course of action themselves.

Thirdly, the person(s) spoken up to needs to react in constructive ways in terms of adequately processing the new information and also in terms of acknowledging the contribution of the person who has spoken up, even if that contribution turns out to be of little practical use. Carroll's (1998) example of an engineering executive at a US nuclear power plant who stated for his plant that "it is against the culture to talk about problems unless you have a solution" is a negative case in point in this respect.

How intricate the dynamics involved in speaking up are can also be seen by looking into the reasons for silence, that is, focusing on the people who do not speak up even when they know they should (Detert and Edmondson 2011). An example is given in Table 2.3 of the responses of aircrew members of a European commercial airline. They had been instructed to think of one specific situation experienced in their current job position in which they had felt they should have spoken up about a safety-relevant issue, but had not (Bienefeld and Grote 2012). The response patterns are interesting in many different ways, but maybe most importantly they show that different professional groups may have quite different reasons for silence, and therefore they also need different kinds of encouragement to speak up. Furthermore, the data shows that high status is not a sufficient condition for raising one's voice, as even captains reported situations in which they did not dare to speak up. Finally, the responses indicate that silence can also be grounded in concerns for others, not least in avoiding overburdening them by adding complications to an already stressful situation.

The three essential prerequisites discussed above for supporting individuals and teams in handling the extra uncertainties involved in speaking up require

Table 2.3 Reasons for silence given by members of aircrews in a European commercial airline

Reasons for silence	Captains (n = 261) (%)	First officers (n = 334) (%)	Pursers (n = 307) (%)	Flight attendants (n = 849) (%)
Status differences	0	11	20	40
Fear of damaging relationships	**53**	**43**	15	42
Feelings of futility	0	**33**	23	**51**
Lack of experience in current job position or on aircraft type	14	13	3	0
Negative impact on others	**24**	24	16	36
Poor relationship with supervisor	0	20	26	35
Fear of punishment	0	23	**67**	**81**
Fear of negative label	3	29	21	6
Perceived conflict efficiency versus safety	21	14	**70**	29
Perceived time pressure	20	11	41	13

Percentages of reasons add up to more than 100 percent, as most participants indicated more than one reason for their silence; numbers in bold represent the two most frequently chosen reasons per occupational group
Source: Adapted from Bienefeld and Grote (2012)

organizational measures aimed at supporting teams, and especially team leaders, in creating a shared understanding of the benefits of speaking up. Additionally, training is necessary to build a repertoire of behaviors needed for speaking up and for adequately reacting when spoken up to. Such trainings are very demanding because they require an atmosphere of psychological safety among the participants, and between participants and instructors, that needs to be created by carefully tailored, non-threatening, instructor interventions. Training contents should include the discussion of hurdles and enablers of speaking up, reflection on the specific social interaction processes involved in speaking up, and also the practicing of appropriate communication algorithms. One powerful vehicle can be structured debriefings as part of simulation-based team trainings and using techniques such as guided team self-correction, open-ended inquiry, and encouragement for perspective-taking (Kolbe et al. 2013).

In sum, speaking up is crucial for safety, exactly because it increases uncertainty by opening up new perspectives for decision making and action. However, a sense of heightened uncertainty—on a personal level as well as concerning the task at hand—is also one of the most salient reasons for people's reluctance to speak up. To counterbalance this uncertainty, a general culture of trust—and more specifically psychological safety—is important but also formal trainings aimed at learning and practicing the behaviors needed for constructive speaking up and adequate reactions to being spoken up to.

Consequences for Error Management

Error management often is contrasted with error avoidance (Frese and Keith 2015), which corresponds with the distinction between minimizing uncertainty and coping with uncertainty (Grote 2009), mentioned above. The arguments for favoring error management also mirror the arguments for helping teams and organizations cope with uncertainty; these arguments are founded on the necessity to build adaptive capacity in the face of "the unexpected" (Weick et al. 1999). In general terms, therefore, one may argue that training individuals and teams in adequate error management should be based on fundamental processes of how people perceive and manage uncertainty. Individual differences in these processes, for instance, based on a general preference to avoid uncertainty, should especially be taken account of and used to tailor individual trainings. Some research evidence exists already that shows such an approach to be particularly effective (Loh et al. 2013). Furthermore, error-management training should be aimed at helping individuals and teams to understand error in the context of an overall balance of stability and flexibility in team and organizational processes. Errors should be encouraged more in situations where flexibility is sought to respond to high levels of uncertainty. This will often prove particularly challenging, though, because errors will even increase uncertainty temporarily.

Regarding the two examples used here to demonstrate the possible benefits of creating uncertainty—flexible rules and speaking up—there is also an apparent connection to be made to error management. Flexible rules entail decision latitude, which has to be adequately used by the respective actors. This obviously introduces opportunities for error, which need to be balanced with the errors committed by pushing for confirming with stricter—but possibly not always applicable—rules (Hale and Borys 2013a). Error management thus concerns not only rule followers but also rule makers. Both need to be empowered, trained, and actively encouraged to leave room for error (Hale and Borys 2013b). Simultaneously, feedback mechanisms have to be established and used that permit the adaptation of rules in view of errors made. Care needs to be taken to not have rule makers always opt for more and tighter rules when errors occur but for them to adhere to flexible rules for those processes that cannot be fully foreseen and specified.

With respect to speaking up, the challenge is to encourage individuals to raise concerns and bring new ideas, which may turn out to be erroneous and help the recipients of these concerns and ideas to take decisions based on them, including the possibility of discarding them as erroneous. The latter additionally needs to happen in ways that maintain the first condition, that is, to not discourage anyone from speaking up in the future. Error-management training can support these processes by looking into the details of these decision and communication processes and practice techniques such as humble inquiry (Schein 2013).

I hope that, with these examples, I have been able to convincingly demonstrate the connection between error management and uncertainty management. Furthermore, the examples should have shown that crucial organizational processes such as rule making and following and speaking up can be viewed in terms of both error and uncertainty management. This dual perspective can enrich organizational measures aimed at improving error management, but it also brings the relevance of error management to the attention of organizational actors involved in rule making and in establishing a climate for speaking up.

References

Air Accident Investigation Branch. 1990. *UK AAIB report 4/90 on the 8 January 1989 accident of a British Midland B737–400 at Kegworth, Leicestershire, England.* Aldershot: Air Accident Investigation Branch.

Anderson, P. 1999. Complexity theory and organization science. *Organization Science* 10: 216–232.

Anderson, N., K. Potocnik, and J. Zhou. 2014. Innovation and creativity in organizations: A state-of-the-science review, prospective commentary, and guiding framework. *Journal of Management* 40: 1297–1333.

Bainbridge, L. 1983. Ironies of automation. *Automatica* 19: 775–779.

Bienefeld, N., and G. Grote. 2012. Silence that may kill: When aircrew members don't speak up and why. *Aviation Psychology and Applied Human Factors* 2: 1–10.

———. 2014. Speaking up in ad Hoc multiteam systems: Individual level effects of psychological safety, status, and leadership within and across teams. *European Journal of Work and Organizational Psychology* 23(6): 930–945.

Carroll, J.S. 1998. Organizational learning activities in high-hazard industries: The logics underlying self-analysis. *Journal of Management Studies* 35: 699–717.

Daft, R.L., and R.H. Lengel. 1984. Information richness: A new approach to managerial behavior and organizational design. In *Research in organizational behavior*, ed. L.L. Cummings and B.M. Staw, vol. 6, 191–233. Homewood: JAI Press.

Dekker, S. 2007. *Just culture – Balancing safety and accountability.* Aldershot: Ashgate.

Detert, J.R., and A. Edmondson. 2011. Implicit voice theories: Taken-for-granted rules of self-censorship at work. *Academy of Management Journal* 54: 461–488.

Edmondson, A. 1999. Psychological safety and learning behavior in work teams. *Administrative Science Quarterly* 44: 350–383.

Edmondson, A.C. 2003. Speaking up in the operating room: How team leaders promote learning in interdisciplinary action teams. *Journal of Management Studies* 40: 1419–1452.

Farber, D.A. 2011. Uncertainty. *The Georgetown Law Journal* 99: 901–959.

Farjoun, M. 2010. Beyond dualism: Stability and change as duality. *Academy of Management Review* 35: 202–225.

Feldman, S.P. 2004. The culture of objectivity: Quantification, uncertainty, and the evaluation of risk at NASA. *Human Relations* 57: 691–718.

Frese, M., and N. Keith. 2015. Action errors, error management and learning in organizations. *Annual Review of Psychology* 66: 661–687.

Galbraith, J. 1973. *Designing complex organizations.* Reading: Addison-Wesley.

Gebert, D., S. Boerner, and E. Kearney. 2010. Fostering team innovation: Why is it important to combine opposing action strategies? *Organization Science* 21: 593–608.

Gersick, C., and J.R. Hackman. 1990. Habitual routines in task-performing groups. *Organizational Behavior and Human Decision Processes* 47: 65–97.

Goodman, P.S., R. Ramanujam, J.S. Carroll, A.C. Edmondson, D.A. Hofmann, and K.M. Sutcliffe. 2011. Organizational errors: Directions for future research. *Research in Organizational Behavior* 31: 151–176.

Grote, G. 2009. *Management of uncertainty. Theory and application in the design of systems and organizations.* London: Springer.

———. 2011. Risk management from an organizational psychology perspective: A decision process for managing uncertainties. *Die Unternehmung* 65: 69–81.

———. 2012. Safety management in different high-risk domains – All the same? *Safety Science* 50: 1983–1992.

———. 2015. Promoting safety by increasing uncertainty – Implications for risk management. *Safety Science* 71: 71–79.

Grote, G., J.C. Weichbrodt, H. Günter, E. Zala-Mezö, and B. Künzle. 2009. Coordination in high-risk organisations: The need for flexible routines. *Cognition, Technology & Work* 11: 17–27.

Grote, G., M. Kolbe, and M.J. Waller. 2012. On the confluence of leadership and coordination in balancing stability and flexibility in teams. Paper presented at the Academy of Management conference, Boston, August.

Hale, A.R., and D. Borys. 2013a. Working to rule or working safety? Part 1: A state of the art review. *Safety Science* 55: 207–221.

———. 2013b. Working to rule or working safety? Part 2: The management of safety rules and procedures. *Safety Science* 55: 222–231.

Hale, A.R., and P. Swuste. 1998. Safety rules: Procedural freedom or action constraint? *Safety Science* 29: 163–177.

Hollnagel, E., D.D. Woods, and N. Leveson. 2006. *Resilience engineering: Concepts and precepts.* Aldershot: Ashgate.

Kahneman, D., and G. Klein. 2009. Conditions for intuitive expertise – A failure to disagree. *American Psychologist* 64: 515–526.

Kahneman, D., and A. Tversky. 1979. Prospect theory: An analysis of decision under risk. *Econometrica* 47: 263–291.

Kerr, N.L., and R.S. Tindale. 2004. Group performance and decision making. *Annual Review of Psychology* 55: 23–655.

Kolbe, M., M.J. Burtscher, J. Wacker, B. Grande, R. Nohynkova, T. Manser, D.R. Spahn, and G. Grote. 2012. Speaking up is related to better team performance in simulated anesthesia inductions. An observational study. *Anesthesia and Analgesia* 115: 1099–1108.

Kolbe, M., M. Weiss, G. Grote, A. Knauth, M. Dambach, D.R. Spahn, and B. Grande. 2013. TeamGAINS: A tool for structured debriefings for simulation-based team trainings. *BMJ Quality & Safety* 22: 541–553.

Leana, C.R., and B. Barry. 2000. Stability and change as simultaneous experiences in organizational life. *Academy of Management Review* 25: 753–759.

Lei, Z., E. Naveh, and Z. Novikov. 2016. Errors in organizations: An integrative review via levels of analysis, temporal dynamism, and priority lenses. *Journal of Management* 42: 1315–1343.

Loh, V., S. Andrews, B. Hesketh, and B. Griffin. 2013. The moderating effect of individual differences in error-management training: Who learns from mistakes? *Human Factors* 55: 435–448.

Manz, C.C., and G.L. Stewart. 1997. Attaining flexible stability by integrating total quality management and socio-technical systems theory. *Organization Science* 8: 59–70.

March, J., M. Schulz, and X. Zhou. 2000. *The dynamics of rules: Change in written organizational codes.* Stanford: Stanford University Press.

Mellers, B.A., A. Schwartz, and A.D.J. Cooke. 1998. Judgment and decision making. *Annual Review of Psychology* 49: 447–477.

Morrison, E.W. 2011. Employee voice behavior: Integration and directions for future research. *The Academy of Management Annals* 5: 373–412.

NAIIC. 2012. *The official report of the Fukushima nuclear accident independent investigation commission.* Tokyo: National Diet of Japan.

Nembhard, I.M., and A.C. Edmondson. 2006. Making it safe: The effects of leader inclusiveness and professional status on psychological safety and improvement efforts in health care teams. *Journal of Organizational Behavior* 27: 941–966.

Nicolini, D., J. Waring, and J. Mengis. 2011. Policy and practice in the use of root cause analysis to investigate clinical adverse events: Mind the gap. *Social Science & Medicine* 73: 217–225.

Paté-Cornell, E. 2012. On "Black Swans" and "Perfect storms": Risk analysis and management when statistics are not enough. *Risk Analysis* 32: 1823–1833.

Perrow, C. 1984. *Normal accidents – Living with high-risk technologies*. New York: Basic Books.

Pian-Smith, M.C.M., R. Simon, R.D. Minehart, M. Podraza, J. Rudolph, T. Walzer, and D. Raemer. 2009. Teaching residents the two-challenge rule: A simulation-based approach to improve education and patient safety. *Simulation in Healthcare* 4: 84–91.

Rasmussen, J. 1997. Risk management in a dynamic society: A modelling problem. *Safety Science* 27: 183–213.

Schein, E.H. 1996. Three cultures of management: The key to organizational learning. *Sloan Management Review* 38: 9–20.

———. 2013. *Humble inquiry: The gentle art of asking instead of telling*. San Francisco: Berrett-Koehler Publishers.

Schöbel, M., and D. Manzey. 2011. Subjective theories of organizing and learning from events. *Safety Science* 49: 47–54.

Shafir, E., and R.A. LeBoeuf. 2002. Rationality. *Annual Review of Psychology* 53: 491–517.

Thompson, J.D. 1967. *Organizations in action*. New York: McGraw-Hill.

Van der Schaaf, T.W., D.A. Lucas, and A.R. Hale, eds. 1991. *Near miss reporting as a safety tool*. Oxford: Butterworth-Heinemann.

Weick, K.E., K.M. Sutcliffe, and D. Obstfeld. 1999. Organizing for high reliability: Processes of collective mindfulness. *Research in Organizational Behavior* 21: 81–123.

3

When Silence Is Not Golden

Immanuel Barshi and Nadine Bienefeld

Who among us has not been faced with a disagreeable situation in which we knew we should say something, and yet we did not? What was the personal risk we saw that caused us to remain silent, even when dealing with safety-relevant issues?

Based on a study of airline cockpit and cabin crew members, the answers include: status differences, fear of damaging relationships, a feeling of futility, lack of experience, concerns about negative impact on others, poor relationship with supervisor, fear of punishment, fear of being viewed negatively, perceived time pressure.

If we want to empower ourselves and others to speak up and minimize errors and incidents, we need to understand those personal perceptions of risk in order to mitigate the worries and fears involved. We must demonstrate that the benefits of speaking up are indeed greater than the perceived personal costs involved. For this purpose, speaking up has to be encouraged constantly—even for minor issues—for people on all organizational levels, and it must be done in an environment that is safe and 100 percent conducive to their input.

However, it is leaders who must help create that environment.

I. Barshi
Mountain View, USA

N. Bienefeld
Zürich, Switzerland

© The Author(s) 2018
J. U. Hagen (ed.), *How Could This Happen?*, https://doi.org/10.1007/978-3-319-76403-0_3

Reporting an error, a potential hazard, or an inadvertent safety violation is a critical aspect of a healthy safety culture. It becomes vital when an incident happens and people ask "How could this happen?" The answer is that it might have happened because nobody spoke up.

> During the course of my pharmaceutical instruction on Sunday afternoons, I was faced with a problem. … I was having instructions in the making of suppositories, … which I was supposed to know how to make for the exam. … Mr. P. the pharmacist was giving me a personal demonstration, and showed me the exact procedure…, then added one metrically calculated drug. He showed me how to turn the suppositories out at the right moment, then told me how to put them into a box and label them professionally as so-and-so *one in a hundred*. He went away then to attend to other duties, but I was worried, because I was convinced that what had gone into those suppositories was 10% and made a dose of *one in ten* in each, not one in a hundred. I went over his calculations and they *were* wrong. In using the metric system he had got his dot in the wrong place. But what was the young student to do? I was the merest novice, he was the best-known pharmacist in the town. I couldn't say to him: "Mr P., *you have made a mistake*." Mr P. the pharmacist was the sort of person who does *not* make a mistake, especially in front of a student. At this moment, re-passing me, he said, "You can put those into stock; we do need them sometimes." Worse and worse. I couldn't let those suppositories go into stock. It was quite a dangerous drug that was being used. … I didn't like it, and what was I to do about it? Even if I suggested the dose was wrong, would he believe me? I was quite sure of the answer to that: he would say, "It's quite all right. Do you think I don't know what I'm doing in matters of this kind?" (Christie 1977)

So describes Agatha Christie in her 1977 autobiography an event that took place during World War One. She was in her mid-20s working in a hospital and caring for the wounded soldiers, learning much about drugs and poisons (something that helped her years later when she turned to writing murder mysteries).

But who among us has not had such an experience? Who among us has not been faced with a disagreeable situation in which we knew we should say something, and yet we did not? Why did we hesitate? Why do we not speak up?

The term itself, "speaking up," already suggests part of the answer. It is often the case that whatever it is we disagree with comes from "higher up," in whatever sense of power hierarchy we might be in. Somebody we perceive to have more power than we do says or does something we disagree with, and if we want to express that disagreement, we must speak "up." Just like the young Agatha Christie, we fear that our protest will be dismissed. What is worse, we fear that we will be ridiculed. Not only our opinion may be dismissed but our very selves as individuals might be dismissed. Even if there is no power hier-archy—as when we see some injustice on the street, some rude behavior toward another person—we often choose to remain silent because we do not want to take the risk. But what is that risk? How do we understand the notion of risk?

When people ask, "What's the risk?" they ask the equivalent of "What are the chances that something bad could happen?" That question has three main components: chances, something, and bad. In the language of risk assessment, "chances" are described in terms of probability or likelihood; the "something" that could happen is called the outcome; and the "badness" of the outcome is talked about as the consequence or the severity. Risk, then, is expressed as a function of likelihood and consequences (or probability and severity) of a given outcome. It is important for us to understand the basics of risk assess-ment to understand people's choices of whether to speak up or to remain silent. What is more, the language of risk assessment could be an important tool in empowering people to speak up, and thus in creating a healthy report-ing culture.

So what is risk assessment? Actually, it is what we do all the time, though we rarely think in terms of a formal risk assessment. Every decision is a choice. Every action can be phrased as a choice: Sitting down is a choice between standing and sitting; scratching the nose is a choice between continuing to suffer the itch or doing something about it. Often, it is only in retrospect, after we have sat down or scratched the nose, that we may even realize that we have made a choice, a decision. Every choice is a form of risk assessment. "Should I run across the street when the pedestrian light is already flashing or wait for the next green light?" "Should I order the spicy Tikka Masala for the first time or go with the mild dhal curry dish that I know and like?" Because risk is relative, risk assessment is a tool to compare options: Standing is worse than sitting (more tiring, less comfortable, less socially acceptable in the given situation); doing nothing about the itch is worse than scratching the nose. This intuitive—and usually implicit, even subconscious—risk assessment is designed to inform the choice: What is less risky—doing nothing or doing something? Among the different things we could do, what is the least risky option?

In our minds, we go through what is called a "cost-benefit analysis." Crossing the street when the pedestrian light is flashing has the potential cost/risk of being caught by the police or being run over by a car, but it also has the benefit of saving time. Trying the Tikka Masala dish runs the risk that it might be too spicy or not to our liking, but it also carries the benefit of discovering a new dish we might like. So, besides choosing the less risky option, we choose the one in which the perceived benefit outweighs the perceived cost.

Common formal methods of risk assessment rely on large amounts of data to calculate the likelihood of a failure (Mauro and Barshi 2009). A thorough understanding of the system involved allows for a careful modeling of different failure scenarios, such that the consequences of a failure can be accurately determined. For instance, a computer manufacturer may need to decide which processor chip to buy for his/her computers. Let us say that there are two different chips that could perform the required computer functions, and they are available from two different suppliers. Given the thousands of chips the computer manufacturer intends to purchase, even a small difference in price per chip translates into a lot of money. So the computer manufacturer has to make a choice. To inform that choice, it requests reliability data from the two chip suppliers, namely, how likely is their chip to fail? If the chip fails, the planned computer is useless, so the computer manufacturer must calculate the risk associated with each chip: The likelihood is given by the reliability data and the consequence is the loss of the computer. Given the wealth of objective data, the manufacturer can make a well-substantiated choice whether to buy one chip or the other. But how well substantiated is the choice of whether to speak up or to remain silent?

The computer chip manufacturer runs multiple reliability tests during the production process and prior to marketing. Once sold, customers provide the manufacturer with feedback about their experiences with the product and the reliability they observe. The manufacturer has a lot of data about the likelihood part of the risk equation. The outcome is clear: a chip failure. The chip either works or it does not; there will not be any multiple possible outcomes, as is usually the case in complex social situations. The consequences of chip failure are clear, too: The device within which the chip is installed would cease to function upon chip failure. There is objective, measurable data to support it all. So the risk is unambiguous, but it is not when it comes to the perceived risks of speaking up. So what are those perceived risks?

Bienefeld and Grote (2012) explored those risks by asking 1751 airline cockpit and cabin crew members to recall one specific situation in which they had felt unable to speak up about a safety-relevant issue (e.g., observed errors or violations of procedures), even though they had felt the need to speak up and later regretted not having spoken up. Participants then chose one or more reasons that motivated their decision to remain silent from a list of 10 reasons (based on Milliken et al. 2003). Table 3.1 shows these reasons, together with illustrating quotes from study participants.

Table 3.1 Reasons for silence

Reasons for silence	Quotes
Status differences (hierarchical structure in the organization)	"Many pursers take on too much power, […] their education is not that different to ours and sometimes they have no idea about what we have to deal with but it feels like there is a two-class society not only between cockpit and cabin but within the cabin crew. They [the pursers] think of themselves as something better. No way I was gonna tell her that she was in the wrong." (Flight Attendant) "Yes, we now have flat hierarchies in the cockpit and they all say that we should speak up. But at the same time, many send subtle signals that they don't really want to hear what one has to say." (First Officer)
Fear of damaging relationships (loss of trust, respect, acceptance, or support)	"I didn't agree and of course it wasn't according to SOPs [standard operating procedures]. But to be the trouble-maker and mess up the team climate on the first day is not a good start to a week of flying together." (First Officer) "Sometimes it's hard to know when you are a colleague and when you are the boss. I generally have a trustful and open relationship with my first officers and I don't want to be the 'four stripes knows it all' type of captain." (Captain)
Feelings of futility (speaking up will not make a difference or recipient will not be responsive)	"Of course I know I should always say something – they tell you in training and in every briefing. But when it comes down to it, they either don't want to hear it or they think we are 'chicken hearts' and simply laugh at us. I've given up." (Flight Attendant) "You know, oftentimes, you are considered a bimbo. It is hard to speak up when you feel you have so little power. […] I don't even try anymore." (Flight Attendant)
Lack of experience in current job position or on aircraft type	"I was the boss and it was me that had the final responsibility but he [first officer] had so many more hours on this aircraft and he seemed confident. […] I was still new in this position. […] I had to grow into it even though before [formal position as first officer] I had seen my speaking up as a responsibility, as my 'raison d'être.'" (Captain).
Concerns about negative impact on others (not wanting to embarrass or upset someone or to get them into trouble)	"I should probably have said something or taken over, but our CRM was good, we had a good team spirit and I just didn't want to be the bad guy." (Captain)

(continued)

Table 3.1 (continued)

Reasons for silence	Quotes
Poor relationship with supervisor (supervisor is unsupportive or distant)	"[…] he was one of these 'hero' commanders! I got the feeling that he believed that first officers are incapable of taking on any kind of responsibility. I feel it is the responsibility of the commander to create a working environment where interventions are possible." (First Officer)
Fear of punishment (not getting promoted or other adverse personal consequences)	"I didn't want to get into trouble and risk a negative entry in my personal file. I am sure she [purser] would have gotten angry if I had told her it was a violation of safety procedures. So I just hoped that I would never have to fly with this one [purser] again." (Flight Attendant)
Fear of being labeled or viewed negatively	"I didn't want the others to think I was a spoilsport […] they all knew the rules, I was no different, why should I take the blame?" (Flight Attendant)
Perceived conflict between efficiency/passenger comfort and safety	"We all know that when it comes down to business, all that counts is on-time departures. If I had delayed that flight […] there could have been a report from the captain. After all, I wasn't certain if I was right and then there's all the hassle with passengers missing their flights, paper work etc. It's just not worth it." (Purser)
Perceived time pressure	"Well there were so many things to be done [during passenger boarding] that by the time I realized I should have said no, the doors were already closed." (Purser)

Source: Adapted from Bienefeld and Grote (2012)

People from different domains give similar reasons for their silence. For instance, Schwappach and Gehring (2014) investigated medical staff's experiences with speaking up about safety concerns and quoted the following:

You cannot do this as a resident. You cannot say 'Professor, we have to discuss this.' That is simply inadequate. That [violation of disinfection rules] needs to be brought up by the chief or a senior. (Senior doctor, ambulatory unit)

Sometimes they [doctors] just slip away, 'You have nothing to tell me.' (Nurse, ambulatory unit)

Eventually, you simply remain silent. What can you do? (Nurse, oncology ward)

Similarly, in various organizations as observed by Milliken et al. (2003):

I raised a concern about some policies and I was told to shut up and that I was becoming a troublemaker. I would have pursued [the issue] further but presently I can't afford to risk my job. This has made me go into a detached mode, making me a 'yes man.' (IT manager)

This particular partner gives me access to a lot of information. I did not want to risk offending him. I did not want to rock the boat and risk losing favor with him. (Research engineer)

As can be easily seen in the quotes above, people choose to remain silent in situations where they know they should speak up because they perceive the cost of speaking up to be greater than its benefit or the risk of speaking up to be greater than the risk of remaining silent. This is why the language of risk assessment can be a powerful tool in helping people speak up.

From the perspective of formal explicit risk assessment, the choice to remain silent is problematic. What data has been used to calculate the likelihood of an adverse outcome? What data has been used to calculate the severity of the consequence? What relationship has been assumed between the likelihood and the consequence to determine the shape of the risk function? The truth is that, all too often, our choices are based on very little, if any, and highly biased data.

We may have an impression that the person we know we should challenge is unlikely to take our opinion seriously, just like young Agatha Christie's impression of the pharmacist. We may have had an experience in which we tried to challenge another person and were hurt by that person's response and so vowed to ourselves to never try that again. Such an experience is likely to bias our choices long after the experience itself, sometimes even throughout our life.

It might be the case that the cultural environment in which we work places a high value on the avoidance of confrontation. We might have bosses or leaders who work hard to maintain the image of not making mistakes. These are all seemingly good reasons to remain silent rather than to speak up; they fall under what Detert and Edmondson (2011) call "implicit voice theories." Our decision is based on the assumption of a very high likelihood of a very bad consequence to ourselves, and possibly others, if we speak up. But what is the risk of remaining silent?

In the case of young Agatha Christie, it was the risk of people being harmed by the high dose of the drug. Silence among aircrews could end up in a catastrophe for everybody on board. For the healthcare professional who felt the professor could not be challenged over violating disinfection rules, it was the risk of a patient developing an infection that could be fatal.

We often excuse our silence by thinking that the situation will get resolved somehow, even without our input. Somebody else will speak up. We tell ourselves that the error we observed is not that serious after all, or the injustice will somehow pass and be forgotten. It is easy to overestimate the risk of speaking up and to underestimate the risk of remaining silent, as this flight attendant found out:

> That day we had this medical case on board I should have intervened. I still think about it often. [...] I should have trusted my gut feeling and told him [the purser] to call for a doctor and inform the cockpit immediately. I am not a medical expert, in fact I had the same standard emergency training as the purser and the other crew members but maybe that passenger would have survived had we reacted more quickly.

These issues concerning speaking up are not limited to upward communication in deliberate hierarchies. People have very subjective perceptions of social power and status. Certain people, regardless of their formal position—they can be peers or subordinates—demonstrate power in subtle ways by the way they talk and act. This can be enough to intimidate others, leading them to not speak up. In the study by Bienefeld (2012), even captains, despite their high status and position of authority, indicated that they, too, were sometimes reluctant to raise safety-relevant concerns or observations. We can see that the subjective perceptions of status influence the decision about whether or not to speak up more strongly than the formal or official hierarchical role.

As demonstrated in the examples above, it would seem obvious that speaking up is important in safety-critical situations. However, if speaking up is not encouraged constantly, even for minor issues, it is not likely to all of a sudden manifest—this is because, all too often, the criticality of a situation is only recognized in hindsight. In the midst of a situation, it is often impossible to tell what the final outcome will be. Thus, sincerely encouraging speaking up is the key to a healthy safety culture.

"Safety culture" might seem like one of those buzzwords or fashionable labels that people throw around without serious intention. However, it can also be a very important aspect of an organization's operational philosophy and everyday actions. Every organization has a safety culture; in some cases it is good, in others less so. A healthy safety culture is one in which people at all levels of the organization feel *psychologically safe*—a term coined by Edmondson (2003)—to take interpersonal risks. However, it is leaders who must help create that environment. Bienefeld and Grote (2014b) showed that when leaders were perceived as inclusive, team members were more likely to speak up because they felt it was psychologically safe to do so. To be perceived as inclusive, leaders must sincerely solicit input, show that they really want to hear the bad news, and truly ask for contradicting opinions. The key is sincerity because people are extremely good at recognizing insincerity. As frontline and low-status employees are inherently suspicious of upper management, management at all levels must work hard to gain the trust of all employees before speaking up can become the norm and the safety culture can become a healthy one. As is always the case in such matters, it starts from the very top. If the most senior manager does not display that sincerity to the next level of management, that level will not be able to gain the trust of the next level down, and so it will continue all the way down the hierarchy to the employees on the shop floor.

But what can leaders do to foster a speaking-up culture? How can leaders create a psychologically safe environment in which all people feel truly invited to speak up?

There are some specific steps leaders can take to be inclusive and to create an environment that encourages speaking up. For instance, leaders can create the right time frame for opportunities to speak up, establish eye contact, and use silence to encourage people to speak. In group interactions, everybody should be invited to express their ideas—the most junior persons should be first because once senior people have spoken, junior people are not likely to contradict them. By using phrases such as "we should…" and "please support me," leaders can reduce the power distance. By acknowledging what is being said and integrating such input into plans and actions, leaders can show that they are honest and sincere. Finally, by creating an "all stop!" or "code red!" procedure for extreme cases, leaders can empower everybody to become a *situational leader* (see Bienefeld and Grote 2014a), someone who will speak up and stop the operation when it is truly critical, when allowing it to continue poses a greater risk than the one involved in speaking up.

The above suggests ways to foster speaking up in a "top down" manner. However, we must also empower a "bottom up" approach that supports people to speak up.

We recently held an international workshop on the topic of speaking up with a group consisting mostly of airline pilots, flight attendants, trainers, and managers. We asked the participants to reflect on situations in which they were able to speak up and what enabled them to do so. Their answers were insightful. People emphasized the importance of choosing the right time and place to speak up, of taking responsibility for one's own role, and of using rational rather than emotional arguments. They mentioned the necessity of showing the other person respect and empathy, and how they connected with the other person while maintaining that person's self-esteem. People also pointed to the importance of diffusing tensions and staying aware of their own sensations and reactions as well as cultural differences. They strongly suggested that one has to check one's facts, not act on rumors, rely on formal limits such as standard operating procedures and regulations, and avoid being judgmental.

In addition to these personal strategies, there are various speaking-up strategies that can be used by people who are—or perceive themselves to be—of low status (e.g., Pian-Smith et al. 2009). Here, we present a stepwise communication tool we call ABC (see Fig. 3.1) and illustrate it with an example from healthcare (Bienefeld 2015).

Bienefeld and Grote (2012) showed that uncertainty of the situation and self-doubt were among the most frequently mentioned reasons for silence. If people are not sure about their own concerns, they should clarify the situation and ask a sincere question without blame or a hidden agenda. Starting on the A for *ask*: If a nurse observes that a doctor is about to apply a medication that the patient might be allergic to, the nurse could say "I'm not sure, have we checked for patient allergies?" Other opening lines could be:

"I am confused/puzzled about …"

"Perhaps I have a different picture of the situation / have learned it differently / haven't noticed …"

"Maybe you can't see it from where you stand, but from where I stand, I can see that…"

"Please help me understand why…"

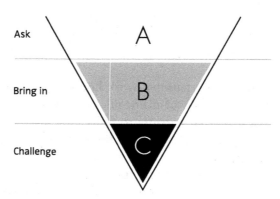

Fig. 3.1 The ABC tool

An honest question opens the door for conversation. Experience shows that most people are willing to listen, when asked sincerely. If asking is successful, steps B and C are no longer necessary.

However, if asking is not successful, people should *bring in* their idea, suggestion, or concern. The nurse in our example could say: "I am concerned that it is unsafe to give this patient a penicillin-like drug, given his known allergy. What are your thoughts?"

The last step—*challenge*—may not be necessary. It should be used if A and B were not successful and the risk of remaining silent is too high, as it would be if safety is the issue. To challenge, people should reinforce their input, obtain support from others if possible, and escalate their concerns. In our example, the nurse could challenge by saying: "Please stop! I think this is a patient safety issue and I would like to call for another doctor."

All patients in hospitals would wish for the medical staff to communicate in such effective ways for the sake of their safety. Passengers on airplanes would want to trust crew members to speak up and save the day, if needed.

Although ABC may seem simple at first, it actually requires a lot of practice because its success depends on having the right attitude, choosing the right words, and hitting the right tone. Depending on the situation, there might be a different time and place for speaking up. The effectiveness of speaking up is often determined by how it is done (e.g., in an assertive rather than a submissive or aggressive manner) (Jentsch and Smith-Jentsch 2001). Also, it is important to distinguish speaking up from whistleblowing or just complaining.

Speaking up is a communication challenge, and part of the challenge is the perception of risk. If we want to empower ourselves and others to speak up, we need communication tools such as ABC, and we need to understand those personal perceptions of risk. We must demonstrate that the benefits of speaking up are indeed greater than the perceived costs involved. It must be clear that the risk of remaining silent is greater than the perceived risk of speaking up.

So what did the young Agatha Christie do when faced with her dilemma and the need to speak up? In her creativity, she actually found a way around speaking:

> There was only one thing for it. Before the suppositories cooled, I tripped, lost my footing, upset the board on which they were reposing, and *trod on them* firmly.
>
> "Mr P.," I said, "I'm terribly sorry; I knocked over those suppositories and stepped on them."

"Dear, dear, dear," he said vexedly. "This one seems all right." He picked up one which had escaped the weight of my beetle-crushers. "It's dirty," I said firmly, and without more ado tipped them all into the waste-bin. "I'm very sorry," I repeated. (Christie 1977)

In doing so, her report of the error had to wait some 50 years before being published, and Mr. P. the pharmacist missed the opportunity to learn, as did all the other people who, at the time, were struggling with the transition from the imperial system of measurement to the metric system—not to mention everybody else who has been struggling with the need to speak up.

Speaking up is much harder than reporting anonymously. The anonymity reduces the risk of direct adverse consequences to the individual reporter, but written reports take time. They can be effective after the fact; they can be helpful in addressing long-term issues. Written reports cannot solve a problem the moment it arises and cannot stop an error chain from rolling once it has started. Only speaking up can. An organization can have a reasonable reporting culture without a strong speaking-up culture, but a good safety culture requires both. Furthermore, a strong speaking-up culture is likely to support a strong reporting culture but not the other way round. Thus, establishing a strong speaking-up culture is a key to building a strong safety culture.

References

Bienefeld, N. 2012. Leadership, boundary-spanning, and voice in high-risk multiteam systems. Unpublished doctoral dissertation, ETH Zurich.

———. 2015. The power of voice. *Talk presented at TEDxZurich*, Switzerland. http://tedxtalks.ted.com/video/The-power-of-voice-Nadine-Bienefeld

Bienefeld, N., and G. Grote. 2012. Silence that may kill: When aircrew members don't speak up and why. *Aviation Psychology and Applied Human Factors* 2 (1): 1–10.

———. 2014a. Shared leadership in multiteam systems: How cockpit and cabin crews lead each other to safety. *Human Factors, the Journal of the Human Factors and Ergonomics Society* 56 (2): 270–286. https://doi.org/10.1177/0018720813 488137.

———. 2014b. Speaking up in multiteam systems: Effects of psychological safety, status, and leadership within and across teams. *European Journal of Work and Organization Psychology* 23 (6): 930–945. https://doi.org/10.1080/1359432X. 2013.808398.

Christie, A. 1977. *An autobiography*. Glasgow: William Collins Sons.

Detert, J.R., and A. Edmondson. 2011. Implicit voice theories: Taken-for-granted rules of self-censorship at work. *Academy of Management Journal* 54 (3): 461–488.

Edmondson, A. 2003. Speaking up in the operating room: How team leaders promote learning in interdisciplinary action teams. *Journal of Management Studies* 40: 1419–1452.

Jentsch, F., and K.A. Smith-Jentsch. 2001. Assertiveness and team performance: More than "Just say no". In *Improving teamwork in organizations: Applications of resource management training*, ed. E. Salas, C.A. Bowers, and E. Edens, 73–94. Mahwah: Lawrence Erlbaum Associates.

Mauro, R., and I. Barshi. 2009. Risk assessment in aviation. Proceedings of the 15th international symposium on aviation psychology, Dayton, OH, 214–219.

Milliken, F.J., E.W. Morrison, and P.F. Hewlin. 2003. An exploratory study of employee silence: Issues that employees don't communicate upward and why. *Journal of Management Studies* 40 (6): 1453–1476.

Pian-Smith, M.C.M., R. Simon, R.D. Minehart, M. Podraza, J. Rudolph, T. Walzer, and D. Raemer. 2009. Teaching residents the two-challenge rule: A simulation-based approach to improve education and patient safety. *Simulation in Healthcare* 4: 84–91.

Schwappach, D., and K. Gehring. 2014. "Saying it without words": A qualitative study of oncology staff's experiences with speaking up about safety concerns. *BMJ Open* 4 (5): 1–8.

4

Executive Perspectives on Strategic Error Management

Vincent Giolito and Paul J. Verdin

We all know stories of CEOs supervising organizations in which grave errors occurred. Those errors challenged the organizations in their strategies, affected their resources, value, sustainable competitive advantage, and endangered their survival. In addition, for poorly managing strategic errors, those executives paid part of the price by losing their positions and reputations.

As a result, executives and academics have begun to recognize that strategic error management is a critical feature of exercising the highest responsibility in an organization, and that it concerns individual behavior, organizational processes, culture, and relationships.

Regardless of whether an organizational error occurs at the top or the bottom of the hierarchy, strategic error management refers to all actions that top executives of an organization undertake (or fail to) in order to disconnect latent errors from actual and potentially adverse consequences, repair the damage done, learn from the errors, and seize the potential new strategic opportunities emerging from the errors.

The first step of effective strategic error management made by a top executive consists of identifying error signals as discrepancies—positive or negative—of clarifying the norm on which the judgment is based and asking for additional information. The acknowledgment of organizational errors is the next step, leading top

V. Giolito • P. J. Verdin
Brussels, Belgium

© The Author(s) 2018
J. U. Hagen (ed.), *How Could This Happen?*, https://doi.org/10.1007/978-3-319-76403-0_4

executives to mentally and individually construct an organizational story that includes the error, and then share this story with others. Of particular importance for successful strategic error management is the relationship between the executive team and the board of directors. However, engaging the whole team requires a "we" culture instead of a leadership style based on an individual personification of power.

In the fall of 2008, Fortis, the leading Belgian bank and one of the five largest in Europe, collapsed and was taken over by banking authorities after attempting a takeover with insufficient funding (Giolito and Verdin 2016b). Value destruction amounted to €20 billion. The chairman had to leave, as had the CEO a few weeks earlier. In late 2016, Deutsche Bank, the leading German lender, agreed to pay $7.2 billion in penalties and relief to consumers for settling a probe launched by US authorities on alleged mis-selling securities (Wells and Gray 2016). The sum amounted to close to half the bank's market capitalization at the time. The co-CEOs, who oversaw the operations, had already been fired and replaced. Also in 2016, Wells Fargo, then the most valuable US bank, lost its title along with billions of dollars in market capitalization after an enquiry revealed employees routinely opened fake customer accounts to attain individual objectives (Gray 2016). After a ruthless audition with a US Senate panel, the CEO stepped down. Outside the banking industry, such mishaps routinely occur as well. In 2015, Volkswagen, then the leading carmaker globally, was accused of massive fraud involving antipollution devices. It lost $25 billion of market value overnight and its CEO was forced to quit (Bryant and Sharman 2015).

A common thread runs across those stories—and myriads more. Top executives were supervising organizations in which errors occurred; those errors eventually challenged the organizations in their strategy, that is, their major goals, including mere survival. In addition, for poorly managing strategic errors, those executives paid part of the price by losing their positions and reputations.

Despite the impact of such episodes on the organizations and individuals concerned and the attention they draw from mainstream media and the public at large, and although seminal works from Shimizu and Hitt (2004, 2011) laid the ground for a vast research agenda based on a new comprehension of organizational errors (Goodman et al. 2011; Hofmann and Frese 2011b), strategic error management has received relatively little attention from scholarly research and from the broader academic and management community. Recent contributions have focused on *why* top executives commit errors (Hunter et al. 2011), complementing psychological explanations at the individual (Lovallo and Kahneman 2003; Tversky and Kahneman 1973) and collective levels (Baron 2005; Janis 1997; Staw 1981). Other studies have focused on *how* errors were managed at the organizational—not executive—level by delineating factors either conducive to errors morphing into catastrophes (Perrow 1999; Shrivastava 1987) or to organizations safely coping with high-risk environments (e.g., Roberts 1990b; Weick and Sutcliffe 2007). Still other studies have delved into the mechanisms by which organizations learn from errors only when it is too late (e.g., Haunschild and Sullivan 2002). However, to a large extent, research has ignored the role of leaders, and specifically top executives, who are expected to shape the organizations they represent

(Carpenter et al. 2004; Hambrick and Mason 1984) in handling the "here and now" of organizational errors and particularly those with strategic consequences (Edmondson and Verdin, this volume).

Thus, the purpose of this chapter is threefold. First, we attempt to make the case for studying strategic error management, that is, the management of organizational errors by top executives. To that end, we share insights gained from a private colloquium gathering top executives overseeing organizations with tens of thousands of employees combined and leading scholars from the error-management community. Second, building on our own qualitative research based on interviews of executives and case studies in the financial sector, this chapter offers a number of definitions that build on and refine extant literature, alongside of a brief description of a framework for effective strategic error management that complements and develops prior insights (e.g., Shimizu and Hitt 2004). Our model, which we refer to as the "AAA" model of strategic error management, specifically identifies error acknowledgment as a pivotal step for executives to reverse negative error spirals. It is depicted in Fig. 4.1. Third, we offer a number of avenues for future research and implications for practitioners.

Relevance of Strategic Error Management

That errors occur frequently in organizations has been the starting point for a small community of researchers over the past 20 years. Examples abound, from Excel spreadsheets used in companies, in which the probability of errors range from 50 to 80 percent (Panko 1998, 2008) to operating rooms in hospitals and flight decks, where pilots are observed making several mistakes in every flight hour (Hagen 2013). Research has also illustrated the severity of error consequences. Studies show medical errors are the third leading cause of death in the United States (Makary and Daniel 2016). Detailed analysis of industrial disasters—for example, the Columbia and Challenger space shuttles, the Deepwater Horizon oil spill, the Chernobyl nuclear accident, the Tenerife air crash—delineates how small errors combined and developed nefarious spirals (Hoffman and Devereaux Jennings 2011; Perrow 1999; Starbuck and Milliken 1988; Weick 1990). Seminal research by Reason (1990, 2000) identifies two distinct and complementary—rather than contradictory—approaches to error management. The first approach is *error avoidance*, by which managers attempt to preemptively identify major risks and design devices and processes that thwart errors. The second approach is *error management*, which consists of intercepting and rectifying errors as they occur (Hofmann and Frese 2011a).

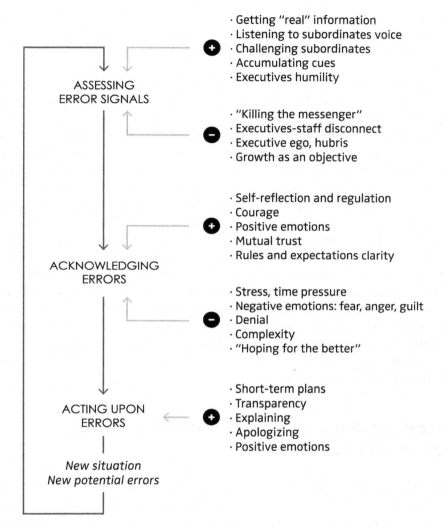

Fig. 4.1 The "AAA" model of strategic error management. (Note: Light gray lines denote enablers (+) and barriers (−) to effective strategic error management. Source: Authors)

However present error avoidance may be in their minds—in part due to a mantra of teaching the right way of doing things in business schools—our research shows that error management remains a critical part of the duty of top executives. As the CEO of a major financial group told us in an interview,

> [If the] problem is just to know whether the organization can survive, it is once every 4 or 5 years. If [it is whether] the organization is going to remain one of

the best performing in its sector … Around 10 times every year, there are real questions to ask ourselves regarding: if we want to stay ahead of the race, what do we do to correct that? (Giolito and Verdin 2016b)

The relevance of strategic error management was confirmed when we invited a panel of top academics, CEOs, and chairmen for a colloquium as part of our research. The leading executives on our panel employed more than 500,000 people and had a combined value of tens of billions of euros. One chairman recounted how a succession of errors in the strategy, the choice of high-ranking managers, and tardy corrective action led the organization to the brink of insolvency. A CEO detailed how his company had to manage strategic errors made by a key supplier. A third executive still regretted not having convinced a board of directors to renounce a projected merger that eventually resulted in the collapse of a major financial group. In the conversation with academics, the executives on the panel converged toward at least three shifts in the comprehension of strategic error management: Errors and error management should be viewed as a process, not an event; a cultural lens rather than a structural lens on organizational errors is conducive to effective error management; and interpersonal and team relationships, particularly in a top management team, make for a better approach to managing errors than the classic search for individual responsibility (Giolito and Verdin 2016a).

From an Event to a Process View of Strategic Error Management

People generally tend to think of errors as discrete events—and managers are no exception. A person in the organization, possibly an executive, took the wrong decision. Or perhaps it was a team decision: Several people acting within their roles and with the best intentions made a poor choice. In any case, it is tempting to link adverse outcomes to one single error, one single person, if only because of the availability bias: People tend to attribute causality to other people and events that are readily available in mind (Tversky and Kahneman 1973). In that view, as one participant noted, errors "are an ex-post reconstruction of an event as having been an error" and help with learning later on. Yet, in the view of strategic error management, errors may be better understood as a process in its own right.

Executives and academics on our panel suggested that there may be no such thing as a big organizational error: More often there are only sequences of small errors poorly managed. In documented cases of industrial catastrophes, error signals—weak and strong—arise long before what will later be analyzed as the major event. "From the outset, we knew something was wrong," recalled an executive whose company came close to default. In that process, erroneous decisions are intertwined with good decisions. All decisions, good and bad, are evaluated by comparison to general references: A strategy, a set of goals, professional guidelines, and also the regulatory and competitive environment. Many decisions may appear erroneous when measured against one set of references, whereas they align with other references. Participants in our colloquium highlighted the importance of conflicting priorities as being a crucial factor for errors. In addition, strategies, goals, guidelines, and environments shift over time, changing right into wrong decisions and vice versa, sometimes leading to reinterpreting the past or retroactively applying new rules or expectations on past events and decisions.

From a Structural Lens to a Cultural Lens on Strategic Error Management

Structure in organizations refers to the set of roles within which people are supposed to operate and interact. A typical "good" structure aims at preventing errors, for example, the double-checks or the "four-eyes principle" before important decisions; think also of a transposition of software that asks users to confirm they indeed want to delete files. Yet, as colloquium participants pointed out, structure offers no guarantee against errors. Experience shows that strategic errors occur even when all rules are respected, as discussed later in the definitions of lower- and higher-order errors. Then, an escalation of commitment prevents undoing the errors (Staw 1981), all the more so due to error contexts triggering strong and negative emotions (Huy 2012; Vuori and Huy 2015). Guilt, shame, and fear in turn lead to counterproductive behaviors such as denial and cover-ups (Giolito and Verdin 2016c; Shimizu and Hitt 2004). A second source of trouble with structure is that it may eventually hinder organizational success, particularly in a dynamic context (Eisenhardt 1989a). A colloquium participant shared his experience: "We put so many processes in place – such as who needs to do what, at which moment … Now we find ourselves in a situation in which our very structure becomes a barrier for innovation. We become risk-averse" (Giolito and Verdin 2016a).

Within a given structure, effective error management may hinge more on organizational culture, that is, "a pattern of shared basic assumptions" (Schein

2004) and beliefs that people hold about how to do the work and cooperate with each other as a result of belonging to the same group or organization. People derive their behaviors and attitudes from individual and—critically— organizational culture as enacted by organizational members, individually and collectively (Bandura 1977, 1991). More than structure, organizational culture may explain both error frequency and the quality of error management. One colloquium participant summed up: "Some organizational cultures drive people crazy. If you grow up in a shame culture, like when you get humiliated if you say something stupid in class, you are not going to acknowledge errors. If you have guilt, you are more likely to try to fix things or to cover up and hope for the better" (Giolito and Verdin 2016a).

In other words, creating or maintaining the wrong culture may constitute the biggest error of all. Organizational cultures in which people feel psychologically safe believe that they may speak their minds when it comes to important organizational outcomes such as safety, thereby promoting effective strategic error management (Edmondson 1999; Nembhard and Edmondson 2006). A participant in our colloquium cited a consulting firm in which people have not only the right but also "the obligation to dissent." Even the most junior person should express their opinion regarding matters of collective interest. In another firm, people are evaluated on the quality of their "critical conversation," referring to their ability to raise important points.

When people share a belief of mutual trust, they are more prone to acknowledge errors, even their own, and pass on the task of correcting errors to someone else. One participant recounted: "When someone commits an error, it is difficult to stay objective and analyze the situation. In our organization, we advocate that people involved in the error should not try to solve it by themselves. With negative emotions linked to the error, they can make bad decisions. You should call a colleague" (Giolito and Verdin 2016a).

From a Focus on Individuals to Teams and Relationships

In organizations, the very phrase "strategic errors" is inevitably associated with the word "ego." Ego may be thought of as an overreliance on intuition: Individuals believe that they essentially can solve any situation by themselves. Participants in our colloquium noted that a CEO's ego is encouraged by a number of factors in the environment, for example, the media exemplifying "the CEO of the year." Ego goes hand in hand with a need for control, potentially up to the point that top executives develop the illusion that they can control everything in the organization—in other words, they can eliminate errors. "How to fight ego?" one participant in our colloquium asked. The first answer that emerged revolved around personal qualities of leaders. "Top executives should balance between system 1 and system 2 thinking," said one participant referencing the works of psychologist Daniel Kahneman (2012), in which system 1 denotes quasi-automatic thinking and system 2 involves deliberate intellectual effort. "It's all about leadership" was a sentence voiced by both academic and executive participants of our colloquium.

Yet, leadership characteristics that foster effective strategic error management may appear paradoxical, with unlikely combinations of empathy and boldness. For example, one panel participant advocated "confident humility": An executive has to be humble enough to listen and adjust to others' opinions, yet confident enough to make bold decisions when necessary. Humility might lead top executives to undergo recurrent error-management training, it was suggested, as large error episodes are possibly too rare to get sufficient experience (March et al. 1991).

Leadership is a relationship, however, and CEOs should be aware of human nature to the point that they understand how their behavior impacts this relationship with the rest of the organization. Here again, there may be a paradox, as the need for alignment competes with the need for checks and balances. However, frequent and transparent dialogue should be an efficient way to detect error signals early on, recognize the errors, and act in time. "Many people believe that if they disagree with others, it will damage the relationship, but it is just a mental model. Yet there can be another mental model in which disagreement is going to improve the relationship" (Giolito and Verdin 2016a).

Because corporate strategy and governance are tightly linked, of particular importance is the relationship between the executive team and the board of directors. In addition, beyond the executives' personal relationships with individuals, an important factor for efficient error management may also reside in teams. Recalling an experience of personally making a strategic mistake, one participant shared how the solution was found only because he openly shared with colleagues (see also Edmondson 1999). Whether in a top management team or on a board of directors, a transparent functioning allows one "to be open and acknowledge that an error was made, and to engage the whole team to solve it." As one of our participants put it, "it is a 'we' feeling" instead of a personification of power.

In sum, as executives and academics recognize that strategic error management becomes a critical feature of exercising the highest responsibility in an organization, their thinking on the matter tends to coalesce on a triple shift toward processes, culture, and relationships. Taking stock of those insights and extant research, we sought to better identify key building blocks and relationships for what may emerge as a theory of strategic error management.

Refined Definitions for Strategic Error Management

The model we offer for strategic error management builds on a body of research initiated by psychologists (e.g., Reason 1990; Tversky and Kahneman 1973) and organizational scholars (e.g., Perrow 1999; Roberts 1990a; Weick et al. 2005). Specifically, our works were inspired by the small research community that focuses on organizational errors and error management and proposed the initial building blocks of theory (Frese and Keith 2015; Goodman et al. 2011; Hofmann and Frese 2011b; Lei et al. 2016). In addition to our panel, our own grounded-theory research (Corbin and Strauss 1990; Glaser and Strauss 1967; Suddaby 2006) consisted of a number of case studies (Eisenhardt 1989b; Eisenhardt and Graebner 2007), particularly of collapses and near-collapses of banks in Europe since 2007, and the content analysis of a series of interviews with 20 top executives in large European financial organizations representing close to one million employees and a market value of several hundred billion euros (Giolito and Verdin 2016b). From there we derived a number of constructs that clarify prior conceptualization and help integrate them in the fields of strategy and upper echelons theory (Carpenter et al. 2004; Felin 2005; Hambrick and Mason 1984; Teece 2007; Whittington 1996; Whittington and Cailluet 2008; Whittington et al. 2006).

Organizational Errors

Developing prior insights (Goodman et al. 2011; Hofmann and Frese 2011a), we refer to organizational errors as decisions by organizational actors that unintentionally represent a double deviation from (a) organizationally specified rules or norms of action and (b) the organization's objectives and goals. Our level of analysis here is not the erroneous decision of any individual but that of the organization, be it a two-member team or a multinational corporation. For an illustration based on the Tenerife air disaster in 1977 (Weick 1990), when the crew of an aircraft neglect to properly check clearance for takeoff, it is a collective deviation from safety procedures. The crew does so unintentionally, in part because they thought clearance was self-evident while they were under time pressure to complete their flight on a tight schedule. The

negligence results in a disaster, as the aircraft hits another jet on the runway—
a major deviation from everything that is expected of a regular airline.

A single initial deviation from organizationally prescribed rules and norms
that may *potentially* lead to adverse consequences at the organizational level
may be analyzed as a *latent error* (Ramanujam 2003; Ramanujam and
Goodman 2003). The error remains latent unless other factors favor or trigger
the consequences, which may take just seconds or years, if not decades. In the
Tenerife air disaster, the negligence regarding takeoff clearance is a latent error
that would have remained inconsequential if not for the heavy fog preventing
the crew from seeing the other jet on the runway. It is worth noting that, in
organizational errors, individual actors exert their roles in good faith. In the
air disaster again, it is the interaction among the crew and between the crew
and other highly trained actors—for example, air traffic control, crew of other
aircraft—following the initial erroneous decision to take off that brings about
the catastrophe (Weick 1990).

Lower- and Higher-Order Errors

Complementing prior taxonomies of organizational errors based either on the
level of cognitive control (Hofmann and Frese 2011a) or temporality and pri-
oritization (Lei et al. 2016), we introduce a distinction between lower-order and
higher-order errors. Lower-order errors refer to deviations from clear and concrete rules and norms. Higher-order errors refer to situations in which an organizational rule itself is "wrong," that is, it deviates from higher principles, which
may range from legal principles to commonsense rules including safety of people and organizational survival. Lei and associates (2016), among others, aptly
singled out the role of conflicting rules in organizational errors. A final reference
to the Tenerife air disaster (Weick 1990) may clarify those points.

In airlines, "safety first" is a cardinal rule, from which derive a number of
detailed procedures, for example, the obligation to double-check clearance. In
Tenerife, it appears that the rest of the crew did not react when the captain
decided to take off without proper clearance. The crew complied to the rule
of hierarchy and not the rule of safety. In airlines, the deviation that separates
the rule in-practice (hierarchy) from the rule (safety) represents a higher-order
error that the entire industry has been fighting against for decades through
crew resource management (Hagen 2013, 2014). For another example in
business settings, investigations into rogue trading scandals often reveal that
the culture on the trading desks—beyond the mindset of the specific individual involved in intentional, fraudulent behavior—is concerned with

making money by any means possible rather than abiding by legal rules, let alone commonsense principles of prudence (Giolito and Verdin 2016b).

Strategic Errors

Strategic error is a "lay construct" (Wright and Cropanzano 2004) rather than a precise, well-defined, and well-researched concept. In the perspective of strategic error management, we refer to strategic errors as all organizational errors that cast doubts on the strategy of an organization, that is, its key goals (including survival and preservation of its independence), its resources (e.g., critical competencies and capability for profit), and more generally its sustainable competitive advantage (e.g., Barney 1991). Based on that definition, strategic errors first include errors in strategy decisions—such as when Kodak repeatedly refuses to invest in digital photography or Nokia fails to convert to smartphones—up to their respective and ultimate demise (D'Aprix 2012; Vuori and Huy 2015). In such occurrences, top executives are at the origin of the error as often as a team is (Eubanks and Mumford 2010; Hunter et al. 2011; Shimizu and Hitt 2011). Second, strategic errors encompass organizational errors that originate at lower levels of the hierarchy but eventually result in adverse consequences for the entire organization. Examples range from disasters in industrial facilities (e.g., Hoffman and Devereaux Jennings 2011) to "rogue trading" scandals in banks (e.g., Gumbel 2008).

Strategic Error Management

Regardless of whether the organizational error occurred at the top or the bottom of the hierarchy, strategic error management refers to all actions that top executives of an organization undertake (or fail to) in order to disconnect latent errors from actual and potential adverse consequences, repair the damage done, learn from the errors, and seize potential new strategic opportunities emerging from the errors (Frese and Keith 2015). When the magnitude of the errors challenges an organization's strategy, it falls on CEOs to step in and make critical decisions. Hagen (2014) aptly proposed a parallel between flight deck critical situations and strategic error management.

Our research suggests that, notwithstanding many similarities, top executives' handling of organizational errors differs in a number of ways (Giolito 2015). First, as they carry the responsibility for the entire organization, they face an extreme level of complexity, all the more so when the organization is highly interconnected with its environment on a daily—sometimes hourly—basis, as is the case with banks. Complexity is compounded by the fact that indicators of effective error management are diverse, from preservation of profit to organizational reputation, and new stakeholders emerge during the error-management process, for example, politicians and the media. Second, top executives mostly rely on indirect and "soft" leadership skills in teams, where they cannot take for granted that all interests neatly align with their own and the organization's. Lastly, top executives by definition have little or no experience of strategic error management (March et al. 1991), let alone any specific training (Giolito and Verdin 2016a).

A Theoretical Model for Strategic Error Management

Beyond refining definitions, our research on top executives led us to delineate a theoretical model for effective strategic error management (see Fig. 4.1). We identified a three-step cycle that we refer to as "triple A," standing for Assessing error signals, Acknowledging errors, and Acting upon errors (Giolito and Verdin 2016b, c). Top executives who are able to iteratively follow the steps may spare their organizations the most damaging consequences stemming from organizational errors.

Assessing Error Signals

For top executives, the first step in strategic error management consists of identifying error signals, that is, information that is intuitively discrepant with prior assumptions. Error signals remind us of the discrepant cues that sensemaking theory pointed to (e.g., Weick 1988). In our framework, however, error signals refer to pieces of information perceived by top executives that are only consistent with there being a latent and hidden organizational error. Error signals are discrepancies, positive or negative. Executives we interviewed in our investigation insisted that when things go too well beyond expectations and understanding, a latent error is likely. For example, the CEO of a banking group recalled that one division reported record profits for a number of years, without disclosing the exact nature of its competitive advantage over peers in the same business. Eventually, he discovered that those profits essentially came from highly speculative operations far from the group's core activity, combined with sloppy accounting. Or, in the words of another

CEO: "If there's an entity where I never see an audit report or a compliance report issue raised, I'm much more scared than [with] those entities that sometimes have an unsatisfactory audit report. Because it's not possible. It's not possible that everything is OK."

Effective strategic error management requires top executives to mentally take note of such signals while clarifying the norm they base their judgment on and asking for additional information. This process may best be described as intuitive (Dane and Pratt 2007; Hodgkinson et al. 2009; Salas et al. 2010). Oftentimes, higher-order errors are signaled by the actual occurrence of a lower-order error. For example, that a trader violates his limits without sanction, that is, a lower-order error, signals a higher-order error consisting of a culture of making profit, regardless of the risks. Simultaneously, top executives actively assess the magnitude and the timeframe of the potential consequences that underlying latent errors may carry. This process relies on imagination exercises, in the form of "What if?" questions, including worst-case scenarios. It is more deliberate than when contrasted to automatic thinking (Kahneman 2012). Deliberation is essentially individual, although it may involve some dialogue with people top executives trust. It eventually leads them to draw the conclusion that something is wrong.

Acknowledging Errors

Interviews with CEOs, case studies, and our panel discussion converged to identify the acknowledgment of organizational errors by top executives as the critical step in effective strategic error management (Giolito and Verdin 2016c). Acknowledging errors refers to top executives mentally and individually constructing an organizational story that includes the error, then sharing this story with others. In that story, both the referent rule and the deviation are identified: Top executives clarify and contrast what should have been done against what has been done. To overcome reluctance and inertia (Shimizu and Hitt 2005), it helps when this story can be categorized into typical errors, that is, "explained" by the organization complying with other, legitimate priorities (Lei et al. 2016). For example, faced with the obligation of recalling millions of defective cars, the CEO of Toyota explained the lack of quality control as the result of a strategic focus on production growth.

The acknowledgment must be shared. Depending on the potential consequences of the error, the audience may be limited to closest associates or spread throughout the organization or beyond. An essential condition for effective strategic error management is that error acknowledgment emanates from the top of the organization, as noted by a CEO recounting an episode that cost his insurance group millions of euros in penalties. "I wrote to all staff to say: One, we haven't done what was to be done; and two, we are going to admit together that, today, the development of our company hinges on our capability to be at the right level of compliance. Of course it's me, as the CEO, who says that, because otherwise it's not true" (Giolito and Verdin 2016b).

Another condition resides in presenting the error as being collective and organizational. We noted significant differences in the final outcomes of organizational errors between those where executives attributed wrongful decisions to the organization and those where executives identified one individual as the sole guilty party. Specifically, reputation damages appear to be much lower in the former case. A participant on our panel summarized: Acknowledging errors as organizational "contributes to create an organizational culture of 'we' instead of 'I' and 'they'" (Giolito and Verdin 2016a). It also helps to defuse negative emotions generated by strategic errors and change (Vuori and Huy 2015). As an example of acknowledging collective errors, a CEO on our panel recalled himself taking full responsibility on behalf of his firm for a mistake inadvertently made by one collaborator on the shop floor level.

Acting Upon Errors

Telling a new organizational story that includes errors allows top executives to make a number of decisions that break with prior strategy and escape typical effects of commitment escalation (Staw 1976, 1981; Staw et al. 1997). Our research showed the action phase of strategic error management as being somewhat less cognitively and organizationally complex than the previous two, as executives again face problem-solving issues they are used to dealing with. However, we drew several complementary insights. First, communicating about the error constitutes an important part of action—far beyond initial error acknowledgment. "The first thing is that you inform everyone there's a big incident. You inform the constituents that there's a big incident. And you explain the way you want to approach it" (Giolito and Verdin 2016b).

Communication may involve an apology to the victims and the stakeholders of the error, as apologizing has been shown to be associated with lower adverse consequences, even when the organization faces civil criminal charges (Cohen 2000; Ho and Liu 2011; Schweitzer et al. 2015).

Second, acting upon errors provides top executives with new room for maneuver and often opens up new opportunities. Of particular importance is the possibility for strategic change, as illustrated by a chairman in the banking industry. "In no more than 10 days [after public acknowledgment], we changed the CEO and we completed an important spinoff, and then we launched the refinancing plan and the public offering in the stock market. We hadn't been able to make this happen in the previous five years" (Giolito and Verdin 2016a).

Finally, the action phase should be understood not as an ending but a new beginning. We refer to our AAA model not as a linear process but as an iterative cycle, where actions taken to effectively manage strategic errors create a new organizational situation with new rules and, hence, new potential deviations, that is, new and inevitable errors.

Discussion and Directions for Research and Practice

Based on empirical research conducted in the banking industry in particular, the aim of this chapter is to show the relevance of strategic error management and offer a number of theoretical insights. We found top executives extremely concerned with strategic error management and, perhaps surprisingly, relatively open to sharing their experiences of organizational errors, including errors of their own. Our findings tend to confirm that error management on the part of top executives might be as important for organizations as it is for professionals in high-risk activities such as flying planes and surgical operations. Refining extant definitions, we also identified a model of effective strategic error management that includes error acknowledgment as a pivotal point by which top executives—building on the initial assessment of error signals—may act appropriately to disconnect latent errors from potentially disastrous organizational consequences.

By highlighting error acknowledgment, we complement prior frameworks developed by sensemaking theory (e.g., Weick 1988). More specifically, we developed prior works on errors at the top of the hierarchy that identified barriers and enablers to error management (Shimizu and Hitt 2004). Adding error acknowledgment to the mechanisms of strategic error management brings about a more refined understanding of strategic errors in the broader sense. It also helps bridge sensemaking and sensegiving at the executive level (Gioia and Chittipeddi 1991; Weick et al. 2005), as acknowledging errors actually consists of giving a new sense to the organizational story for its members and stakeholders. In that regard, strategic error management might also be analyzed as a decisive stage for strategic change. Additionally, in corporate and business settings, proposing strategic error management as a critical element of executives' roles sheds new light on the development of dynamic capabilities that allow organizations to successfully navigate in fast-changing environments (Eisenhardt 1989a; Teece 2007).

Implications for Research

Our developments, based on grounded-theory investigations, may mark a milestone in the research cycle on strategic error management. With constructs now being defined with more precision, we would invite scholars to consider going beyond qualitative studies and begin the endeavor of laying the ground for investigations based on statistical methods (Edmondson and McManus 2007). This quantitative endeavor might be undertaken in two ways. First, researchers may want to build instruments for making constructs such as error signal assessment and error acknowledgment observable and measurable variables, for example, by developing scales for surveying executives and organizations or even imagining more inventive research designs. With the latter suggestion in mind, scholars may take inspiration from studies that gathered data on seemingly controversial topics from poorly accessible sources: For instance, Hayward and Hambrick (1997) measured executive hubris by classifying CEO exposure in the media. A second avenue for quantitative studies may reside in the statistical analysis of aggregated episodes of error management, following the way paved by Haunschild and Sullivan (2002) and Shimizu and Hitt (2005). In parallel, we naturally encourage colleagues to pursue qualitative studies with the aim of gaining a fine-grained understanding of personal, interpersonal, and organizational dynamics that enable or thwart effective strategic error management. Ethnography might help, possibly associated with consulting work in the tradition of action research (e.g., Argyris 1988).

Implications for Practice

As strategic error management is shown to be an important part of organizational strategy, top executives may want to include it more explicitly in their approach to their roles. We would encourage them to recognize that errors make for an inevitable part of organizational life, whatever the precautions taken ex ante and, for that very reason, be prepared to handle errors in a process-based view. Our AAA model may be of help here, as it invites organizational actors to (a) manage strategic errors based on their potential consequences for the organization, with the aim of removing connotations of individual guilt and shame that trigger reflexes of denial and cover-up and, by contrast, precisely delineating relevant rules and deviations; (b) transparently acknowledge organizational, strategic errors as a by-product of ordinary organizational life, thus fostering a collective and collaborative problem-solving approach; and (c) take appropriate action based on new strategic stories, while being prepared to seize unexpected opportunities—and remaining aware that the future inevitably will entail new organizational errors. A final recommendation may be addressed to consultants and business educators for integrating strategic error management in their work in the form of training, simulations, and case-based exercises.

Conclusion

As part of the broader effort for developing knowledge on error management, we set out to focus on top executives and strategic errors. An underlying characteristic of our research is its positioning at the intersection of a number of disciplines, specifically strategy and managerial cognition. We believe that, in the future, both research and practice will benefit from insights developed in other areas, such as leadership. We can only encourage readers in that direction.

References

Argyris, C. 1988. Crafting a theory of practice: The case of organizational paradoxes. In *Paradox and transformation: Toward a theory of change in organization and management*, ed. R.E. Quinn and K.S. Cameron, 255–278. Cambridge, MA: Ballinger Publishing.

Bandura, A. 1977. *Social learning theory*. Englewood Cliffs: Prentice Hall.

———. 1991. Social cognitive theory of self-regulation. *Organizational Behavior and Human Decision Processes* 50 (2): 248–287.

Barney, J. 1991. Firm resources and sustained competitive advantage. *Journal of Management* 17 (1): 99–120.

Baron, R.S. 2005. So right it's wrong: Groupthink and the ubiquitous nature of polarized group decision making. *Advances in Experimental Social Psychology* 37: 219–253.

Bryant, C., and A. Sharman. 2015. Martin Winterkorn resigns as VW boss over emissions scandal. *Financial Times*, September 23. https://www.ft.com/content/d2288862-61d1-11e5-97e9-7f0bf5e7177b

Carpenter, M., M. Geletkanycz, and G. Sanders. 2004. Upper echelons research revisited: Antecedents, elements, and consequences of top management team composition. *Journal of Management* 30 (6): 749–778. https://doi.org/10.1016/j.jm.2004.06.001.

Cohen, J.R. 2000. Apology and organizations: exploring an example from medical practice. *Fordham Urban Law Journal* 27: 1447–1482.

Corbin, J.M., and A. Strauss. 1990. Grounded theory research: Procedures, canons, and evaluative criteria. *Qualitative Sociology* 13 (1): 3–21.

D'Aprix, R. 2012. Kodak's demise: Denial and truth in a difficult world. *Strategic Communication Management* 16 (3): 10.

Dane, E., and M.G. Pratt. 2007. Exploring intuition and its role in managerial decision making. *Academy of Management Review* 32 (1): 33–54.

Edmondson, A. 1999. Psychological safety and learning behavior in work teams. *Administrative Science Quarterly* 44 (2): 350–383.

Edmondson, A.C., and S.E. McManus. 2007. Methodological fit in management field research. *Academy of Management Review* 32 (4): 1246–1264.

Eisenhardt, K.M. 1989a. Making fast strategic decisions in high-velocity environments. *Academy of Management Journal* 32 (3): 543–576.

———. 1989b. Building theories from case study research. *Academy of Management Review* 14 (4): 532–550.

Eisenhardt, K.M., and M.E. Graebner. 2007. Theory building from cases: Opportunities and challenges. *Academy of Management Journal* 50 (1): 25–32.

Eubanks, D.L., and M.D. Mumford. 2010. Leader errors and the influence on performance: An investigation of differing levels of impact. *The Leadership Quarterly* 21 (5): 809–825. https://doi.org/10.1016/j.leaqua.2010.07.009.

Felin, T. 2005. Strategic organization: A field in search of micro-foundations. *Strategic Organization* 3 (4): 441–455. https://doi.org/10.1177/1476127005055796.

Frese, M., and N. Keith. 2015. Action errors, error management, and learning in organizations. *Annual Review of Psychology* 66 (1): 661–687. https://doi.org/10.1146/annurev-psych-010814-015205.

Gioia, D.A., and K. Chittipeddi. 1991. Sensemaking and sensegiving in strategic change initiation. *Strategic Management Journal* 12 (6): 433–448.

Giolito, V.J. 2015. *Managing organizational errors: Three theoretical lenses on a bank collapse.* Brussels: Solvay Brussels School of Economics & Management Working Paper. https://dipot.ulb.ac.be/dspace/bitstream/2013/208371/3/wp15033.pdf

Giolito, V.J., and P. Verdin. 2016a. *From wrong to right – Error management conference and summit report.* Brussels: Solvay Brussels School of Economics & Management. https://www.dropbox.com/s/usbfwk7tx948pwb/160926%20l%20Error%20Mgt%20Summit%20Report.pdf?dl=0

———. 2016b. From wrong to right: A multi-source investigation of organizational error management by top executives. Presented at the AOM annual meeting, Anaheim.

———. 2016c. From wrong to right: The critical role of error acknowledgment in managing strategic errors. Presented at the strategic management society annual meeting, Berlin.

Glaser, B., and A. Strauss. 1967. *The discovery of grounded theory. Strategies for qualitative research.* Mill Valley: The Sociology Press.

Goodman, P.S., R. Ramanujam, J.S. Carroll, A.C. Edmondson, D.A. Hofmann, and K.M. Sutcliffe. 2011. Organizational errors: Directions for future research. *Research in Organizational Behavior* 31: 151–176. https://doi.org/10.1016/j.riob.2011.09.003.

Gray, A. 2016. Wells Fargo loses status as world's most valuable bank. *Financial Times,* September 14. https://www.ft.com/content/cfda2e06-79ba-11e6-97ae-647294649b28

Gumbel, P. 2008. Saving Société Générale. *Fortune* 157 (8): 106–114.

Hagen, J. 2013. *Confronting mistakes: Lessons from the aviation industry when dealing with error.* Houndmills/Basingstoke/Hampshire: Palgrave Macmillan.

———. 2014. Applying airline error management principles on the ground: An interview with Jan U. Hagen, author of confronting mistakes: Lessons from the aviation industry when dealing with error. *Strategic Direction* 30 (2): 34–35. https://doi.org/10.1108/SD-02-2014-0009.

Hambrick, D.C., and P.A. Mason. 1984. Upper echelons: The organization as a reflection of its top managers. *The Academy of Management Review* 9 (2): 193. https://doi.org/10.2307/258434.

Haunschild, P.R., and B.N. Sullivan. 2002. Learning from complexity: Effects of prior accidents and incidents on airlines' learning. *Administrative Science Quarterly* 47 (4): 609–643.

Hayward, M.L., and D.C. Hambrick. 1997. Explaining the premiums paid for large acquisitions: Evidence of CEO hubris. *Administrative Science Quarterly* 42: 103–127.

Ho, B., and E. Liu. 2011. Does sorry work? The impact of apology laws on medical malpractice. *Journal of Risk and Uncertainty* 43 (2): 141–167.

Hodgkinson, G.P., E. Sadler-Smith, L.A. Burke, G. Claxton, and P.R. Sparrow. 2009. Intuition in organizations: Implications for strategic management. *Long Range Planning* 42 (3): 277–297. https://doi.org/10.1016/j.lrp.2009.05.003.

Hoffman, A.J., and P. Devereaux Jennings. 2011. The BP oil spill as a cultural anomaly? Institutional context, conflict, and change. *Journal of Management Inquiry* 20 (2): 100–112. https://doi.org/10.1177/1056492610394940.

Hofmann, D.A., and M. Frese. 2011a. Errors, error taxonomies, error prevention and error management: Laying the groundwork for discussing errors in organizations. In *Errors in organizations*, ed. D.A. Hofmann and M. Frese, 1–44. New York: Psychology Press.

———, eds. 2011b. *Errors in organizations*. New York: Psychology Press.

Hunter, S.T., B.W. Tate, J.L. Dzieweczynski, and K.E. Bedell-Avers. 2011. Leaders make mistakes: A multilevel consideration of why. *The Leadership Quarterly* 22 (2): 239–258. https://doi.org/10.1016/j.leaqua.2011.02.001.

Huy, Q.N. 2012. Emotions in strategic organization: Opportunities for impactful research. *Strategic Organization* 10 (3): 240.

Janis, I.L. 1997. *Groupthink*. Notre Dame: University of Notre Dame Press.

Kahneman, D. 2012. *Thinking, fast and slow*. London: Penguin.

Lei, Z., E. Naveh, and Z. Novikov. 2016. Errors in organizations: An integrative review via level of analysis, temporal dynamism, and priority lenses. *Journal of Management* 2 (5): 1315–1343.

Lovallo, D., and D. Kahneman. 2003. Delusions of success. *Harvard Business Review* 81 (7): 56–63.

Makary, M.A., and M. Daniel. 2016. Medical error – The third leading cause of death in the US. *British Medical Journal*: i2139. https://doi.org/10.1136/bmj.i2139.

March, J.G., L.S. Sproull, and M. Tamuz. 1991. Learning from samples of one or fewer. *Organization Science* 2 (1): 1–13.

Nembhard, I.M., and A.C. Edmondson. 2006. Making it safe: The effects of leader inclusiveness and professional status on psychological safety and improvement efforts in health care teams. *Journal of Organizational Behavior* 27 (7): 941–966. https://doi.org/10.1002/job.413.

Panko, R.R. 1998. What we know about spreadsheet errors. *Journal of Organizational and End User Computing (JOEUC)* 10 (2): 15–21.

———. 2008. Spreadsheet errors: What we know. What we think we can do. *arXiv Preprint arXiv:0802.3457*. http://arxiv.org/abs/0802.3457

Perrow, C. 1999. *Normal accidents – Living with high-risk technologies*. Edition: Updated. Princeton: Princeton University Press.

Ramanujam, R. 2003. The effects of discontinuous change on latent errors in organizations: The moderating role of risk. *Academy of Management Journal* 46 (5): 608–617. https://doi.org/10.2307/30040652.

Ramanujam, R., and P.S. Goodman. 2003. Latent errors and adverse organizational consequences: A conceptualization. *Journal of Organizational Behavior* 24 (7): 815–836. https://doi.org/10.1002/job.218.

Reason, J. 1990. *Human error*. First ed. Cambridge: Cambridge University Press.

———. 2000. Human error: Models and management. *British Medical Journal* 320 (7237): 768–770.

Roberts, K.H. 1990a. Managing high-reliability organizations. *California Management Review* 32 (4): 101.

———. 1990b. Some characteristics of one type of high-reliability organization. *Organization Science* 1 (2): 160–176.

Salas, E., M.A. Rosen, and D. DiazGranados. 2010. Expertise-based intuition and decision making in organizations. *Journal of Management* 36 (4): 941–973. https://doi.org/10.1177/0149206309350084.

Schein, E.H. 2004. *Organizational culture and leadership*. Third ed. San Francisco: Jossey-Bass.

Schweitzer, M.E., A.W. Brooks, and A.D. Galinsky. 2015. The organizational apology. *Harvard Business Review* 93 (9): 44–52.

Shimizu, K., and M.A. Hitt. 2004. Strategic flexibility: Organizational preparedness to reverse ineffective strategic decisions. *The Academy of Management Executive* 18 (4): 44–59.

———. 2005. What constrains or facilitates divestitures of formerly acquired firms? The effects of organizational inertia. *Journal of Management* 31 (1): 50–72. https://doi.org/10.1177/0149206304271381.

———. 2011. Errors at the top of the hierarchy. In *Errors in organizations*, ed. D.A. Hofmann and M. Frese, 199ff. New York: Psychology Press.

Shrivastava, P. 1987. *Bhopal: Anatomy of crisis*. Illustrated ed. Cambridge, MA: Ballinger Publishing.

Starbuck, W.H., and F.J. Milliken. 1988. Challenger: Fine-tuning the odds until something breaks. *Journal of Management Studies* 25 (4): 319–342.

Staw, B.M. 1976. Knee-deep in the big muddy: A study of escalating commitment to a chosen course of action. *Organizational Behavior and Human Performance* 16 (1): 27–44.

———. 1981. The escalation of commitment to a course of action. *The Academy of Management Review* 6 (4): 577. https://doi.org/10.2307/257636.

Staw, B.M., S.G. Barsade, and K.W. Koput. 1997. Escalation at the credit window: A longitudinal study of bank executives' recognition and write-off of problem loans. *Journal of Applied Psychology* 82 (1): 130.

Suddaby, R. 2006. From the editors: What grounded theory is not. *Academy of Management Journal* 49 (4): 633–642.

Teece, D.J. 2007. Explicating dynamic capabilities: The nature and microfoundations of (sustainable) enterprise performance. *Strategic Management Journal* 28 (13): 1319–1350. https://doi.org/10.1002/smj.640.

Tversky, A., and D. Kahneman. 1973. Availability: A heuristic for judging frequency and probability. *Cognitive Psychology* 5 (2): 207–232.

Vuori, T.O., and Q.N. Huy. 2015. Distributed attention and shared emotions in the innovation process: How Nokia lost the smartphone battle. *Administrative Science Quarterly.* https://doi.org/10.1177/0001839215606951.

Weick, K.E. 1988. Enacted sensemaking in crisis situations. *Journal of Management Studies* 25 (4): 305–317.

———. 1990. The vulnerable system: An analysis of the Tenerife air disaster. *Journal of Management* 16 (3): 571–593.

Weick, K.E., and K.M. Sutcliffe. 2007. *Managing the unexpected: Resilient performance in an age of uncertainty.* Second ed. San Francisco: Jossey-Bass.

Weick, K.E., K.M. Sutcliffe, and D. Obstfeld. 2005. Organizing and the process of sensemaking. *Organization Science* 16 (4): 409–421. https://doi.org/10.1287/orsc.1050.0133.

Wells, P., and A. Gray. 2016. Deutsche Bank agrees to pay $7.2bn to settle DoJ probe. *Financial Times*, December 23. https://www.ft.com/content/785232ab-79b1-32de-843d-04c9f680e539

Whittington, R. 1996. Strategy as practice. *Long Range Planning* 29 (5): 731–735.

Whittington, R., and L. Cailluet. 2008. The crafts of strategy. *Long Range Planning* 41 (3): 241–247. https://doi.org/10.1016/j.lrp.2008.03.003.

Whittington, R., E. Molloy, M. Mayer, and A. Smith. 2006. Practices of strategising/organising. *Long Range Planning* 39 (6): 615–629. https://doi.org/10.1016/j.lrp.2006.10.004.

Wright, T.A., and R. Cropanzano. 2004. The role of psychological well-being in job performance. *Organizational Dynamics* 33 (4): 338–351. https://doi.org/10.1016/j.orgdyn.2004.09.002.

5

The Strategic Imperative of Psychological Safety and Organizational Error Management

Amy C. Edmondson and Paul J. Verdin

Despite considerable discussion in the management literature about the need for flexible strategies and agile learning organizations, many—if not most—large organizations and their strategy processes remain top-down, slow to change, and fraught with obstacles to learning. A "strategy-as-learning" approach is presented that contrasts with the dominant conception of strategy-as-planning. Conceptualizing and practicing the work of organizational strategy as a learning process implies that strategy is about developing good questions and thoughtful hypotheses to be tested through execution. This produces a mode of operating called execution-as-learning.

Strategy-as-learning requires psychological safety, which enables speaking up, dissenting, error reporting, candidly discussing risks, and practicing organizational error management. Without these behaviors, especially at the executive levels, organizations are at risk of experiencing avoidable strategic failures.

A. C. Edmondson
Boston, USA

P. J. Verdin
Brussels, Belgium

© The Author(s) 2018
J. U. Hagen (ed.), *How Could This Happen?*, https://doi.org/10.1007/978-3-319-76403-0_5

A growing body of research emphasizes the importance of psychological safety for error management. In particular, in dynamic contexts that benefit from an iterative, improvement-oriented approach, psychological safety fosters operational effectiveness by enabling candid interpersonal interactions, which include proactively seeking help, being open about errors, and experimenting. Most research on errors and psychological safety has taken place in operational contexts rather than in the realm of organizational strategy or strategic management. An aim of this chapter is to examine the need for psychological safety and a learning approach in strategy development, to complement its role in execution and operations management. Our goal is to develop ideas for research and practice to help prevent strategic errors in organizations. To do this, we start with a distinction in the literature between organizational errors and individual human errors and explain why organizational errors have critical strategic importance for organizations. We also review research on organizational errors and conditions that help reduce their occurrence.

We build on this prior research to offer a new perspective on strategy—that it is a dynamic learning process characterized by frequent updating, in which creativity and learning-by-doing are deemed to be as important to success as analysis. We also draw from prior work that distinguishes between "execution-as-efficiency" and "execution-as-learning" to develop the concept of "strategy-as-learning." Strategy-as-learning is an iterative approach to strategy—a leadership mindset and set of practices—that comprises an alternative to conceiving of strategy as an analytic planning exercise.

In the sections that follow, we first conduct a brief review of research on organizational errors and psychological safety. We then present our emerging ideas about strategic errors and why psychological safety may help prevent them or manage them. We reflect on recent, well-publicized examples of organizational errors of strategic proportion occurring at the top in large and respected corporations around the world. These cases suggest the need for a new way of thinking about strategic failures to help reduce or avoid the incidence of major organizational errors. Building on these cases, we articulate a "strategy-as-learning" approach that contrasts with the traditional and still dominant concept of "strategy-as-planning." The latter views strategy formulation and implementation as distinct and separate activities, whereas the former shows them to be inextricably intertwined and more appropriate for today's need for continuous innovation and value creation in dynamic environments. We conclude with a brief discussion of the implications of our ideas and suggest directions for future research.

Organizational Errors and Psychological Safety

Organizational errors are those involving the actions of multiple organizational participants and have the potential to result in adverse organizational outcomes (Goodman et al. 2011). Such errors represent unintended deviations from organizational expectations about how to execute the work and involve multiple individuals acting within formal organizational roles; these errors carry a risk of harm and are primarily caused by organizational conditions, including values and rewards. An organizational error is thus different from an individual error occurring in an organizational context; notably, an organizational error is caused not by idiosyncratic features of one or more individuals (as frequently highlighted in popular academic and practitioner publications; e.g., Russo and Schoemaker 1989; Kahneman 2013; Roxburgh 2003) but rather by conditions present in the organization (Goodman et al. 2011). Organizational errors are not the result of simple human fallibility but rather can be traced to organizational conditions, policies, and even strategies. Error research has examined both kinds of errors—individual and organizational. In this chapter, we consider the latter.

In general, error research examines errors in the context of organizational operations. It has long been recognized that human error can disrupt the successful execution of the tasks and processes that transform inputs into products and services for customers (Reason 1984). Not surprisingly, given the importance of preventing major harm, the error literature is dominated by studies on errors in high-stakes industries and operational settings such as hospitals (Edmondson 1996; Rudolph 2003), airlines (Hackman 2003; Hagen 2013; Salas et al. 2001; Weick 1993), nuclear power (Carroll 1998; Perrow 1982), space exploration (Edmondson et al. 2005; Bohmer et al. 2009), and aircraft carriers (Weick and Roberts 1993). Nonetheless, errors in work execution are possible in any operational setting in which work is carried out by team(s) of people to provide products or services for stakeholders of all kinds, not all of which present the potential for dramatic consequences (e.g., Goodman et al. 2011).

In production and service operations, such as factories or call centers, errors are understood to be inevitable due to human fallibility (Rumelhart 1980; Norman 1981; Reason 1984) and to operational complexity (Perrow 1984). Thus, a key management challenge is finding ways to ensure that there are few errors, and that those that do occur are detected and corrected or contained before they cause harm to workers, customers, or reputations (e.g., Goodman et al. 2011). Importantly, errors sometimes occur without leading to harm, giving rise in the literature to the notion of "latent errors" (Edmondson 1996; Edmondson et al. 2005; Reason 1994).

Much can be learned about error and failure prevention from studies on high-reliability organizations (HROs). Defined as organizations that consistently operate without major adverse outcomes, despite carrying out inherently high-risk work (Roberts and Libuser 1993), HROs are argued to avoid experiencing catastrophic consequences of errors through the exercise of mindfulness and vigilance, among other work practices (Weick et al. 2000).

Among the most important factors affecting error and failure prevention are work design and work climate. Concretely, work design—in manufacturing and service operations—can incorporate fail-safe elements to reduce the likelihood of worker error (Chase and Stewart 1994). The Toyota production system, for example—considered by many to be the gold standard for operational excellence—includes a form of mistake-proofing called *poka-yoke*, which seeks to design tasks in ways that minimize deviation from proper execution, thus making errors less likely (Shingo 1986).

The work climate, in contrast, influences a worker's ability and willingness to detect and report errors and potential errors (Edmondson 1996). A widely employed variable in error research is psychological safety, defined as the degree to which people perceive their work environment as being conducive to speaking up; reporting and highlighting errors; asking for help; offering ideas; and other behaviors that create image risks for individuals (Edmondson 1999, 2003). In a psychologically safe environment, people believe that if they make a mistake, others will not penalize them or think less of them for it. They believe that others will not resent or humiliate them for reporting an error or asking for help, information, or feedback; nor for detecting, reporting, and discussing someone else's error. Psychological safety thus fosters the confidence to report, discuss, manage, and learn from error. Psychological safety also allows people to ask questions when in doubt about a procedure or result, and to team up to solve problems as they occur. Pointing out "what went wrong" in one's own or others' work is never easy, but psychological safety helps to mitigate defensiveness, allowing groups and organizations to talk about, better handle, and learn from errors.

A psychologically safe environment for discussing errors can be readily seen as useful in error management in any operational context that contains interdependent tasks. By confronting the chances and realities of operational errors directly and productively, organizations can reduce the risk of major failures—both safety and economic failures. For this reason, past research on psychological safety started with the assumption that organizations need to learn from their errors, and it emphasized the debilitating effects of interpersonal fear in blocking this goal. Empirical studies in a variety of operational settings have shown that a climate of psychological safety is associated with learning behaviors (Edmondson 1999), quality improvement (Tucker et al. 2007), and organizational and team performance (Baer and Frese 2003; Duhigg 2017; Edmondson 1999).

A robust finding with major implications for error management is that psychological safety tends to be a group-level phenomenon (Edmondson 1996, 1999; Edmondson and Mogelof 2006). Many studies have found that a group of individuals who work together (in a work team or unit) have similar perceptions of psychological safety within groups and significant differences in perceptions of psychological safety between groups, even within the same organization. These findings suggest that psychological safety is significantly influenced by proximal leaders and peers, adding to effects of senior executives or company founders, who play a major role in shaping the culture of an organization.

A seminal study in this line of work investigated medication errors in hospital patient-care units and discovered, unexpectedly, significant differences in nurses' beliefs about the social consequences of reporting medication errors (Edmondson 1996). The construct of team psychological safety was thus discovered by accident; the study had intended to show that better teams made fewer errors. Instead, it was discovered that teams varied in how willing and able they were to reveal and prevent errors, in a manner that was highly correlated with measures of team effectiveness in a well-validated survey. In some of the hospital teams, members openly acknowledged errors and discussed ways to avoid their recurrence; in others, members kept their knowledge of drug errors to themselves.

For example, a nurse in one team explained, "Mistakes are serious, because of the toxicity of the drugs [we use]—so you're never afraid to tell the Nurse Manager." In this statement, she reveals an almost taken-for-granted belief that the workplace is psychologically safe. Specifically, she understands the very real danger inherent in the work means that speaking up is expected and essential. In striking contrast, nurses in other units reported that people tended to hide mistakes. As one put it, "You get put on trial! People get blamed for mistakes" and talking about them was not easy. These responses—elicited in open-ended interviews about what it was like to work in the unit in question—illustrated markedly different beliefs about the psychological safety climate. In the first team, members saw it as self-evident that speaking up is natural and necessary for safety and learning. In the other team, speaking up was viewed as a last resort. From this contrast, the idea that psychological safety is important for detecting errors and learning from them took shape. Subsequent research has formalized the climate variable as being a potential influence on team learning and performance (Edmondson 1999).

This study, along with similar findings in other organizations and industries (Edmondson 1999, 2003; Nembhard and Edmondson 2006), suggests that error management behaviors differ substantially across groups within organizations. Given its importance in speaking up, psychological safety is vital for effective error management. Therefore, to ensure consistent, effective error management, senior executives must work to promote the development of consistently high levels of psychological safety throughout an organization, in part by providing training or coaching for mid- and lower-level managers (Edmondson 2012).

A closely related finding is that status and hierarchy affect psychological safety and, in turn, shape learning and prevention behaviors as well as the real-time management of errors as they occur. The effects of hierarchy on speaking up are well established in the field of aviation—especially in errors and crisis situations in the cockpit—and are the basis for crew resource management (CRM) training. CRM places priority on "the human factor" rather than prioritizing technology or technical skills, which may surprise the outsider, given the technological intensity and high stakes involved in the successful management of commercial airlines. Yet, the recognition of human factors (including interpersonal dynamics) has long been systematically implemented in pilot training and crew management (e.g., see Hagen 2013; Salas et al. 2001).

Specifically, the presence of those with higher status can inhibit the psychological safety of those with lower status—an effect that disappears with more inclusive leadership. Work groups with inclusive leaders are less likely to present status-based differences in psychological safety and more likely to successfully implement improvement or innovation projects (Nembhard and Edmondson 2006; Tucker et al. 2007).

A practical implication of this line of research is that senior executives who appreciate the role that psychological safety plays in error and risk management can invest in the development of leadership competencies throughout the organization. Organizations create and deliver value through distributed, interconnected work activities; the participation of those carrying out this work is essential—especially through sharing what they hear from customers, suppliers, and other sources of information about what may need to change. In sum, senior executives shape the policies and practices through which psychological safety is built, group by group, throughout an organization.

Organizational Errors and Strategic Failures

Organizational errors—involving actions of multiple participants with the potential for adverse organizational outcomes—encompass a wide range of possible failures across parts, levels, or regions of an organization. Most research, however, has focused on errors in operational contexts, as noted earlier, paying particular attention to psychological safety as an explanatory factor in error management. In this section, we consider the potential relevance of psychological safety and error management for strategy formulation and execution.

First, it should be clear that organizational errors occurring in operations may have strategic consequences if they cause harm to people, reputations, or financial performance—sometimes even jeopardizing the very survival of the organization. Second, strategy errors themselves can lead to major organizational failures. Strategy failures are often attributed to inadequate implementation, that is, to failures of execution. Both strategy failures and operational failures, therefore, can have strategic consequences. To illustrate this point, we first draw from recent highly publicized cases of organizational errors to build a foundation for a new strategic perspective and its significance for psychological safety and error management.

Organizational Errors with Strategic Consequences

We first consider organizational errors in operations that may have strategic consequences. Clearly, some organizational errors, if left unchecked, can bring down an entire organization, with obvious strategic implications, as events and public attention may escalate, bringing the potential for harm to organizational reputations, market positions, and financial performance, or the potential of civil or criminal liabilities.

Recent case studies provide telling examples of "operational errors" turning into "strategic errors." A crucial question—for theory and practice—is how strategic errors might be avoided. One possibility is that the better management of operational errors can reduce or prevent strategic errors. As a former CEO of a major global bank put it: "We know that *'sh-- happens'* all the time, [but] how can we make sure it does not hit the fan!?" Some recent cases expose some of the processes and conditions under which such escalation may happen—or be avoided (Roberto et al. 2006; Giles 2013; Giolito 2016; Hamwi et al. 2017).

In one case, a seemingly isolated incident of a rogue trader surpassing his trading limits and taking increasingly risky positions in the financial markets without proper control or correction led to a major disaster at French bank Societé Générale. In another, the shortcuts and cheating by a handful of engineers at Volkswagen led to one of the largest corporate disasters in recent history, almost bringing down one of the largest car companies in the world and costing tens of billions of dollars in actual liabilities and damages as well as loss in market cap.

An operational accident at Deep Water Horizon drilling rig led to one of the largest damages in history ever paid out by an oil company, or any company (Oualhadj and Giolito 2016). A sales practice in a part of Wells Fargo— one of the most admired retail banks in the United States—spiraled into one of the greatest corporate banking scandals of recent history. A potential fire hazard in an externally sourced component (the battery) of the Galaxy 7 smart phone led to a multi-billion dollar loss as well as huge reputation damage for Samsung. The April 2017 dramatic overbooking incident involving a single passenger on a routine commercial flight at United Airlines led to major damage to the airline's corporate reputation and financial value—and a call for a company boycott from a *Wall Street Journal* contributor. Questionable and, to many, objectionable practices to keep a cement plant operating in war-stricken Syria led to a major scandal and the resignation of the CEO at LafargeHolcim.

A myriad of less dramatic strategic mishaps never see the light of day (or the spotlight of the media). For instance, in one case, skipping steps in the research and testing of a new consumer product while everyone involved appeared to be diligently doing their jobs—checking boxes and spreadsheets—left no one in charge and violated basic rules of consumer value, leading to a commercial failure in the launch of a new product at a global fast-moving consumer goods company.

In each of these cases, publicized or not, operational practices led to operational errors that spiraled out of control, bringing major strategic consequences. The original error consisted of either not following established rules or procedures, or, ironically, they occurred *because* people followed established rules or practices that were problematic. Kaupthing Bank, a major casualty during the financial crisis in Iceland, went bankrupt a few weeks after reporting outstanding financial results and key ratio values, following generally accepted standards and practices. These, however, did not consistently reflect the performance of the bank nor its liquidity and ability to be sustainable, even in the short run (Denuit and Schmit 2012).

From these cases, we learn that merely following the rules is inadequate in preventing major failures. Notable examples of errors that stem from following accepted practices and rules include those that stem from unrealistic targets, whether from inappropriate or incomplete scorecards and performance indicators; unwritten ethical standards that are at odds with formal standards; or refusals to consider long-term consequences of short-term actions, such as when selling exploding mortgages and other predatory lending practices. Eventually, organizational errors with strategic consequences are the inevitable result of following flawed—but accepted—practices.

In each of the case studies mentioned in this section, information about deviations from prescribed practice, or about problems stemming from the application of prescribed practice, was available to organization managers and, often, to senior executives—often for quite a long time. The errors were well known at the operational level and were often of the organization's own making (i.e., they were not due to an unexpected external shift or event but rather to internal decisions and practices). Yet, they were not acted upon, whether due to conflicting pressures, unrealistic targets, or shifting ethical standards—all senior management responsibilities. Opportunities existed for managers, middle managers, or top executives to intervene and correct the situations; because this did not happen, or happened too late, major damage was the result.

In short, organizational failures often occur when information is available at the operational level but is not shared with senior management or else is shared but not acted upon by senior management. As Carroll put it, drawing from field research on safety in numerous organizations, very often "workers are worried, supervisors are concerned, managers are mixed, and executives are happy!" (quoted in Giolito and Verdin 2016a).

Considered in the light of prior error research, these cases of strategic error display an apparent lack of psychological safety in the organization that might have enabled participants to speak up about emergent and ongoing errors or concerns. A lack of psychological safety was likely partly responsible for the failures to manage organizational errors in ways that prevented escalation. Seen in this light, how much the top executives actually knew, and when, about a specific event or incident in and of itself becomes of secondary importance to their responsibility as creators or stewards of the organization's culture.

Senior management behaviors (words and actions) have an outsized influence on culture; they embody the values and expected behaviors that others consciously and unconsciously emulate. People look to senior managers for cues as to what actions and messages will be welcome—and which will not. Their words and actions set the tone and the expectations for the entire organization.

As it has been reported in the Volkswagen case, the pressure and fear in the organization resulting from the leadership example and culture emanating from the top seems obvious: For instance, the CEO of Volkswagen was reported to have pressed his staff to come up with a solution, with the veiled threat, *"I have your names!"* (Giolito et al. 2018).

Contrast this with the real-life situation where the CEO of the international operation of a major US bank refused to reveal to headquarters the name of his employees who had just committed a multi-million dollar mistake in a major stock transaction, explaining, "It was my mistake. I am the CEO so I am responsible." In so doing, he created immense loyalty among employees and created a climate of psychological safety that later served him—and the entire bank—remarkably well in handling subsequent crises.

Likewise, the famous quote during the successful resolution of NASA's Apollo 13 crisis, "Failure is not an option!" is often misused in corporate contexts to suggest that failure is unacceptable. This use contrasts with the meaning of what was said by the Apollo mission leader, Gene Krantz—that failure can be avoided through extreme vigilance and ingenious problem solving. When misused, the phrase risks breeding a culture that is ironically more vulnerable to dramatic failures because of its intolerance to acknowledging or reporting errors and problems (Edmondson 1996; Roberto et al. 2006). In learning organizations, people distinguish between types of failure—for example, recognizing the difference between preventable and intelligent failures—and embrace intelligent failures as vital sources of innovation (Edmondson 2011).

Many notable case studies on organizational errors point to the critical role of culture in enabling people to invite, report, acknowledge, and act on emerging errors and error signals (e.g., Roberto et al. 2006). Setting the wrong culture can be seen as a strategic error by senior executives, as stated by some CEOs and chairmen of major financial institutions (Giolito and Verdin 2016b; Edmondson and Verdin 2017).

Psychological safety for error management at the top—or more specifically within senior management and executive teams—may play a crucial role in shaping the quality of executive decision making and strategic management. Its absence can be seen in the case of the Fortis banking group when, together with the Royal Bank of Scotland and Santander, it took part in the hostile takeover of ABN Amro—the largest banking acquisition in history at the time—and subsequently was dismantled as one of the largest "victims" of the financial crisis. Even though the acquisition itself might have been questioned as a sound strategic move (perhaps comprising a straightforward strategy error, as discussed in the following section), no less important were the series of mistakes at the executive levels—foremost being the "implementation errors" in carrying out the acquisition. In particular, in the wake of emerging and growing signals of distress and dysfunction, the executives seem to have ignored sound principles in securing the proper financing that brought down the entire banking group, in a culture that did not allow for much probing or questioning, pursuing alternative views, or taking account of the subsequent important signals and cues that emerged as indications of a larger crisis (Giolito and Verdin 2017).

Contrast this to the culture subsequently created by the CEO of insurance group Ageas—ironically the technical successor of what remained of the failed Fortis group. Ageas essentially has been practicing the principles of servant-leadership and fostering psychological safety at the top and across the entire organization, first and foremost through leading by example and fostering a culture of openness and trust. "All our employees get the chance to have their say, irrespective of their department or position. At the same time, we expect our people to take initiative and not wait until somebody tells them what to do. As a result, and in contrast to the past, the distance between the basis and the top [is] now a lot shorter" (interview with CEO of Ageas, TIJD Connect, May 2017).

In short, psychological safety may be an essential condition for deviations (or "errors") to be noticed, detected, assessed, acknowledged, and acted upon before they have a chance to gain momentum, spread, and produce strategic consequences. This is true not only at lower operational levels and in small groups but also for senior executives and the organizational culture. This is because psychological safety enables speaking up, error reporting, dissenting, and candidly discussing risks. Without these behaviors, especially at the executive levels, organizations are at risk of strategic failures that could have been avoided.

A Traditional View of Strategy Failures

We see another important role for psychological safety and error management in minimizing organizational strategy failures, as distinct from operational errors that spiral out of control. In practice, many (if not most) strategy failures are attributed to failures in implementation. Clearly, even great strategies can be poorly implemented, thereby failing to deliver results.

Survey studies indeed frequently report that strategies fail due to poor implementation. One study found that up to 70 percent of strategic plans and strategies were not successfully implemented (Sterling 2003). A survey by the

Economist (The Economist Intelligence Unit 2013) found that 60 percent of firms struggled to bridge the gap between "formulation" and "implementation." A recent large-scale survey by PwC's "Strategy&" group reported that two out of three executives admit their company's capabilities do not adequately support execution of the company's strategy (Leinwand and Mainardi 2016). Although this data comprises perceptual measures, the level of agreement that strategic failure is typically a matter of execution (e.g., see Huy 2016; Martin 2010; Sull et al. 2015) is striking.

Failure of implementation is usually seen as being distinct from the situation when the strategy itself is faulty—such as when it is based on inadequate data, poor analysis, or flawed logic. More specifically, a strategy may be flawed because it is not well-aligned with the company's market and competitive context, customer needs, or core competences and capabilities. However, the distinction between "formulation" and "implementation" may not always be easily drawn.

To begin with, what shows up as an implementation problem may, in fact, be traceable to poor strategy formulation that produces a "bad" strategy (as has been argued, e.g., in Rumelt 2012). Second, a "good" strategy may only be good at one moment in time; market dynamism can quickly convert a good strategy into a flawed one.

However, for the sake of argument, we first accept the premise that formulation and implementation are separable activities to draw a map of possibilities, yielding three types of strategic failure, as depicted in Fig. 5.1: a flawed strategy well implemented; a good strategy poorly implemented; or a flawed strategy with poor implementation. Strategic success, in this map, requires both a sound strategy concept and effective implementation (upper-right quadrant).

As appealing as this simple framework may seem, we suggest that it falls short in an environment characterized by high levels of uncertainty and ambiguity. We thus suggest a new perspective that finds the distinction between

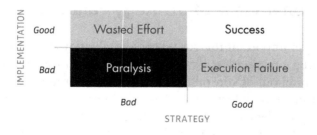

Fig. 5.1 Three types of strategic failure

formulation and execution of strategy hard to draw, and more importantly, counterproductive. That is, the distinction itself may be a contributing factor in a strategic failure in a complex, dynamic market.

To understand why, consider that the conventional approach to tackling the implementation problem—itself based on the premise that poor implementation explains the failure—amounts to a checklist to help senior management overcome well-recognized obstacles to effective execution. With checklist items such as "sharing a vision," "communicating," "gaining buy-in," "cascading," "alignment," "providing resources," "securing talent," "motivating people," "monitoring progress," "promoting accountability," or "performance evaluation," such advice amounts to exhortations to managers to work hard and to get others engaged in working hard, as suggested or implied in various publications (The Economist Intelligence Unit 2013; Meyer 2013; Vuori and Huy 2016).

Frequently identified obstacles to execution may not comprise an accurate diagnosis of the challenge (Verdin et al. 2011). Even when obstacles have been properly identified, overcoming them may not be a matter of simple exhortation and effort. Oftentimes, more complex phenomena are at work that are much more complicated to untangle and manage. They require changes in behavior, which is not easy, given that behavior is affected by shifting and ambiguous forces in complex organizations. Often, therefore, managers are put in positions where there are conflicting demands and mixed messages, constituting a different analysis of why implementation fails. Solving the implementation problem is unlikely to succeed using "command-and-control" and an "execution-as-efficiency" mode; rather, what is needed is an "execution-as-learning" approach that relies on trial-and-error and constructive feedback between thinking and doing, deciding and executing, across various layers and departments of the organization. Furthermore, perhaps it is the very distinction between formulation and implementation that is at least partly responsible for the poor record of "strategy implementation," as explored in the next section.

Beyond Formulation Versus Implementation

An alternative explanation for strategy implementation failures thus has do with the way the concepts of strategy and implementation have been framed in much of the academic and practitioner literature on strategy. We suggest that the distinction between formulating and implementing strategy is itself problematic.

Starting from a concept of strategy that first can be "decided" and developed (at the top) and subsequently rolled out or implemented (throughout the organization) creates at least two potential risks. First, by distinguishing "formulation" from "implementation," we lose the opportunity to leverage insights from the field during the formulation process, as well as to alter the strategy. Second, the implementation mode implied by this distinction tends to take the form of command-and-control or a top-down approach in which answers are set by those in charge, and doers implement those answers. Such an approach is increasingly seen as being inadequate for the complex nature of today's markets and succeeding through innovation.

Research on "teaming" and error management has shown that complex and especially innovative projects require quite different "execution" approaches than for standard or routine projects (Edmondson 2012). It seems that strategy implementation is all too often treated in an "execution-as-efficiency" mode, which assumes that leaders have the answers (the strategy has been set and decided), change is indeed a huge challenge, feedback is one way, and the goal is to get the results or benefits that are presumed there to be captured (value capturing). This mode is increasingly at odds with the requirements of today's highly dynamic and uncertain environment, which demands a strategy driven by value creation (Verdin and Tackx 2015; Tackx et al. 2016).

A growing number of strategy scholars suggest that successful strategy today is less and less about defending a competitive position or about building a "sustainable advantage" against the "forces of competition." As McGrath (2013) has written, "The dominant idea in the field of strategy—that success consists of establishing a unique competitive position, sustained for long periods of time—is no longer relevant for most businesses." Strategy is presented instead as a means of continuously creating and innovating value to customers—the basis of highly visible calls for "value innovation" (Kim and Mauborgne 1999) or "disruptive innovation" (Christensen and Overdorf 2000). "Instead of seeing business—and strategy and business education—as a matter of figuring out how to defeat one's known rivals and protect oneself against competition through structural barriers," writes Denning (2012), "it must aim to add value to customers through continuous innovation and finding new ways of delighting its customers."

This demands a kind of strategy that builds on the foundations laid by the "resource-based view" of strategy (Wernerfelt 1984), brings in the concept of "the learning organization" (Garvin et al. 2008; Senge 2010), and "is less and less about a rigid plan ... [but rather] about developing a general direction built around deep and uniquely strong capabilities, that constantly learn, improve, test and adjust in manageable increments to the changing market"

(Zook and Allen 2012). As one CEO remarked in a Duke Corporate Education study in the wake of the financial crisis and ensuing economic fallout: "I am going to do a 5-year plan and then measure myself against that plan? I think this is going out the window" (Duke Corporate Education 2013).

In this changing context, leaders set the direction, putting certain processes in motion as a starting point—as hypotheses to be tested. People understand that constant small changes are a way of life, and feedback is a two-way dialogue up and down the hierarchy. In execution-as-learning, employee involvement in thinking and doing is essential; employees throughout the organization are engaged in experimentation and problem solving with an aim to create long-term value, above and beyond easy and short-term value gains (Edmondson 2012).

An execution-as-learning approach to strategy implementation requires the creation of psychological safety to support a learning culture throughout the organization. In a psychologically safe climate, errors are a source of learning-by-doing and a process of adapting the course of the strategic actions to the changing requirements in the field, the market, or the shop floor. In short, psychological safety and error management practices may contribute to successful strategic management. To begin with, psychological safety matters in any context in which uncertainty is present. Risk-aversion is natural; when people must act without knowing if the results will be positive, psychological safety can help them proceed, despite the risk. Furthermore, strategy management in an uncertain world is a collaborative process, which brings interpersonal risks, which can be reduced by a climate of psychological safety. Finally, because ideas can be sourced from lower levels in the organization, people need to feel safe in order to speak up. By conceptualizing strategy formulation as a learning process, we thus propose that psychological safety will play a role in its success.

Strategy-as-Learning

Conceptualizing and practicing the work of organizational strategy as a learning process implies that the strategy will not constitute a set of *premeditated decisions* and well-reasoned answers to "strategic" issues setting out a pre-conceived *course of action*. Instead, strategy formulation and execution together must comprise a framework of guiding principles, a sense of direction, and a set of questions to be defined, refined, and iteratively answered.

Limits to the traditional concepts and approaches to "strategic planning" have been discussed in various strands in the literature, notably in the late 1980s and early 1990s in influential works by Mintzberg (1993), Pascale (1984), Hamel and Prahalad (2010), and Hayes (1985), to name a few. Some of these works were inspired by the "unorthodox" winning strategies practiced by a wave of successful Japanese companies at the time. Widely documented success stories of companies such as Komatsu, Honda, and Toyota in markets previously dominated by Caterpillar, Harley-Davidson, and General Motors, which had traditional approaches to strategic planning, provided support for alternative views of strategy. These came to be called by terms such as "emergent strategies" or "entrepreneurial strategy." They also gave rise to the notions of "strategic intent" (instead of plan) and "learning-by-doing" or "crafting strategy." The basic idea was to shift toward developing a strategy in the field as you go (Mintzberg 1987).

There is growing interest in alternative views of strategy, reflecting the belief that traditional strategic planning approaches no longer work in a turbulent, dynamic marketplace. For instance, recent research on "sense-making" and "sense-giving" (Giolito 2017; Maitlis and Christianson 2014; Weick 1993; Weick et al. 2005) explores a realistic, complex interaction pattern between thinking and acting, knowing and doing, providing yet another basis for questioning the "formulation-implementation" model. The concepts of "strategic conversation" and "story-telling" add another perspective (Liedtka and Rosenblum 1996), as do recent contributions on "open strategy" and "strategy co-creation" (Tackx and Verdin 2014; Nketia 2016). More generally, interest in "strategy-as-practice" is on the rise in the academic community, providing further support for the view that a realistic, constructive, dynamic concept of strategy is needed (Vaara and Whittington 2012). What these alternative views of strategy seem to have in common is an organic, dynamic, flexible approach that avoids the stark distinction between implementation and formulation.

Although a learning approach to strategy is thus not entirely new (see Mintzberg 1990) and has been discussed more recently (Pietersen 2010a, b), there is room to better identify its characteristics and key components, as well as to consider the conditions under which senior executives can effectively shape and lead strategy as a learning process. We propose that prior research on psychological safety and error management may prove highly relevant in the development and actual use of a "strategy-as-learning" approach.

Toward that end, we propose a simple framework, depicted in Table 5.1, to contrast the primary features of strategy-as-learning with the traditional notion of strategic planning. Among other features, our framework highlights

Table 5.1 Strategy-as-planning versus strategy-as-learning

	Strategy-as-planning	Strategy-as-learning
Senior executive role	Analysis and planning	Articulate vision and purpose
	Decision making	Frame and question
Middle management role	Cascade	Coach
	Monitor	Collect
	Measure	Process
Field employee role	Implement	Sense and provide feedback
	Execute	Experiment and create
Assumptions about the environment	Stable	Volatile
	Predictable	Uncertain
	Critical variables are known	Ambiguous
Strategy formulation activities	Analyze, plan, decide	Develop hypotheses
	Forecast	Test hypotheses
	React	Create
View of error	A deviation from a plan	A source of data
	To be avoided, minimized, corrected, or written off	Signal of an opportunity
		A trigger for new hypotheses
View of failure	"Not an option"	"Intelligent failure" welcome

key differences between the old and new approaches for executives and other managers at different levels in the organization.

A learning perspective incorporates and embraces the notion that strategy is essentially a continuously creative process in an environment that has been often characterized by the shorthand VUCA (volatile, uncertain, complex, and ambiguous). This creative process starts from the need for continued value creation for customers and markets, which requires continuous learning, adaptation, experimentation, and testing. We can contrast this process with strategy, defined as a set of decisions made at the top in the organization on the basis of a forecast of a sufficiently predictable environment, to be subsequently cascaded and executed at lower levels.

The role of (senior) management in such a process is fundamentally different from those in a planning or command-and-control framework. It consists of setting the direction, defining the purpose of the organization, and framing the issues—and especially the relevant questions—rather than providing all the answers, in order to realize that purpose. The critical role for leaders and managers, therefore, is to focus on questioning rather than answering, as has recently been recognized in a variety of contexts—even though the implications for a fundamentally different "implementation" approach have not always been fully appreciated (Kachaner et al. 2015).

Middle management's role becomes one of coaching, collecting, and processing information and input rather than cascading, monitoring, and measuring, which make sense in a planning and implementing process.

Fundamentally, strategy-as-learning invites field and frontline associates to provide essential input and feedback, leaving vital operational decisions to them where possible.

Strategy making is thus not about providing answers to pre-conceived questions but rather about developing and adapting the right questions and helping to advance hypotheses to be tested. The answers and decisions are left to those who are best placed to act and think as well as to learn by doing. Errors then are not so much deviations from the plan to be corrected as they are sources of data and information to help people alter their hypotheses. Errors are thus a source of learning—and sometimes a source of innovation. Strategy-as-learning takes a different approach to—and even bypasses—the execution problem by avoiding an artificial distinction between formulation and implementation to begin with. Similarly, failure is not something to avoid at all costs ("not an option") but rather something that must be celebrated when it results from experiments in new territory and brings valuable—if still disappointing—information to the organization.

Returning to the logic of Fig. 5.1, we might imagine a zig-zagging or spiral path from the paralysis of a bad strategy with bad implementation toward the upper-right zone of success. Instead of embracing the old logic (that organizations must first develop a "good strategy," then rigorously enforce its implementation), we instead recognize that strategic management in a dynamic context is necessarily flexible and iterative. No less important, it also seeks to help create a better strategy by incorporating some of the fundamental changes taking place in the field of strategy that, as mentioned above, call into question the traditional concepts of defensive "value capturing" based on industry analysis, and competitive positioning, in favor of an approach requiring continuous value creation.

Implications and Directions for Future Research

This chapter seeks to connect research on psychological safety and organizational errors to the theory and practice of strategic management. We argued that research showing that psychological safety fosters operational effectiveness by enabling candid interpersonal interactions can be applied to the work of organizational strategy making. Our goal was to explore the strategic relevance of past research on psychological safety and organizational error management, as well as on execution-as-learning as an approach to operations. Execution-as-learning can be seen to help solve the so-called implementation problem frequently noted in both strategy research and practice, by suggesting an iterative tweak-as-you-go approach to execution that may promote greater implementation success.

Taken a step further, however, execution-as-learning suggests a new way of thinking about strategy, which we referred to as strategy-as-learning. This is a deliberate contrast to the notion of strategy as a plan to be developed and then implemented—an approach that is still, even if sometimes implicitly, dominant in much of the corporate and consulting world as well as in strategy textbooks and teaching.

As discussed, a strategy-as-learning approach views strategy as (the dynamic result of) an ongoing process rather than as the outcome of a top-down plan to be implemented by others. In this view, strategy happens through "learning-by-doing"—in interactions between the "thinking" and the "doing," consistent with observations in the sense-making literature. We concur that this is a more realistic model than the "thinking-doing" mode assumed in many approaches to strategy development currently being practiced.

Strategy-as-learning invites senior management to take a role as orchestrators, directors, and guardians of a process. They provide guidelines and formulate questions. The answers are developed through concrete steps, measures, and experiments in the field in a kind of ongoing conversation with the market and with technological possibilities. Top management's role is to ensure a consistent and coherent purpose and vision over time and throughout the organization as well as to allocate resources for everyone in the organization to act.

The result, when well-practiced, may be a more relevant, coherent, dynamic strategy, which is connected to the operations and drives toward a relentless search for customer value creation. This search lies at the heart of sustainable strategy in today's dynamic and competitive environment. Today's markets call for a strategy-as-learning approach more than ever. We argue that the findings and insights from research on psychological safety and organizational error management can be put to good use in developing such an approach further.

Much research is needed to convert our framework and ideas into robust empirical findings or management practices. For instance, we need to clarify and study the roles, responsibilities, and leadership requirements at various levels of an organization for practicing strategy-as-learning. Research is also needed to better understand the obstacles to building psychological safety and practicing effective error management at the executive levels. Furthermore, research is needed to design and test practices for avoiding, eliminating, and overcoming these obstacles. A multiple-case study design may be one way to build understanding of how strategy and error management practices can interact and work together to build robust, strategic execution.

Finally, our topic lends itself to action research because strategy-as-learning is rarely found in actual practice in today's organizations. Despite considerable discussions in the management literature about agile organizations or about learning organizations, many—if not most—large organizations are top-down, slow to change, and fraught with obstacles to learning. When a phenomenon of interest does not exist, researchers must seek ways to first create the phenomenon as part of the research. Referred to as "action research," this approach gives the researcher the responsibility to design and test new knowledge about what actions work to create the desired changes.

Treating strategy as a learning process is compelling intellectually, but it faces noteworthy hurdles created by enduring habits of thought and hierarchy that reinforce a natural human preference for certainty, plans, and straightforward directives. Strategy-as-learning invites members of organizations to act as scientists—detecting, hypothesizing, experimenting, and learning—despite the very real intellectual and emotional challenges embedded in each of these activities. Our framework must be considered merely a starting point for asking new questions, conducting new research, and developing tools that may help bring these ideas into more tangible and robust forms in the future.

Acknowledgments We gratefully acknowledge the superb research assistance of Marie Godts, Charles Hoffreumon and Irene Ingardi (SBS-EM), the support of the Baillet-Latour Chair in Error Management at SBS-EM (ULB) and its senior research fellow Dr. Vincent Giolito, and the Harvard Business School Division of Research.

References

Baer, M., and M. Frese. 2003. Innovation is not enough: Climates for initiative and psychological safety, process innovations, and firm performance. *Journal of Organizational Behavior* 24 (1): 45–68.

Bohmer, R., L.R. Feldman, E.M. Ferlins, and A.C. Edmondson. 2009. *Columbia's final mission*. Brighton, MA: Harvard Business Press. https://hbr.org/product/columbia-s-final-mission/304090-PDF-ENG

Carroll, J.S. 1998. Organizational learning activities in high-hazard industries: The logics underlying self-analysis. *Journal of Management Studies* 35 (6): 699–717.

Chase, R.B., and D.M. Stewart. 1994. Make your service fall-safe. *Sloan Management Review* 35 (3): 35.

Christensen, C.M., and M. Overdorf. 2000. Meeting the challenge of disruptive change. *Harvard Business Review* 78 (2): 66–77.

Denning, S. 2012. The one force that really matters. *Forbes*. https://www.forbes.com/sites/stevedenning/2012/11/20/what-killed-michael-porters-monitor-group-the-one-force-that-really-matters/#5d868aa2747b

Denuit, T., and M. Schmit. 2012. *Managing growth and value creation – The Kaupthing case*. Solvay Brussels School of Economics & Management Case Study, Brussels.

Duhigg, C. 2017. *Smarter faster better: The transformative power of real productivity*. New York, NY: Random House.

Duke Corporate Education. 2013. *Leading in context* (CEO Study). http://www.dukece.com/wp-content/uploads/2015/06/LeadingInContext_web_newlogo.pdf

Edmondson, A., and P. Verdin. 2017. Your strategy should be a hypothesis you constantly adjust. *Harvard Business Review*. Retrieved from https://hbr.org/2017/11/your-strategy-should-be-a-hypothesis-you-constantly-adjust

Edmondson, A.C. 1996. Learning from mistakes is easier said than done: Group and organizational influences on the detection and correction of human error. *The Journal of Applied Behavioral Science* 32 (1): 5–28.

———. 1999. Psychological safety and learning behavior in work teams. *Administrative Science Quarterly* 44 (2): 350–383.

———. 2003. Speaking up in the operating room: How team leaders promote learning in interdisciplinary action teams. *Journal of Management Studies* 40 (6): 1419–1452.

———. 2011. Strategies for learning from failure. *Harvard Business Review* 89 (4): 48–55. (April 2012).

———. 2012. *Teaming: How organizations learn, innovate, and compete in the knowledge economy*. New York: Wiley.

Edmondson, A.C., and J.P. Mogelof. 2006. Explaining psychological safety in innovation teams: Organizational culture, team dynamics, or personality. *Creativity and Innovation in Organizational Teams*, 109–136.

Edmondson, A.C., M.A. Roberto, R.M. Bohmer, E.M. Ferlins, and L.R. Feldman. 2005. The recovery window: Organizational learning following ambiguous threats. In *Organization at the limit: Lessons from the Columbia disaster*, ed. W. Starbuck and M. Farjoun. Hoboken: Wiley-Blackwell.

Garvin, D.A., A.C. Edmondson, and F. Gino. 2008. Is yours a learning organization? *Harvard Business Review* 86 (3): 109.

Giles, D.L. 2013. *The Deepwater Horizon oil spill: The politics of crisis response*. Cambridge, MA: Harvard Kennedy School Case Study.

Giolito, V., and P. Verdin. 2017. *Fortis and ABN-AMRO: Managing the largest acquisition in the banking industry*. Case Study. Thecasecentre.Org. Retrieved from https://www.thecasecentre.org/programmeAdmin/products/view?id=140732

Giolito, V., P. Verdin, M. Hamwi, and Y. Oulaladj. (2018). *Volkswagen Über Alles*. Case Study. Thecasecentre.Org. Retrieved from https://www.thecasecentre.org/main/products/view?&id=150604

Giolito, V.J. 2016. *Société Générale & Kerviel: Managing huge operational errors*. Solvay Brussels School of Economics & Management Case Study, Brussels.

———. 2017. *Sensemaking and sensegiving in strategic error management*. Solvay Brussels School of Economics & Management Working Paper, Brussels.

Giolito, V.J., and P. Verdin. 2016a. *From wrong to right – Error management conference and summit report*. Solvay Brussels School of Economics & Management, Brussels.

———. 2016b. From wrong to right: A multi-source investigation of organizational error management by top executives. Presented at the AOM annual meeting, Anaheim.

Goodman, P.S., R. Ramanujam, J.S. Carroll, A.C. Edmondson, D.A. Hofmann, and K.M. Sutcliffe. 2011. Organizational errors: Directions for future research. *Research in Organizational Behavior* 31: 151–176.

Hackman, J.R. 2003. Learning more by crossing levels: Evidence from airplanes, hospitals, and orchestras. *Journal of Organizational Behavior* 24 (8): 905–922.

Hagen, J. 2013. *Confronting mistakes: Lessons from the aviation industry when dealing with error*. Houndmills/Basingstoke/Hampshire: Palgrave Macmillan.

Hamel, G., and C.K. Prahalad. 2010. *Strategic intent*. Brighton, MA: Harvard Business Press.

Hamwi, M., Y. Oualhadj, V. Giolito, and P. Verdin. 2017. *Making Volkswagen great again*. Solvay Brussels School of Economics & Management Case Study, Brussels.

Hayes, R.H. 1985. Strategic planning – Forward in reverse? *Harvard Business Review*, November 1. https://hbr.org/1985/11/strategic-planning-forward-in-reverse

Huy, Q. N. (2016). Five reasons most companies fail at strategy execution. *INSEAD Blog*, January 4. http://knowledge.insead.edu/blog/insead-blog/five-reasons-most-companies-fail-at-strategy-execution-4441

Kachaner, N., K. King, and S. Stewart. 2015. Four best practices for strategic planning. *BCG Perspectives*, April. https://www.bcgperspectives.com/content/articles/strategic-planning-business-unit-strategy-four-best-practices-strategic-planning/

Kahneman, D. 2013. *Thinking, fast and slow* (Reprint). New York: Farrar Straus Giroux.

Kim, W.C., and R. Mauborgne. 1999. Strategy, value innovation, and the knowledge economy. *Sloan Management Review* 40 (3): 41.

Leinwand, P., and C.R. Mainardi 2016. *Strategy that works: How winning companies close the strategy-to-execution gap*. Brighton, MA: Harvard Business Review Press.

Liedtka, J.M., and J.W. Rosenblum. 1996. Shaping conversations: Making strategy, managing change. *California Management Review* 39 (1): 141–157.

Maitlis, S., and M. Christianson. 2014. Sensemaking in organizations: Taking stock and moving forward. *The Academy of Management Annals* 8 (1): 57–125.

Martin, R.L. 2010. The execution trap. *Harvard Business Review*.

McGrath, R. 2013. Transient advantage. *Harvard Business Review*.

Meyer, T. 2013. Why strategy implementation often fails. *Human Capital Review*. http://www.humancapitalreview.org/content/default.asp?Article_ID=1165&ArticlePage_ID=2312&cntPage=5

Mintzberg, H. 1987. Crafting strategy. *Harvard Business Review*, July. https://hbr.org/1987/07/crafting-strategy

———. 1990. Strategy formation: Schools of thought. *Perspectives on Strategic Management* 1968: 105–235.

———. 1993. The pitfalls of strategic planning. *California Management Review* 36 (1): 32–47. https://doi.org/10.2307/41165733.

Nembhard, I.M., and A.C. Edmondson. 2006. Making it safe: The effects of leader inclusiveness and professional status on psychological safety and improvement efforts in health care teams. *Journal of Organizational Behavior* 27 (7): 941–966.

Nketia, B.A. 2016. The influence of open strategizing on organizational members' commitment to strategy. *Social and Behavioral Sciences*, (235): 473–483. http://creativecommons.org/licenses/by-nc-nd/4.0/

Norman, D.A. 1981. Categorization of action slips. *Psychological Review* 88 (1): 1.

Oualhadj, Y., and V. Giolito. 2016. How do executives of big companies manage errors: The case of BP and the Deepwater Horizon explosion in 2010. Solvay Brussels School of Economics & Management Master Thesis, Brussels.

Pascale, R.T. 1984. Perspectives on strategy: The real story behind Honda's success. *California Management Review* 26 (3): 47–72. https://doi.org/10.2307/41165080.

Perrow, C. 1982. President's Commission and the normal accident. In *Accident at Three Mile Island: The Human Dimensions*. https://inis.iaea.org/search/search.aspx?orig_q=RN:13677929

———. 1984. *Normal accidents: Living with high risk systems*. New York: Basic Books.

Pietersen, W. 2010a. *Strategic learning: How to be smarter than your competition and turn key insights into competitive advantage*. New York: Wiley.

———. 2010b. Strategy as learning. *The European Business Review* 22 (4): 24–27.

Reason, J. 1984. Lapses of attention in everyday life. In *Varieties of attention*, ed. R. Parasuraman and D.R. Davies, 515–549. Orlando: Academic Press.

———. 1994. Latent errors and systems disasters. In *Social issues in computing*, 128–176. McGraw-Hill. http://dl.acm.org/citation.cfm?id=174851

Roberto, M.R., R.M.J. Bohmer, and A.C. Edmondson. 2006. Facing ambiguous threats. *Harvard Business Review* 84 (11): 106–113.

Roberts, K.H., and C. Libuser. 1993. From Bhopal to banking: Organizational design can mitigate risk. *Organizational Dynamics* 21 (4): 15–26.

Roxburgh, C. (2003). Hidden flaws in strategy. *McKinsey Quarterly* (2) (May): 26–39.

Rudolph, J.W. 2003. *Into the big muddy and out again: Error persistence and crisis management in the operating room*. Chestnut Hill: Boston College. http://escholarship.bc.edu/dissertations/AAI3103269.

Rumelhart, D.E. 1980. Schemata: The building blocks of cognition. In *Theoretical issues in reading comprehension: Perspectives from cognitive psychology, linguistics, artificial intelligence and education*, ed. R.J. Spiro, B.C. Bruce, and W.F. Brewer, 33–58. Hillsdale: Lawrence Erlbaum Associates.

Rumelt, R.P. 2012. Good strategy/bad strategy: The difference and why it matters. *Strategic Direction* 28 (8). http://www.emeraldinsight.com/doi/full/10.1108/sd.2012.05628haa.002.

Russo, J.E., and P.J. Schoemaker. 1989. *Decision traps*. New York, NY: Simon & Schuster.

Salas, E., C.A. Bowers, and E. Edens. 2001. *Improving teamwork in organizations: Applications of resource management training*. Boca Raton, FL: CRC Press.

Senge, P.M. 2010. *The fifth discipline: The art and practice of the learning organization: First edition*. New York, NY: Random House.

Shingo, S. 1986. *Zero quality control: Source inspection and the poka-yoke system.* Boca Raton, FL: CRC Press.

Sterling, J. 2003. Translating strategy into effective implementation: Dispelling the myths and highlighting what works. *Strategy & Leadership* 31 (3): 27–34. https://doi.org/10.1108/10878570310472737.

Sull, D., R. Homkes, and C. Sull. 2015. Why strategy execution unravels and what to do about it. *Harvard Business Review.* http://www.apdata.com/upload/file/HRadar_Ed4_Why_strategy_execution_unravels.pdf

Tackx, K., and P. Verdin (2014). *Can co-creation lead to better strategy? An exploratory research.* Universite Libre de Bruxelles Working Papers 14–027.

Tackx, K., S. Rothenberger, and P. Verdin. 2016. Is advertising for losers? An empirical study from a value creation and value capturing perspective. *European Management Journal.* http://www.sciencedirect.com/science/article/pii/S0263237316300913

The Economist Intelligence Unit. 2013. *Why good strategies fail.* Economist Intelligence Unit Perspective. https://www.eiuperspectives.economist.com/strategy-leadership/why-good-strategies-fail

Tucker, A.L., I.M. Nembhard, and A.C. Edmondson. 2007. Implementing new practices: An empirical study of organizational learning in hospital intensive care units. *Management Science* 53 (6): 894–907.

Vaara, E., and R. Whittington. 2012. Strategy-as-practice: Taking social practices seriously. *Academy of Management Annals* 6 (1): 285–336.

Verdin, P., and K. Tackx. 2015. *Are you creating or capturing value? A dynamic framework for sustainable strategy.* Harvard Kennedy School Working Paper 36. https://www.hks.harvard.edu/centers/mrcbg/publications/awp/awp36

Verdin, P., E. Cabocel, J. Celens, and F. Faelli. 2011. Making change work. What managers, executives and staff tell us that really matters. *Review of Business & Economics* 56: 244–269.

Vuori, T.O., and Q.N. Huy. 2016. Distributed attention and shared emotions in the innovation process: How Nokia lost the smartphone battle. *Administrative Science Quarterly* 61 (1): 9–51. https://doi.org/10.1177/0001839215606951.

Weick, K.E. 1993. The collapse of sensemaking in organizations: The Mann Gulch disaster. *Administrative Science Quarterly* 38: 628–652.

Weick, K.E., and K.H. Roberts. 1993. Collective mind in organizations: Heedful interrelating on flight decks. *Administrative Science Quarterly* 38: 357–381.

Weick, K.E., K.M. Sutcliffe, and D. Obstfeld. 2000. High reliability: The power of mindfulness. *Leader to Leader* 17 (07).

———. 2005. Organizing and the process of sensemaking. *Organization Science* 16 (4): 409–421.

Wernerfelt, B. 1984. A resource-based view of the firm. *Strategic Management Journal* 5 (2): 171–180.

Zook, C., and J. Allen. 2012. *Repeatability: Build enduring businesses for a world of constant change.* Brighton, MA: Harvard Business Press.

6

Learning Failures As the Ultimate Root Causes of Accidents

Nicolas Dechy, Yves Dien, Eric Marsden, and Jean-Marie Rousseau

A learning process fails when one or more of its stages are deficient and when the same events or similar events recur. Learning deficiencies always involve different levels of the socio-technical system in a hierarchical dimension.

In mature industries, accidents often act as a trigger, showing that certain beliefs were incorrect and that some fundamental, implicit assumptions concerning the safety of the system were wrong. This requires a search for new models that better represent reality—a process that can turn out to be both painful and expensive, and may therefore be rejected. As a result, people are in denial. They tell themselves that accidents could not happen to them and refuse to accept the risk to which they may be exposed. At an organizational and institutional level, group-think phenomena or commitment biases can lead to collective denials.

However, a number of major accidents have been preceded by warnings raised by people familiar with the respective systems and who attempted, unsuccessfully, to alert actors who had the ability to prevent a danger they perceived. Very often, the dissenting opinions and whistleblowers were not heard due to cultures in which bad news was not welcome, criticism was frowned upon, or where a "shoot the messenger" attitude prevailed.

N. Dechy • J.-M. Rousseau
Fontenay-aux-Roses, France

Y. Dien
Paris, France

E. Marsden
Toulouse, France

© The Author(s) 2018
J. U. Hagen (ed.), *How Could This Happen?*, https://doi.org/10.1007/978-3-319-76403-0_6

Although there are many situations in system design and daily operations in which engineers and managers prioritize safety over production/cost goals, a lot of evidence in accident cases suggests that safety is not receiving sufficient attention. Performance pressures and individual adaptation push systems in the direction of failure and lead organizations to gradually reduce their safety margins and take on more risk. This migration—or drift into failure, normalization of deviance, and the associated erosion of safety margins—tends to be a slow process, during which multiple steps occur over an extended period of time. As these steps are usually small, they often go unnoticed, a "new normal" is repeatedly established, and no significant problems are noticed until it is too late.

This chapter describes why the failure to learn the lessons from incidents and accidents is a common weakness in safety management and a significant causal factor of many accidents. Most major accidents are caused by a combination of multiple direct and root causes, but the failure to learn is, in fact, often one of the recurring root causes.

In safety management, the goal of analyzing an incident is to understand what, how, and why it happened a certain way; the goal of learning from an incident is to avoid the recurrence of a similar one. This may happen within or outside of the organization, within another organization, or even in another industrial sector.

Since the 1980s, high-hazard industries have established processes to learn lessons from incidents and implement these findings in system designs and operations. This is recognized today to be a key safety function that is requested within regulatory safety management systems. Most industries devote significant resources to these processes and have developed several tools and methods to investigate the events and learn lessons (Carroll et al. 2003; Frei et al. 2003; Sklet 2004; Kingston et al. 2007; ESReDA 2009; Ferjencik 2011; Dechy et al. 2012; Dien et al. 2012; Hagen 2013; Ramanujam and Carroll 2013; Marsden 2014; Drupsteen and Guldenmund 2014; Rousseau et al. 2014; Blatter et al. 2016).

However, this pillar of prevention strategy is not always as effective as expected. There are safety-relevant incidents that are not detected, notified, or reported upon, internally or externally. There can be a lack of depth in the analysis. Corrective actions may be superficial or not implemented in due time in order to prevent the recurrence of a similar event. There may be whistleblowers no one listens to. It can also be that the memory of some lessons is lost or that the resources dedicated to the learning process are not adequate.

Several accident investigations often find the learning processes to be deficient. This weakness is a recurring root cause, among others such as production pressures, organizational complexities, regulatory complacency, human-resources deficiencies, and also blindness, deafness, or denial from a part of the management (Dien et al. 2004, 2012; Rousseau and Largier 2008; Dechy et al. 2011a; ESReDA 2015; Starbuck and Baumard 2005).

Let us illustrate some of the failures to learn, especially the weaknesses in the internal reporting processes of a company and their interactions with control authorities. Indeed, an important characteristic of a learning organization is its ability to create a culture and work climate in which reporting potentially safety-relevant events—including errors and mistakes—becomes systematic. If a work climate/culture leads to fear of blame and discourages people from raising questions and expressing concerns, the basis for learning is not given.

In all industries, severe incidents have to be reported to the control authorities. In some industries—such as aviation and nuclear power—the control authorities conduct inspections and regulatory assessments of the safety management systems, including the learning systems. Open and transparent discussions are necessary for the regulators to exercise control in an informed manner. However, reporting is not always systematic and does not always lead to adequate measures being taken by a company's management and the regulatory authority. We explain some causes of this problem later.

The four following case studies that were chosen as examples of (internal and external) underreporting comprise major accidents in different industries, countries, and periods of time. The accident-investigation reports often provide very detailed accounts of root causes and connect issues that, when brought together, allow us to identify and learn from some organizational patterns of failure.

Industrial Accidents

The Crash of the McDonnell Douglas DC-10 at Ermenonville, 1974

On March 3, 1974, a DC-10 crashed in a forest close to the Paris Orly International Airport shortly after takeoff. The door of the cargo compartment had opened suddenly, causing a decompression of the cargo compartment, which led to the rupture of the floor of the plane, damaging vital control cables. Another reason for this accident, though, was the failure to learn, with special problems regarding the internal and external reporting (Eddy et al. 1976; McIntyre 2000; Llory 1996).

- Already during pre-certification ground tests of the DC-10 in 1970, a sudden, explosive opening of the cargo compartment door had taken place.
- A major near miss due to almost the same problem occurred in Windsor (Canada) in June 1972. A crash was avoided because the plane had only 56 passengers and the pilot was highly experienced and trained. The damage to the floor, due to the depressurization of the cargo compartment, was limited, and some electrical commands remained operational, allowing the pilot to maintain control.
- After the 1970 ground test and the 1972 Windsor incident, a manager of the subcontractor Convair of McDonnell Douglas—in charge of the engineering design of the door-locking mechanisms—wrote the so-called

Applegate memorandum, pointing to the risks relating to the cargo compartment door.

- Some training pilots at McDonnell Douglas warned their management that the start of operations of the DC-10s sold to Turkish Airlines was premature.
- After the 1972 near miss in Windsor, due to the pressure of the American and Dutch control authorities, McDonnell Douglas had to divulge to the Federal Aviation Administration (FAA) that "there had been about one hundred airline reports of the door failing to close properly during the 10 months of DC-10 service" (McIntyre 2000). The FAA was found to have been lax in analyzing the answers of McDonnell Douglas regarding this situation.
- After the accident nearby Paris, detailed statistics showed that 100 DC-10 incidents dealing with the door mechanism had been recorded in the six months prior to the 1974 crash, giving evidence of a very high rate of incidents related to the opening or closing of the door (3.3 incidents per plane per year) and to the door in general, with a rate of 20 incidents per plane per year.

Learning Failures in Radiotherapy: Therac 25

Between 1985 and 1987, six severe incidents with four fatal accidents occurred in the United States and Canada involving excessive radiation being emitted by a cancer treatment machine, the Therac 25. Since 1983, the machine had been installed in 11 treatment centers (5 in the United States, 6 in Canada) without incident. There were several causes of these accidents, including software failures (Leveson and Turner 1993; Leveson 1995; Llory and Montmayeul 2010).

We do not know much about the first three incidents, which occurred in three different centers. After the fourth incident, the investigation from the center did not find the cause nor did they manage to re-create the incident, despite the presence of engineers from the manufacturer, Atomic Energy Canada Limited (AECL). Instead, they assured everybody that the machine could not cause over-irradiation and that no accidents had occurred.

However, three weeks later, another incident in the same center allowed the hospital radiologist to find the anomaly and re-create it in front of AECL engineers. After the sixth accident in 1987, other software bugs were found.

The AECL engineers were convinced that no over-irradiation could occur as a result of their design. For them, the incidents had to do with incorrect use of the machine. As it turned out, the software bug was a new problem, underestimated due to the engineers' overconfidence in technology.

By now we know that software is difficult to test and often impossible to fully check. However, the AECL engineers ignored the most basic quality assurance procedures and safe-design principles, such as redundancy and defense-in-depth applied within other industries.

Given that they denied having problems, the AECL was deficient in informing other user centers about the incidents or anomalies when they occurred—an attitude that prevented the emergence of collective risk awareness.

After the fifth incident, the American Association of Physicist in Medicine set up a user club and organized meetings with the three stakeholders—that is, users, designers, and control authorities from the United States and Canada—to exchange experiences and discuss the incidents. They learned that some users had implemented supplementary mechanical barriers to add controls.

The lack of reaction of the US control authorities was at first explained by their lack of competencies and risk awareness regarding software issues. However, the geographical dispersion of the users in the United States and the rule that the system designer was required to inform the control authority had diluted the warning signs coming from users. Later, the control authorities changed their reporting requirements so that users could report events both to the control authority and the system designers.

Learning from Failures at the Davis-Besse Nuclear Power Plant

In March 2002, more than 20 years after the Three Mile Island accident in 1979, another incident in the US nuclear industry provided striking safety lessons.

A cavity the size of a football was found in the upper section of the nuclear reactor vessel during a planned outage. Due to corrosion, the cavity had perforated 6.63 inches of carbon steel over several years, reaching the stainless steel layer of the vessel (Department of Energy 2005). This last layer had resisted the primary circuit pressure of 2500 psi-172 bars, though it was not designed to do so. The corrosion was activated by the boric acid used in the primary circuit that was leaking through a crack located at the crossing of top pipes. The plant was within two inches of a severe accident, namely, a loss of primary coolant circuit function.

The task force of the operator, FirstEnergy Nuclear Operating Company (FENOC), investigated the causes of the incident and identified several organizational and managerial flaws (Myers 2002) showing the multiplicity of causes. Among them were that FENOC's top management was production-oriented rather than safety-oriented, and that organizational changes were conducted without assessing their safety impact. The deficiencies regarding the learning process were numerous (Department of Energy 2005) and contributed to the underestimation of risks, despite the fact that the vessel corrosion had been known for years.

Already in the 1980s, the risk of the crossing rods potentially cracking was known. In 1991, it led to an incident in a French nuclear power plant (Llory and Montmayeul 2010). In 1993, the Nuclear Regulatory Commission (NRC) asked for a corrective action plan. The industry answered that there was hardly any risk involved and problems would be discovered through inspections. The NRC accepted this statement but required more monitoring and asked operators to develop techniques to better detect irregularities.

In 2001, a group of inspectors found extensive cracks at the Oconee Nuclear Power Plant. Mandated by the NRC, the Electric Power Research Institute then classified the most vulnerable plants. These were those that had been designed by Babcock and Wilcox, just as the Oconee and Davis-Besse plants had been.

In November 2001, cracking had been identified in all the Babcock and Wilcox nuclear power plants, except in the Davis-Besse plant, which had decided not to shut down for an inspection, despite the fact that the NRC had required one before the end of 2001. FENOC wanted to postpone the inspection until the planned outage in March 2002 and convinced the NRC to wait for the outage to inspect the risks related to cracking.

After the incident, the FENOC, the NRC (2002), and the Department of Energy (2005) enumerated the learning failures:

- *A lack of learning from internal events*: There was a long list of leaks at Davis-Besse, a large number of which were not examined in depth, evaluated, or corrected. The focus was on treating symptoms rather than identifying root causes. In addition, reports of leaks were not kept in the archives, and no adequate risk analyses were performed.
- *A lack of external learning on the national and international levels with poor benchmarking on the boric acid issues*: Interviews with operators showed that they did not know about some of the lessons of the incidents that occurred in the 1980s in other US plants and, as a consequence, believed that the corrosion risk was rather low, despite the deposit of dry boric acid on the vessel.

- Some employees were aware of the isolated symptoms and the risks related to extensive corrosion of the vessel but did not alert managers to take precautionary measures: The management relied excessively on the findings of the resident inspectors to identify (serious) issues. All independent control functions (internal quality assurance, system engineers, resident inspectors, local commission of the plant) missed the degradation of the reactor vessel signaled by dry boric acid deposits as well as the increase of primary circuit leaks between 1996 and 2002.
- An ineffective corrective action program in which recurring problems were not treated, including the underestimation of deficiencies: There were superficial analyses of the causes, in particular of the boric acid deposits that indicated leaks in 1996, 1998, and 2000. All pertinent reports were downgraded as "normal," which implied that no root-cause identifications or corrective actions were necessary. Within the operator, there was an agreement on a "well-defined" problem, namely leaks at the flange, without verification through inspection, which was the key to downgrading the risk. A corrective action item could be considered as completed and closed by referring to a document on recurring issues such as boric acid deposits, or by work that was limited to a removal of the deposits. All this amounted to insufficient evidence for an unplanned shutdown.
- All these severe and recurring deficiencies, in particular the final delay of the inspection, were allowed by the regulator, the NRC: The NRC had sufficient evidence to require an inspection or a shutdown, but it accepted the compromise for a delay requested by FENOC. This is what we can call regulatory complacency.

Learning Failures at the Texas City Refinery

At BP's Texas City Refinery, an explosion, followed by a fire, occurred in March 2005 during the startup of an isomerization unit (ISOM), killing 15 workers. Several components, including safety devices, had not been functioning adequately, and a sequence of actions had been taken that led to the accident. Several failures to learn were identified after the accident (U.S. Chemical Safety and Hazard Investigation Board 2007; Hopkins 2010):

- The US Chemical Safety and Hazard Investigation Board (CSB) noted that "[m]any of the safety problems that led to the March 23, 2005, disaster were recurring problems that had been previously identified in audits and investigations. [...] In the 30 years before the ISOM incident, the Texas City site suffered 23 fatalities. In 2004 alone three major incidents caused three fatalities. Shortly after the ISOM incident, two additional incidents occurred [...]."

- There was a repeated failure to analyze (exhaustively and in depth) severe incidents that could have, in other circumstances, caused catastrophic effects.
- The CSB also noted a failure to implement an effective learning system, despite several audits pointing to its deficiencies: "BP had not implemented an effective incident investigation management system to capture appropriate lessons learned and implement needed changes."
- BP and the petroleum industry did not learn from their incidents and violated a number of standards.
- BP did not learn from a series of incidents nor from an accident that occurred at BP Grangemouth in Scotland. All were investigated by the Health and Safety Executive, the UK control authority. Several of the root causes identified were similar to those of the Texas City accident.
- The CSB observed that several managers were aware of the degraded state of the refinery. For example, the new director of BP's South Houston Integrated Site (consisting of five BP businesses, including the Texas City site) observed in 2002 that the Texas City Refinery infrastructure and equipment were "in complete decline."
- In March 2004, a $30 million accident occurred on site, and many learning failures were identified by the dedicated investigators, especially in reporting (see later in the paragraph on reporting and learning culture).
- Corrective actions and change management were poor and declining at Texas City, as noted by CSB: "Texas City had serious problems with unresolved PSM [process safety management] action items. [...] At the end of 2004, the Texas City site had closed only 33 percent of its PSM incident investigation action items; the ISOM unit closed 31 percent."
- Concerns were growing and were also shared by the BP management. A November 2004 internal presentation made for BP management titled "Safety Reality" was intended as a wakeup call for the Texas City site supervisors. It stated that the plant needed a safety transformation and included a slide titled "Texas City is not a safe place to work."
- In late 2004, the BP management called for a safety culture assessment to be performed by a consulting company called Telos. The assessment identified some of the key root causes that would lead to the March 2005 accident. Here are extracts from the CSB report (U.S. Chemical Safety and Hazard Investigation Board 2007): "Production and budget compliance

gets recognized and rewarded before anything else at Texas City. [...] The pressure for production, time pressure, and understaffing are the major causes of accidents at Texas City. [...] There is an exceptional degree of fear of catastrophic incidents at Texas City."

Analysis

Structuring the Numerous Failures to Learn

The accidents described are far from being the only ones that highlight the difficulties of learning from failure. Other accidents, such as Three Mile Island (1979), the Ladbroke Grove trains collision (1999), and the Space Shuttle Columbia explosion (2003), show additional features of the failure to learn (Cullen 2000; Columbia Accident Investigation Board 2003; Llory 1996, 1999; Dechy et al. 2011a).

When analyzing learning failures as being contributing causes of accidents, we found deficiencies at nine key stages of the learning process (Dechy et al. 2009):

1. the definition of the learning system and policy[1]
2. the detection of the event or recognition of the safety threat
3. the collection of adequate data
4. the analysis[2] of the event(s)
5. the definition of the corrective measures
6. the implementation of the corrective measures
7. the assessment and long-term monitoring of the effectiveness of corrective measures
8. the memorizing and recording of the event, its lessons, its treatment, and its follow-up
9. the communication of the lessons to be learned by stakeholders and potentially interested parties

A learning process fails when one or more of its stages are deficient and when the same events or similar events recur, since one of the objectives that

---

[1] Types of events to be treated, allocation of resources, relationships between the entities implied in the learning process.

[2] To understand the direct and root causes of the event requires the collection and the interpretation of objective and subjective data; at this stage, one also considers the real and potential consequences of the event.

was assigned to the learning process has not been reached (Dien and Llory 2005). This has been clearly demonstrated in the accidents analyzed above—not with just one but rather multiple failures within the learning process at different stages.

At the very least, there was the inability to implement an adequate learning policy (Texas City); detect events (Davis-Besse); analyze events or trends (DC-10, Therac 25, Davis-Besse, Texas City); or implement effective corrective actions (DC-10, Therac 25, Davis-Besse, Texas City).

The learning steps always involve different levels of the socio-technical system in a hierarchical dimension, but other elements as well. Indeed, we also highlighted deficiencies in the learning process from external events, systems, and countries (Therac 25, Davis-Besse, Texas City), which led us to consider that there was another learning policy and full learning process to manage. Indeed, inter-organizational learning requires a dedicated will and the ability to translate the lessons and corrective actions from a first system into the context of a second system in order to compensate for the loss of context (Koornneef 2000).

In addition, we have found repeated learning deficiencies over a long period of time, based on responses to single incidents rather than groups of similar ones (DC-10, Therac 25, Davis-Besse, Texas City). High-hazard companies should be able to gain insights from history in order to identify trends, patterns, recurring events, or differences in order to detect new lessons that could have been missed during the first analysis. Such analyses means reopening old cases and requires a system such as an event database to maintain records. These types of deficiencies point to the importance of a third dimension of the learning policy: the historical dimension (Dechy et al. 2009), which is situated on the third dimension of organizational analysis (Dien et al. 2004, 2012).

We suggest that the learning process should also be analyzed along a fourth dimension, namely communication (Dechy et al. 2009), a dimension that is transverse from and shared by the three others (vertical, transversal, historical). Indeed, learning systems are there to process information, extract it from a context related to the event, and formalize lessons in different formats such as reports, databases, safety alerts, and stories. They involve several actors with their inputs and biases. Expert judgment also means using the right rhetoric to convince others of a threat to safety.

These dimensions are summarized in Fig. 6.1, which provides a framework for the improvement of actions at each stage of the learning process and an awareness of potential deficiencies to address in an audit, for example.

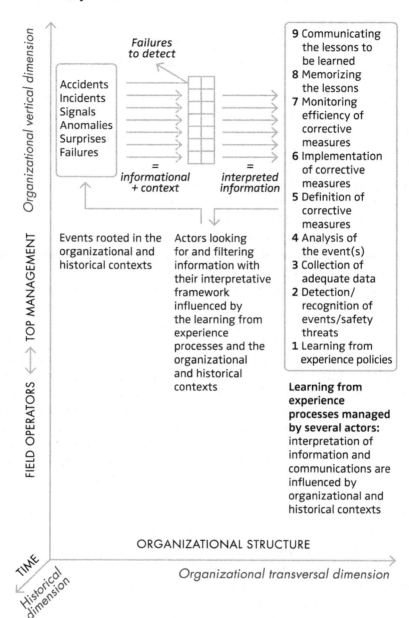

Fig. 6.1 The learning-process issues in four organizational dimensions. (Source: Adapted from Dechy et al. 2009)

Underlying Patterns of Underreporting and Lack of Reaction to Warning Signs

Above, we provided examples and a framework of what, where, and how the failure to learn can happen and be observed. These elements can be seen as symptoms of underlying problems, similar to the distinction between symptoms and pathologies of learning barriers made by the European Safety, Reliability & Data Association project group on dynamic learning (see Fig. 6.2; for further developments, see chapters 3 and 4 of ESReDA 2015).

The objective of the following discussion then is to deepen the analysis and look for some underlying patterns and potential syndromes of learning failures. We have therefore divided our remaining analysis into four parts: the role of beliefs and safety models; the role of reporting and learning culture; the role of the regulators; and the way in which safety concerns are integrated into the decision-making process and trade-offs dealing with the question: Is safety really first?

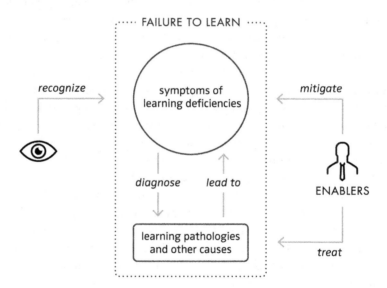

Fig. 6.2 Symptoms and pathogens related to failure to learn. (Source: ESReDA 2015)

Beliefs and Safety Models

In mature industries, accidents too often act as a trigger, showing us that our beliefs were incorrect, that some fundamental, implicit assumptions we made concerning the safety of the system were wrong.

Accidents are often defined in terms of their technical origins or their physical impacts (damages, emergency response). Turner (1978, in Turner and Pidgeon 1997) defines them in sociological terms: "a significant disruption or collapse of the existing cultural beliefs and norms about hazards."The end of an accident is achieved for Turner when the wrong beliefs about safety have been changed.

More generally, failure indicates that our existing models of the world are inadequate, requiring a search for new models that better represent reality (Cyert and March 1963). This challenge of the status quo can turn out to be expensive, which can then lead to people not looking closely enough into warnings that something is not quite as it should be.

Often, there are biases we have and share with colleagues. Sometimes we are in denial and tell ourselves that "it couldn't happen to us." On an individual level, denial is related to cognitive dissonance, a psychological phenomenon in which people refuse to accept or face the risk to which they are exposed. At an organizational and institutional level, group-think phenomena or commitment biases can lead to collective denials.

A general trend has been observed in several process-driven industries showing the pursuit of the wrong kind of excellence. System, industrial, or process safety is too complex to be monitored through safety or key performance indicators only. Several organizations have confused safety excellence with occupational safety indicators, such as injury rates, which are easier to measure (see McNamara's fallacy in Kingston et al. 2011).

In 2000, there was a severe accident at the BP refinery of Grangemouth in Scotland. It was investigated in depth by the UK Health and Safety Executive (HSE). Three senior BP process safety engineers, including the BP Texas City process safety manager, were aware that "traditional indicators such as 'days away from work' do not provide a good indication of process safety performance" (U.S. Chemical Safety and Hazard Investigation Board 2007).

However, this lesson was not learned by BP, because its Texas City Refinery was perceived by top managers as having a good safety record, based on the injury-rate indicator, which was improving. At the same time though, there was contradictory evidence on process safety, which was undergoing a severe degradation, as noted in the CSB report on the accident: "During this same period, loss of containment incidents, a process safety metric tracked but not managed by BP, increased 52 percent from 399 to 607 per year."

Reporting and Learning Culture

A learning policy defines which types of events must be reported. Criteria are determined—some of them with the regulatory authority. Most of them are objective, but others are based on a subjective judgment regarding their relevance for reporting or for learning. The reporting depends on the voluntary input of people who have time constraints. Both the formal and informal reporting channels are affected by the organization's work climate and, more broadly, its culture. This can cause underreporting of safety-relevant events, create biases in the information provided, and affect the way in which people discuss safety concerns.

A number of major accidents have been preceded by warnings raised by people familiar with the respective systems and who attempted, unsuccessfully, to alert actors who had an ability to prevent the danger they perceived. Very often, the dissenting opinions and whistleblowers were not heard due to cultures in which bad news was not welcome, criticism was frowned upon, or where a "shoot the messenger" attitude prevailed. The DC-10 accident provides an example: Both the Applegate memorandum from the subcontractor and the warnings from the McDonnell Douglas trainers were ignored by the company's management.

In addition, in the absence of psychological safety (Edmondson 1999), people will hesitate to speak up when they have questions or concerns related to safety. This can lead to the underreporting of incidents and to investigation reports of poor quality since people do not feel safe mentioning possible anomalies that may have contributed to the event. It can create poor analyses of underlying factors, as it is easier to point the finger at faulty equipment rather than a poor decision made by a unit manager.

In many workplace situations, people do not dare to raise their concerns. They prefer to be silent and to withhold their ideas as well as concerns about procedures and processes. They have developed "self-protective implicit voice theories"—that is, self-censorship. This is usually based on taken-for-granted beliefs about speaking up at work and whether it is accepted or not—beliefs that they have internalized as a result of their interactions with authority over the years (Detert and Edmondson 2011).

One year before the Texas City Refinery accident in 2015, a $30 million accident occurred. Investigators found that "[t]he incentives used in this workplace may encourage hiding mistakes. [...] We work under pressures that lead us to miss or ignore early indicators of potential problems. [...] Bad news is not encouraged" (U.S. Chemical Safety and Hazard Investigation Board 2007). As an additional indication of the direct effects of financial pressures, the PSM manager indicated that the closure rate of corrective actions had fallen since the incentive metric had been removed in 2003 from the formula used to calculate bonuses (U.S. Chemical Safety and Hazard Investigation Board 2007; Hopkins 2010).

Although it is known that to err is to be human, we still find it difficult to be confronted with mistakes, as they are mostly associated with shame and embarrassment. It explains why 88 percent of managers prefer to talk privately about their employees' mistakes rather than have an open discussion (Hagen 2013). Learning from mistakes requires an open and a just culture in which blame is considered to be counterproductive (Reason 1997; Dekker 2008).

In addition, the cultures of some nations contain strong customs about uttering or receiving criticism. The same goes for suggestions for improvement, which can be seen as the implicit criticism of the people who created a system or structure. In this instance, Fukushima comes to mind (Diet 2012).

The Regulators

Control authorities react both to mandatory reportable events and to the findings of their inspections (scheduled and unscheduled). The way they react to reportable events and safety alerts and how they prioritize them are key aspects of their role. Organizational learning is mostly thought of as a component of risk management, but it is also a component of risk governance.

At the Davis-Besse Nuclear Power Plant, plant managers relied on the resident inspector to take corrective actions. This lack of a proactive attitude, which nearly led to a severe accident, was a key factor.

Sometimes there are regulatory authorities who promote the wrong safety models, that is, some regulators use indicators of occupational safety to determine inspection priorities for hazardous plants. At Texas City, the US Occupational Safety and Health Administration decided, on the basis of these indicators, to focus on the construction work that had led to injuries and fatalities, rather than inspect the refineries. More generally, the effects of norms and regulations may lead some actors to play the compliance game, such as that found in bureaucratic quality approaches, but compliance is not safety. There is not sufficient time available for inspectors to go deeper than what is formalized and shown.

Another issue that shows up at the regulatory level in the accidents outlined above is organizational complexity, which hampers the learning process. It has to do with the inter-organizational dimensions when there are several operators or if several countries are involved.

A particular task of control authorities is to make sure that operators learn from each other, not just to check if internal learning is good enough. Actually, there are many institutional and cultural obstacles to the sharing of information and lessons between sites, firms in the same industry, and (even more) between industry sectors. The pathology is self-centeredness (ESReDA 2015). Several factors contribute to it. The major ones are geographic dispersion, which fragments the safety alerts reported to the control authority, and the way integration processes are handled. Among our case studies, Therac 25, Davis-Besse, and DC-10 are good examples.

However, complacency among the control authorities is often a root cause of accidents. The Davis-Besse Nuclear Power Plant is particularly intriguing, as the US NRC had all the evidence to conclude that the level of risk was high and that they should have required its immediate shutdown. The near miss of an accident occurring at Davis-Besse had, at the time, a strong negative impact on the credibility of the NRC. Similarly, the US FAA did not react after the first incidents involving the failures of the DC-10 cargo door locks and was found to have been complacent.

Is Safety Really First?

Given the accident case study approach we have chosen, the answer to this question is no. Although there are likely many situations in system design and daily operations in which engineers and managers prioritize safety over production/cost goals (Rousseau 2008; Hayes 2015), a lot of evidence in accident cases suggests that safety is not receiving sufficient attention. Let us look at some patterns related to the "safety first" motto and the extent to which it is implemented.

A first issue is the effect of conflicting messages. When management's "front-stage" (Goffman 1959) slogans concerning safety and the reality of decisions or "back-stage" actions do not match, management messages lose their credibility. Langåker (2007) has analyzed the importance of compatibility between front-stage and back-stage messages regarding the effectiveness of organizational learning. In fact, mottos such as "safety first" can be counterproductive, as only a few people really believe in them. In reality, production comes first. Safety induces direct costs, which influence short-term economic results. It should be remembered, though, that in high-risk industries, non-safety can eventually induce higher costs. Trevor Kletz used to recall: "[T]here's an old saying, if you think safety is expensive, try an accident. Accident cost a lot of money. And not only in damage to plant and in claims for injury, but also for the loss of the company's reputation." With the Texas City Refinery, BP faced a $1.5 billion accident and several billions in claims after the Macondo blowout in 2010 and the oil spill in the Gulf of Mexico.

Let us look again at the accident at BP's Grangemouth refinery in Scotland. The UK HSE investigation showed an overemphasis on short-term costs and production, which led to unsafe compromises, causing long-term issues such as plant reliability.

Only a few years after the accident, the US CSB found that BP managers—including the company's top management—were not aware of, or had not understood, the lessons of Grangemouth. No changes were made to BP's approach to safety.

Similar findings were made later by the safety culture assessment conducted by Telos consulting group weeks before the 2005 accident at Texas City: "The Business Unit Leader said that seeing the brutal facts so clearly defined was hard to digest, including the concern around the conflict between production and safety. 'The evidence was strong and clear and I accept my responsibility for the results'" (U.S. Chemical Safety and Hazard Investigation Board 2007).

Surprisingly, when presenting the results to all plant supervisors on March 17, 2005 (a week before the major accident), the same business unit leader manager stated (U.S. Chemical Safety and Hazard Investigation Board 2007) that the site had gotten off to a good start in 2005 with safety performance[3] that might "be the best ever." He added that Texas City had "the best profitability ever in its history last year" with more than $1 billion in profit, "more than any other refinery in the BP system." As concluded by the board chairperson of the US Chemical Safety Board in front of the US House of Representatives, the levels of investment in and maintenance of infrastructure were too low, which explained the profitability and "left it vulnerable to a catastrophe" (Merritt 2007).

The 2005 Texas City Refinery explosion is a particularly pathologic example of the impact of production and financial pressures on safety, but the accidents of Therac 25, Davis-Besse, and the DC-10s also show that years of production pressure can defeat safety measures, and that warning signs are often ignored. Most of these severe problems were recognized by employees and disclosed by some. Managerial actions could have taken place long before the accidents.

---

[3] Safety performance in terms of lost time injury rate.

These cases may look extreme. Indeed, in daily management, things are more complex and the boundaries are blurred, as technical, human, and organizational factors are levers of global performance, including production, quality, reliability, and safety. Also, problems can be difficult to root out, but even these can be found, investigated, and assessed (e.g., Rousseau 2008; Dechy et al. 2011b, 2016).

Performance pressures and individual adaptation push systems in the direction of failure and lead organizations to gradually reduce their safety margins and take on more risk. This migration (Rasmussen 1997; Rasmussen and Svedung 2000; Amalberti et al. 2006)—or drift into failure (Snook 2000), normalization of deviance (Vaughan 1996), and the associated erosion of safety margins—tends to be a slow process, during which multiple steps occur over an extended period of time. As these steps are usually small, they often go unnoticed, a "new normal" is repeatedly established, and no significant problems are noticed until it is too late.

At Davis-Besse, top managers relied too much on past successes to be able to consider that their decision making might have been inadequate. They did not distinguish between a reliable and a safe system (Llory and Dien 2006).

A common issue is the level of evidence of a threat to safety and when it demands action. Unfortunately, and as exemplified by the NASA space shuttle accidents of Challenger in 1986 (Vaughan 1996) and Columbia in 2003 (Columbia Accident Investigation Board 2003), the burden of proof is put on the "safety attorneys" who want to stop production, instead of requiring the "production attorneys" to provide evidence that everything is under control and "safe to fail."

Conclusion

In order to study an activity as complex as learning safety lessons from critical incidents—which combines technical, human, organizational, and societal dimensions—we should look empirically at the detailed accounts that are especially provided by accident investigators. This case study approach may seem tedious, but reports of crises and accidents shed light on performance features and deficiencies that were partly hidden in the "dark side" of organizations (Vaughan 1996) or hard to see for most, but not all.

Some researchers (Llory 1996) even argue that accidents are the "royal road" (referring to Freud's metaphor about dreams being the royal road to the unconscious) to discovering the real (mal)functioning of organizations. Other researchers refer to the "gift of failure" (Wilpert in Carroll and Fahlbruch

2011), because incidents offer an opportunity to learn about safe and unsafe operations, generate productive conversations across stakeholders, and bring about beneficial changes to technology, organizations, and mental models. It is an alternative strategy that is at least complementary to the study of normal operations advocated by high-reliability organizations and resilience engineering (e.g., Bourrier 2011; Hollnagel et al. 2006).

The systematic study of more than a hundred accidents shows a disturbing pattern: The root causes of accidents recur independent of the industrial sector, the organizational culture, and the period in which the accident occurred. This empirical finding is important, as this recurrence opens the possibility of capitalizing on the lessons from accidents. Those recurring root causes of industrial accidents have been analyzed and defined as the pathogenic (organizational) factors (Reason 1997; Dien et al. 2004; Rousseau and Largier 2008; Llory et Montmayeul 2010).

We propose to develop the "knowledge and culture of accidents" and promote its transfer through a culture of learning, especially for organizational analysis and diagnosis of safety management (Dechy et al. 2010, 2016; Dien et al. 2012). In our view, the knowledge provided by the lessons of accidents is put to insufficient use. This process has just started and should receive more support from high-risk industries and regulators.

By discussing accident case studies and emphasizing common factors, we want to demonstrate how we can better use the lessons from accidents instead of failing to learn from them. We should remember Santayana's (1905) warning: "Those who cannot remember the past are condemned to repeat it."

One of the main questions organizations need to answer is: Does the learning failure situation belong to a failure of reporting or of analyzing and implementing corrective measures? We have provided examples and a framework for monitoring learning deficiencies that should help managers to improve their learning process. It shows that from blindness—linked to reporting and analysis deficiencies—it should shift to an issue of deafness or even denial in responding to warning signs, implementing corrective actions, and avoiding the "too little, too late" syndrome recalled by Merritt (2007).

Safety through lessons learned from incidents requires avoiding the cultivation of a bureaucratic approach (an office mentality and sticking to procedures), and instead to go beyond official rules and transcend boundaries. Should we become complacent, we should remind ourselves that prior to Three Mile Island, there was a similar accident in Switzerland, but it was not mandatory to inform the American safety authorities about events occurring abroad. This task (on generic lessons) has still not been perfectly achieved within industries, and even less between industries.

References

Amalberti, R., C. Vincent, Y. Auroy, and G. De Saint-Maurice. 2006. Violations and migrations in health care: A framework for understanding and management. *Journal of Quality and Safety in Health Care* 15 (1): i66–i71.

Blatter, C., N. Dechy, and S. Garandel (2016). Vers un retour d'expérience prenant en compte les facteurs organisationnels et humains. *édité par l'IMdR*. http://www.imdr.fr

Bourrier, M. 2011. The legacy of the high-reliability organization project. *Journal of Contingencies and Crisis Management* 19 (1): 9–13.

Carroll, J., and B. Fahlbruch. 2011. Honoring B. Wilpert, "The gift of failure: New approaches to analyzing and learning from events and near-misses". *Safety Science* 49 (1): 1–106.

Carroll, J.S., J.W. Rudolph, and S. Hatakenaka. 2003. Learning from organizational experience. In *Blackwell handbook of organizational learning and knowledge management*, ed. M. Easterby-Smith and M.A. Lyles, 575–600. Malden: Blackwell.

Columbia Accident Investigation Board. 2003. *Report*. Vol. 1. Washington, DC: National Aeronautics and Space Administration. http://caib.nasa.gov

Cullen, W. D. [Lord] 2000. *The Ladbroke Grove rail inquiry*. Part 1 and part 2 reports. Norwich: HSE Books, Her Majesty's Stationery Office. [Report Part 2: 2001].

Cyert, R.M., and J.G. March. 1963. *A behavioural theory of the firm*. Cambridge, MA: Blackwell.

Dechy, N., Y. Dien, and M. Llory. 2009. *Les échecs organisationnels du retour d'expérience*. INERIS report N°DRA-08-95321-15660A, 23/12/2008. http://www.ineris.fr

———. 2010. For a culture of accidents dedicated to industrial safety. *Congrès λμ17 de l'IMdR*. La Rochelle, October 5–7.

Dechy, N., J.-M. Rousseau, and F. Jeffroy. 2011a. Learning lessons from accidents with a human and organisational factors perspective: Deficiencies and failures of operating experience feedback systems. EUROSAFE 2011 conference, Paris.

Dechy, N., J.-M. Rousseau, and M. Llory. 2011b. Are organizational audits of safety that different from organizational investigation of accidents? ESREL conference, Troyes, France, September 18–22.

Dechy, N., Y. Dien, E. Funnemark, S. Roed-Larsen, J. Stoop, T. Valvisto, and A.-L. Vetere Arellano, on behalf of ESReDA Accident Investigation Working Group. 2012. Results and lessons learned from the ESReDA's accident investigation working group. *Safety Science* 50 (6): 1380–1391.

Dechy, N., J.-M. Rousseau, Y. Dien, M. Llory, and R. Montmayeul. 2016. Learning lessons from TMI to Fukushima and other industrial accidents: Keys for assessing safety management practice. Proceedings of the IAEA international conference on human and organizational aspects of assuring nuclear safety – Exploring 30 years of safety culture. Proceedings of the IAEA conference on the 30 years of safety culture. Vienna, Austria, February 22–26.

Dekker, S. 2008. *Just culture: Balancing safety and accountability*. Aldershot: Ashgate.

Department Of Energy. 2005. Action plan on lessons learned from the Columbia Space Shuttle accident and Davis-Besse reactor pressure-vessel head corrosion event. https://ehss.energy.gov/deprep/2005/TB05L29F.PDF

Detert, J.R., and A.C. Edmondson. 2011. Implicit voice theories: Taken-for-granted rules of self-censorship at work. *Academy of Management Journal* 54 (3): 461–488. https://doi.org/10.5465/AMJ.2011.61967925.

Dien, Y., and M. Llory. 2005. Veille technologique et scientifique, accidents, incidents et crises – Les "marqueurs" de facteurs organisationnels pathogènes: Cas de la NASA à partir des données de l'accident de la navette Columbia – rapport EDF R&D HT-52/05/020/A.

Dien, Y., M. Llory, and R. Montmayeul. 2004. Organisational accidents investigation methodology and lessons learned. *Journal of Hazardous Materials* 111: 147–153.

Dien, Y., N. Dechy, and E. Guillaume. 2012. Accident investigation: From searching direct causes to finding in-depth causes. Problem of analysis or/and of analyst? *Safety Science* 50 (6): 1398–1407.

Drupsteen, L., and F.W. Guldenmund. 2014. What is learning? A review of the safety literature to define learning from incidents, accidents and disasters. *Journal of Contingencies and Crisis Management* 22 (2): 81–96.

Eddy, P., E. Potter, and B. Page. 1976. *Destination disaster*. London: Hart-Davis, MacGibbon.

Edmondson, A.C. 1999. Psychological safety and learning behavior in work teams. *Administrative Science Quarterly* 44 (2): 350–383. https://doi.org/10.2307/2666999.

ESReDA. 2009. Guidelines for safety investigation of accidents. http://www.esreda.org

———. 2015. Barriers to *learning from incidents and accidents*. ESReDA technical report, coordinated by E. Marsden. http://www.esreda.org

Ferjencik, M. 2011. An integrated approach to the analysis of incident causes. *Safety Science* 49: 886–905.

Frei, R., J. Kingston, F. Koornneef, and P. Schallier. 2003. Investigation tools in context. Proceedings of the JRC/ESReDA 24th seminar on "Safety investigation of accidents." Petten: The Netherlands, May 12–13. http://www.nri.eu.com

Goffman, E. 1959. *The presentation of self in everyday life*. New York: Doubleday.

Hagen, J. 2013. *Confronting mistakes: Lessons from the aviation industry when dealing with errors*. Houndmills/Basingstoke/Hampshire: Palgrave Macmillan.

Hayes, J. 2015. Taking responsibility for public safety: How engineers seek to minimise disaster incubation in design of hazardous facilities. *Safety Science* 77: 48–56.

Hollnagel, E., D.D. Woods, and N.C. Leveson, eds. 2006. *Resilience engineering: Concepts and precepts*. Aldershot: Ashgate.

Hopkins, A. 2010. *Failure to learn: The BP Texas City refinery disaster*. Sydney: CCH Australia.

Kingston, J., R. Frei, F. Koornneef, and P. Schallier. 2007. *Defining operational readiness to investigate (DORI)*. White paper 1.

Kingston J., Y. Dien, and N. Dechy. 2011. Safer access to space and hard lessons from soft sciences: Organisational failures and challenges learned from space and technological disasters. Proceedings of the space access international conference, Paris, France, September 21–23.

Koornneef, F. 2000. Organised learning from small-scale incidents. PhD thesis, Delft, The Netherlands, Delft University Press.

Langåker, L. 2007. An inquiry into the front roads and back alleys of organisational learning. Proceedings of the organization learning, knowledge and capabilities conference. London, Ontario. http://www2.warwick.ac.uk/fac/soc/wbs/conf/olkc/archive/olkc2/papers/langaker_and_nylehn.pdf

Leveson, N. 1995. *Safeware, system safety and computers – A guide to preventing accidents and losses caused by technology*. Boston: Addison-Wesley.

Leveson, N., and C. Turner. 1993. An investigation of the Therac-25 accidents, 0018-9162/93/0700-0018 – IEEE. *Computer* 26 (7.) (July): 18–41.

Llory, M. 1996. *Accidents industriels: le coût du silence, Opérateurs privés de parole et cadres introuvables*. Paris: Éditions L'Harmattan.

———. 1999. *L'accident de la centrale nucléaire de Three Mile Island*. Paris: Éditions L'Harmattan.

Llory, M., and Y. Dien. 2006. Les systèmes sociotechniques à risques: Une nécessaire distinction entre fiabilité et sécurité. Performances n°30, n°31, n°32.

Llory, M., and R. Montmayeul. 2010. L'accident et l'organisation. Editions Préventique.

Marsden, E. 2014. Ed. Groupe de travail REX FonCSI coordonné par E. Marsden, Quelques bonnes questions à se poser sur son dispositif de retour d'expérience, Les cahiers de sécurité industrielle, n° 2014–01. http://www.foncsi.org

McIntyre, G. 2000. *Patterns in safety thinking – A literature guide to air transportation safety*. Aldershot: Ashgate.

Merritt, C.W. 2007. Testimony of Carolyn W. Merritt, U.S. CSB, Before the US House of Representatives. Committee on energy and commerce, subcommittee on investigations and oversight, May 16.

Myers, L. 2002. Management and human root causes, Davis-Besse Nuclear Power Station. FENOC, August 15.

National Diet of Japan. 2012. The official report of the Fukushima nuclear accident independent investigation commission. Executive summary. Tokyo: National Diet of Japan.

Nuclear Regulatory Commission. 2002. Issues "Lessons learned" task force report on agency's handling of Davis-Besse reactor vessel head damage. *NRC News*, US Nuclear Regulatory Commission.

Ramanujam R., and J. Carroll. 2013. Learning from failure. In *Grote and Carroll (2013), Safety management in context – Cross-industry learning for theory and praxis*.

June 19–21, 2013. White Book edited by Swiss Re Centre for Global Dialogue. http://www.swissre.com/cgd

Rasmussen, J. 1997. Risk management in a dynamic society: A modelling problem. *Safety Science* 27 (2/3): 183–213.

Rasmussen, J., and I. Svedung. 2000. *Proactive risk management in a dynamic society.* Technical report. Karlstad: Swedish Rescue Services Agency. https://www.msb.se/ribdata/filer/pdf/16252.pdf

Reason, J. 1997. *Managing the risks of organizational accidents.* Aldershot: Ashgate.

Rousseau, J.-M. 2008. Safety management in a competitiveness context. EUROSAFE forum proceedings, Paris, France, November 3–4.

Rousseau, J.-M., and A. Largier. 2008. Conduire un diagnostic organisationnel par la recherche de facteurs pathogènes, Techniques de l'Ingénieur AG 1576.

Rousseau J.-M. et al. 2014. Faire du REX aujourd'hui: pourquoi? comment? – Repères pour un retour d'expérience événementiel source d'apprentissages, rapport IRSN PSN-SRDS/2014–00019. http://www.irsn.fr

Santayana, G. 1905. *The life of reason.* Ithaca: Cornell University Library.

Sklet, S. 2004. Comparison of some selected methods for accident investigation. *Journal of Hazardous Materials* 111 (1–3): 29–37.

Snook, S.A. 2000. *Friendly fire, the accidental shootdown of US Black Hawks over Northern Iraq.* Princeton: Princeton University Press.

Starbuck, W.H., and P. Baumard. 2005. Learning from failures: Why it may not happen. *Long Range Planning* 38: 281–298.

Turner, B., and N. Pidgeon. 1997. *Man-made disasters.* Second ed. Oxford: Butterworth Heinemann. [First edition: Turner, B. (1978). Wykeham Publications].

US Chemical Safety and Hazard Investigation Board. 2007. *Investigation report, refinery explosion and fire, BP – Texas City.* Texas, March 23, 2005. Report no 2005-04-I-TX. http://www.csb.gov

Vaughan, D. 1996. *The challenger launch decision. Risky technology, culture, and deviance at NASA.* Chicago: University of Chicago Press.

7

Understanding Safety Management Through Strategic Design, Political, and Cultural Approaches

John S. Carroll

The reporting of accidents, near misses, errors, surprises, and opportunities for improvement is a key component within both safety management systems and safety culture. But to understand how reporting occurs, and when it fails to occur, we must consider the organizational and institutional context within which reporting functions.

As professional groups have distinct goals, experiences, and expertise that shape their judgments, we need more than one lens when discussing the failure or success of error reporting.

Looking through the strategic design lens, reporting should be part of everyone's job description and is another task that people in an organization must fulfill. Therefore, the reporting system should be easy to use, regardless of whether it is a paper document, a web portal, a discussion with the supervisor, or an Employee Concerns Program. Expectations have to be set and communicated to the workforce, and measures have to be available to assess results.

Examined through the political lens, reporting systems are intertwined with power, status, and relationships. In this context, a report is no longer a communication of errors, but it may place some workers or managers at risk of looking bad or being blamed. These problems are not solved by having a well-designed reporting system. The stakeholder conflicts we are dealing with here need to be addressed rather than being dismissed as impediments to successful error reporting.

J. S. Carroll
Cambridge, USA

© The Author(s) 2018   **129**
J. U. Hagen (ed.), *How Could This Happen?*, https://doi.org/10.1007/978-3-319-76403-0_7

Reporting becomes a cultural habit or routine when we see others reporting, and these role models tell stories about having an impact from their reporting. When we see that reporting helps address common problems, then it becomes meaningful in a way that is not just part of our job description but also becomes embedded into the culture for sustained impact.

In analyzing an event, the ideas from each lens are not so much added together as they are compared against each other and combined to achieve a more comprehensive analysis from multiple perspectives. Most importantly, a richer analysis suggests more ways to intervene to bring change, support change, overcome resistance, and achieve the desired outcomes.

Safety management is an evolving set of concepts, tools, and practices. Although we are making considerable advances in addressing the complexities of technologies, human behavior, and organizational systems, considerable work remains, requiring a necessary openness to multiple ideas. Recent approaches range from formal safety management systems that rely on organizational structures and rules, to high-reliability organizing and safety-culture concepts that focus on human cognition and organizational culture. This chapter offers three perspectives, or "lenses," on organizations—namely, strategic design, political, and cultural lenses—that can be used to map out and analyze safety management approaches. Using the lenses sequentially and in combination offers a comprehensive and systemic view of safety management. The example of error reporting is used to illustrate organizational practices and design opportunities arising from the use of all three lenses.

Introduction

Decades ago, Rasmussen (1990) noted that explanations for accidents in organizations had gone through historical phases, first focusing on technology and then on human error by frontline workers (what Reason [1990] called the "sharp end"). He predicted the focus would move upstream (in time and status) to implicate designers and managers. Indeed, recent and increasingly widespread approaches to safety focus on safety management systems and safety culture (e.g., Reason 1997), which comprise structures and processes within the responsibilities of senior levels of management.

Although the progression may appear as progress, Rasmussen noted that investigators tend to see what they are prepared to see, that is, what they expect to find based on shared mental models in their environments. But those mental models are not universal, even in a single time period. For example, Schein (1996), Carroll (1998), and Rasmussen (1993, 1997) suggest that professional groups have distinct goals, experiences, and expertise that shape their judgments. Academic disciplines bring varied values, goals, and paradigms with overlapping, yet distinct theories and models. Engineers, operators, and managers have different understandings of a production plant. Scientists, community members, lawyers, designers, consultants, and risk analysts have different perspectives and different criteria for what constitutes a good explanation of an accident and how to avoid future accidents.

We could react to these variations in at least two basic ways. First, we could consider safety management (or any kind of management) to be an immature field at this point in history and believe that a comprehensive and valid "systems" theory will someday arise to surpass or bypass current approaches. Of course, until then, we have to make do with what we have. Second, we could accept that there will *never* be one accepted universal theory or approach, and therefore we need to cultivate multiple viewpoints and build capabilities and habits to combine diverse approaches to address particular situations. Although it may sound as if these views are the same—given current practice, which lacks the "one right way"—the former leans toward a competition among approaches and disparagement of other views, whereas the latter leans toward interdependence, interdisciplinary inquiry and dialogue, collaboration, and growth.

My argument is that there is now, and will be for the foreseeable future, a need for individuals and collectives to have a "conceptual toolbox" rather than a single tool. As Weick (1992, cited in Anderson 2007) notes,

> the idea of a conceptual toolbox fits quite well with the notion of requisite variety; it takes variety (in the toolbox) to sense and register variety in the world.... And conceptual toolboxes increase the chance that at least one of your explanations will converge with the explanation of someone else, hence, agreement and collaboration are made possible.... Any conceptual tool creates blind spots. More tools means the potential for offsetting some of the blind spots.... A big toolbox means that you retain adaptability and do NOT fall into the trap wherein adaptation precludes adaptability.

Accordingly, I suggest that we accept the necessity of using multiple approaches to enrich our understanding and stimulate ideas for improvement. In this chapter, I use a framework for organizational analysis called "The Three Lenses," which offers three perspectives on organizations: strategic design, political, and cultural lenses (Ancona et al. 2004). I first briefly describe the three lenses before illustrating the framework through analysis of a key process in safety management: the reporting of accidents, near misses, errors, surprises, and opportunities for improvement. I then examine safety management more broadly through the three lenses and suggest directions forward for both research and management practice.

The Three Lenses

As summarized in Fig. 7.1, each of the three lenses distills the essence of related theories that share ideas about human nature, the functions of organizations, the meaning of organizing, the information needed to make sense of an organization, and ways to bring about change. By using all the lenses to analyze an organization or problem, we gain new insights and a richer understanding of organizational dynamics and human behavior within organizations.

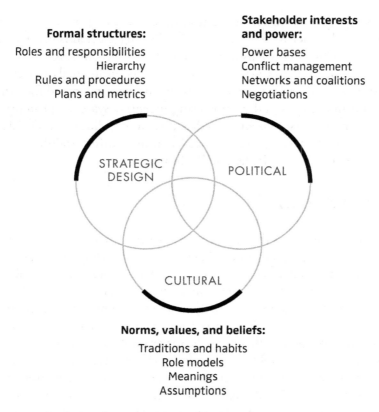

Formal structures:

Roles and responsibilities
Hierarchy
Rules and procedures
Plans and metrics

**Stakeholder interests
and power:**

Power bases
Conflict management
Networks and coalitions
Negotiations

STRATEGIC
DESIGN

POLITICAL

CULTURAL

Norms, values, and beliefs:

Traditions and habits
Role models
Meanings
Assumptions

Fig. 7.1 Organizations as human systems—the three lenses

The Strategic Design Lens

The strategic design lens views an organization as a kind of machine that has been designed to achieve goals by carrying out tasks. The organizational vision or purpose is implemented through a strategy for achieving that vision, based on an assessment of fit between opportunities, threats, and capabilities. Action comes about through planning. An airline, for example, would have a strategy of moving passengers via aircraft between destinations in order to meet its goals of profit, growth, service, and so forth. People, money, equipment, and information are assigned using logical principles of efficiency and effectiveness to achieve organizational goals.

Every organization uses grouping of people and tasks—typically by specialty, geography, product, or customer—to facilitate the flow of materials and information. An airline has to organize operations and crews, maintenance, sales, and other functions by hiring and contracting various types of expertise and locating them where needed. When people are grouped together, information is transmitted more readily within the group, but information also has to flow across boundaries using linking mechanisms, including the management hierarchy, liaison roles, task forces, accounting and IT systems, planning processes, and meetings. Since specific individuals and groups may have different values and goals, alignment mechanisms coordinate the efforts of diverse individuals and groups using incentive systems (promotions, pay, bonuses, better assignments, medals), resource allocation decisions, and human resource development processes around hiring, training, mentoring, and job rotation (e.g., Nadler and Tushman 1997).

The Political Lens

The political lens views the organization as a contested struggle for power (the ability to get things done) among stakeholders with different goals and underlying interests (Pfeffer 2010). Because organizations pursue multiple goals (e.g., production, safety, environment, worker satisfaction, profit, growth, innovation), conflicts are continually arising and being handled. Organizations often translate goal conflicts into conflicts between managers and groups assigned to champion different goals, for example, production and safety. An airline pilot, for example, may receive different messages from operations managers seeking on-time performance and fuel-cost reduction and safety managers seeking reduced risk from weather and air traffic hazards.

Groups with similar interests and goals combine to form coalitions that advocate their side of important issues. External parties such as shareholders (whose goal is profits) and regulators (whose goal is safety) may align with different internal factions. Goals and strategies are either imposed by a guiding coalition or negotiated among interest groups. Individuals and groups have different sources of power or power bases, including a formal position or authority; control over scarce resources; rules and regulations; information and expertise; seniority; relationships with others; skill with manipulating symbols and persuading others; and personal energy and charisma. As the environment shifts or new strategies are developed, groups that have the capabilities to deal with these new demands may gain power, but existing power holders may resist losing their power and status by delaying and subverting any change.

The Cultural Lens

The cultural lens assumes that people take action as a function of the meanings they assign to situations. Cultural elements—the symbols, stories, and experiences from which meanings are derived—are shared among members of a culture and transmitted to new members. Cultures develop over time as groups address important problems and pass on their traditions. Two airlines in the same industry, for example, could have quite distinct corporate cultures with divergent focuses on costs versus service and short-term versus long-term issues, and different understandings of leadership, excellence, expertise, and cooperation.

Cultures can be thought of in layers, with visible symbols or artifacts that are easily observed at the surface layer, articulated values and beliefs that are written and discussed just under the surface, and a deep layer of assumptions and meanings that are more difficult to bring to the surface (Schein 2016). Culture is a way of life; it is what we do around here and why we do it. Action comes about through habit and routine. Organizational cultures may be relatively uniform or fragmented into geographical, hierarchical, occupational, or departmental subcultures. For example, do the pilots and mechanics identify more strongly with their airline or with their occupational group? Does headquarters have an executive culture that is different from local operations (see Schein 1996)?

The Reporting of Problems, Incidents, Near Misses, and Opportunities for Improvement

The reporting of accidents, near misses, errors, surprises, and opportunities for improvement is a key component within both safety management systems and safety culture. But to understand how reporting occurs, and when it fails to occur, we must consider the organizational and institutional context within which reporting functions. We first briefly describe formal and informal reporting systems and their place in safety management, use each lens to consider the issue of reporting, and bring the lenses together with some additional thoughts and recommendations.

Organizations need everyone to speak up about problems and opportunities. Risks are dynamic, which means that the conditions and actions leading up to an accident change over time. A risk may emerge and then subside, for example, when a particular mechanic with inadequate training is performing a particular repair—right then the plant is vulnerable, but that vulnerability may disappear with the next inspection or repair. If that repair happens while another system is unavailable due to testing or upgrading, and a supervisor out for training is replaced temporarily by another person with less knowledge of systems, suddenly there is a potential confluence of weaknesses or defects that could assemble into an accident. But if nothing triggers that accident or enough defenses remain, the entire situation could evaporate and never appear the same way again. There are untold numbers of such events and behaviors occurring that open and close windows of vulnerability. If the system is allowed to drift toward failure (Dekker 2011) without an awareness of vulnerabilities or actions to control them (Leveson 2012), then more and more weaknesses will exist for longer periods of time. But if these weaknesses are appreciated, searched for, detected early, and acted upon quickly, then the organization can reduce these opportunities and guide the system away from vulnerable states. Such self-correction or self-improvement requires hazard awareness, vigilance, reporting, speaking up (see Edmondson 1999), and corrective actions.

There are many examples of formal and informal reporting systems. Aviation has a confidential system for reporting near misses and then accumulating these "weak signals" to detect problems with particular airplanes, airports, regions, and so on. Nuclear power plants encourage employees to report huge numbers of problems, which then go into a triage system to prioritize further investigation and corrective action. In the Toyota Production System, employees are empowered to "pull the cord" to stop production whenever something is beyond acceptable boundaries. Inspections, audits, and engaged supervision add layers of monitoring and feedback that can result in the reporting of problems.

There is a deep belief that accidents are preventable and safety is achievable. Investigations of accidents reveal that there were signals of trouble and people knew something was wrong, but they either failed to speak up or were not listened to. It is easy to know in hindsight what signals should have been heeded, but it is far more difficult to deal with hundreds or thousands of reports, most of which appear trivial or "normal" until the accident happens (Vaughan 1996). There are many potential answers to this problem that have been tried in various industries. Our hope in this chapter is to understand better why things go well or go wrong and what can be done to improve the odds.

Reporting Through the Strategic Design Lens

As Schwartz (2011) suggests, when managers want to get something done in organizations, they typically write rules (policies, procedures) and/or establish incentives (rewards and punishments). Managers also create organizational structures in the form of tasks, roles and responsibilities, hierarchical relationships (lines of authority), and department structures. These actions focus on the strategic design elements of grouping, linking, and aligning. In short, managers set goals, make people accountable, measure progress, and reward those who produce the right results. This is indeed the underlying logic of safety management systems, which require organizations to iteratively set goals and measure progress, and then raise the goals as performance improves.

Reporting can also be managed the same way. Looking through the strategic design lens, reporting should be an expectation for everyone's job description, another task they must fulfill. The reporting system should be easy to use, regardless of whether it is a paper document, a web portal, a discussion with the supervisor, a discussion with the Employee Concerns Program, and so on. The resources have to be made available; someone has to be placed in charge and accountable for results; expectations have to be set and communicated to the workforce; measures have to be available to assess results (e.g., number of reports, categories of reports, categories of report makers); and employees should be rewarded for reporting (with praise, good catch awards, gift certificates, etc.). If reports are not forthcoming in the desired numbers and quality, then the organization should reinforce the importance of reporting in training, instruct supervisors to encourage and coach reporting, make the systems easier to use, and increase the incentives to report (bigger rewards, part of promotion consideration).

The aviation reporting system is a good example of strong incentives to report, in that many voluntarily reported errors are forgiven, but failure to report becomes an extremely serious action subject to severe sanctions. The Nuclear Regulatory Commission also takes into account whether a problem was self-reported by a power plant, which is much more desirable for everyone than having the problem discovered through an external audit or investigation after an accident. In essence, every defect or problem is not only a test of the organization's quality and safety, but also a test of its ability to detect and report its own issues. Consistent with Leveson (2015), it is also a test of assumptions about the functioning of the feedback and control system that maintains safety.

Reporting Through the Political Lens

Managers may be surprised to discover that the elaborate reporting systems they have put in place are not generating a large number of reports, and that incidents continue to occur even though workers should have been reporting precursors to the incidents early enough to avoid more serious issues. The reporting system exists, expectations have been communicated, rewards have been given out, but not much is being reported. Sometimes, a lot may be reported, but it looks like unimportant, low-level stuff, not the important vulnerabilities and near misses that the system is designed to reveal.

Examined through the political lens, reporting systems are intertwined with power, status, and relationships. A report is not simply a communication of facts about the plant, but most likely places some workers or managers at risk of looking bad or being blamed for a problem. Problem reports create work, possibly even for the reporter of the problem (OK, thanks for telling us, now go fix it), or more likely for others who may or may not appreciate the extra tasks. Problem reporting can upend the hierarchy by empowering the lowest-level worker to make complaints, even if their manager is the focus of the complaints. It also may empower those who do not understand what they are reporting—challenging and diminishing the authority of the subject matter experts. In nuclear power plants, a confidential report to the Employee Concerns Program bypasses the supervisory hierarchy and affords that employee legal protection against "harassment, intimidation, retaliation, or discrimination." This sounds great except when an employee who knows they are at risk of being fired decides to make claims about safety concerns, which places them in protected status. In short, rules intended to promote reporting for all the right reasons become a source of power capable of being misused.

Even when reporting systems are confidential, it is likely that people will find out eventually about who reported what. Those connected to the reporting individual in a network of relationships may feel betrayed, in that their friend has "told" on them or just created more paperwork or busywork. Or they may feel disrespected, in that their expertise was not trusted, and the reporting individual believed they knew more about the situation and took it upon themselves to make trouble. Even those not personally connected to the reporting individual may feel that there is an "us versus them" dynamic in which members of some groups are using the reporting system to take action against other groups, as when engineers report on operators or vice versa. Or, workers may feel a "chilling effect" when their manager or managers in general are discouraging reporting.

The key to understanding the political lens is recognizing that not every employee or manager shares the goals of the plant or of the owners of the plant. Instead, they may be seeking to make their jobs easier, or more interesting, or more important. Or they may be seeking friendships and belonging at work. Or they may have values and principles about safety, environment, or quality that are not aligned fully (or not perceived to be aligned fully) with the trade-offs made by senior managers. Reporting then gets conflated with the goals of particular stakeholders, for example, reporting too little so as not to damage relationships with others or reporting too much while pushing a personal agenda.

None of the above problems are entirely unpredictable or unmanageable. However, they are not removed just by having a well-designed reporting system. The way in which that system is implemented—and the preexisting aspects of the organization into which it is placed—can subvert even the best strategic design.

Reporting Through the Cultural Lens

Management wants reporting to be a habit or routine—it is the way we do business and a key component of safety culture (Reason 1997). Reporting because your supervisor tells you to report, or because you could get a $50 gift certificate, or because it is part of your job responsibilities and affects your bonus—these are all reasonable motivations. However, there are other, possibly more powerful motivations, such as reporting because we are helping our team, because it makes work better, or because it makes the organization safer and more productive. Reporting becomes a habit or routine when we see others reporting routinely, and these role models tell stories about having an impact from their reporting. When we see that reporting helps address common problems, then it becomes meaningful in a way that is very different from a monetary incentive and embedded into the culture for sustained impact (see Schein 2016).

In contrast, many reporting systems are "black holes" from the viewpoint of the workforce—reports go in and nothing comes out. Report makers do not hear what is done about their report; they do not see changes they imagined would occur; they do not know why decisions were made to do nothing at this time; they may not even be thanked. The feeling is that they were not heard, not respected, not appreciated. Management does not listen; management does not care. These cultural meanings are very different from what was intended when setting up the reporting system. It may be the case that reports were taken seriously and changes planned, but no one informed those making the reports. As a result, it should not be surprising that reporting dries up due to a lack of visible feedback and improvement. Worse, the ill feelings create cynicism and fan intergroup tensions.

People want to contribute to something bigger than themselves. Skilled leaders know how to articulate a purpose that engages the mind and the heart. Those leaders have to be familiar with, or in dialogue with, the various stakeholders. In short, they have to listen and care. Paul O'Neill at Alcoa made worker safety the focus of his strategy. It was something that everyone could get behind, except Wall Street analysts who thought he was nuts and told their investors to sell Alcoa. But it was also an indirect approach to production improvement: By analyzing and changing the habits that affected worker safety, Alcoa was reexamining and restructuring its inefficient and dangerous production process (Duhigg 2014). Safety improved, but so did production efficiency, innovation, morale, and profits. Unlike the negative side effects of beneficial intentions, these were positive effects intended and delivered by a focus on worker well-being.

Putting the Lenses Together: So What?

The point of the three-lenses analysis is to offer insight, not confusion. We can look separately through each lens in order to be comprehensive, but in order to see the system as a whole, we have to put the lenses together to consider the interconnections. A reporting system does not exist on its own. It has to relate to: the people who will report as well as those who will handle reports; the technology of reporting and the technology of work; the organization in which the reporting system must exist; and the external context of stakeholders and institutions. Both engineers and managers share a mindset favoring the strategic design lens: They see the world as rational and controllable. Strategic design thinking is important and necessary, but it is not sufficient to achieve success. We must also make a deliberate effort to think about the political and cultural bases for—and implications of—actions. Implementation of new technologies, including information technologies, reporting technologies, and so forth, often fail to achieve the desired results due to implementation failures: right technology, wrong way of introducing it. Sometimes the desired improvements require multiple rounds of action and feedback—if the organization expects success on the first round, the resources and engagement may not be sufficient to sustain efforts beyond the initial phase (Repenning and Sterman 2001; Tyre and Orlikowski 1994).

An interesting example is the SUBSAFE program in the US Navy, which emerged after the catastrophic loss of the USS *Thresher* nuclear submarine in 1963 (Sullivan 2003). The *Thresher* sank and imploded when welds gave way, salt water soaked electronic controls, and the sub could not surface. The SUBSAFE program was developed in a matter of months to ensure that subs would be able to maintain hull integrity and operability of crucial systems to allow control and recovery. The program involved a very detailed set of design requirements and audits. But included in the program was a requirement that any failure to meet specification had to be reported within 24 hours to the admiral in charge of operations. Although this may seem like a straightforward strategic design requirement with rules and incentives, consider how the organization would have to change in order to make this possible. In most organizations, there is no possibility that some event occurring on the shop floor of a factory is going to make its way to the CEO in 24 hours. For that to happen, everyone would have to be vigilant, motivated, and prepared to report quickly. Level after level of hierarchy would have to be ready to process a signal and pass it along. Anyone on vacation or not available would have to be on call or to have someone on call. The entire organization would be upended and reprioritized by this need to get this one piece of information up to the top in such a short period of time. New habits would develop and new meanings arise from this one requirement, along with new assumptions about what is possible and effective. But such a requirement has to be carefully chosen to be achievable, of course, otherwise the leader loses credibility, the organization begins to ignore or subvert the requirement, and we are left with a less manageable and more cynical workforce.

It is tempting to see the political and cultural issues as problems that can be solved through a strategic design lens. Those issues could be addressed by clear roles, rules, responsibilities, and incentives. Strong leaders could try to articulate and mandate the desired safety culture by setting clear expectations and combining inspiration and rewards. However, it is a rare leader indeed who can take a purely top-down approach to change (Beer and Nohria 2000; Schein 2016) by assuming that there is a recipe for leadership and design that will work anywhere. Instead, some degree of inquiry and engagement is necessary to find out the political and cultural realities, enlist key stakeholders and opinion leaders in the change process, and act in ways that build momentum, ultimately shifting the political and cultural landscape.

Take, for example, the aviation reporting system. The key insight that led to a high degree of reporting was to address the fear that reports would be used against pilots. This fear arose from both political and cultural sources. Pilots are a powerful stakeholder group, with key expertise needed by the airlines and a strong union voice. Investigations of accidents typically focused on pilot error, with differences of opinion arising from different stakeholder groups. Mistrust and defensiveness became part of the culture. It is not surprising that a voluntary reporting system produced few reports. What was needed was a confidential reporting system that pilots could trust. That was achieved by engaging a trusted third party, NASA, to receive the reports and maintain confidentiality. Of course, that confidentiality was not absolute, but agreements had to be negotiated about exactly when the reports could be identifiable in order to meet goals of safety and fairness (Reason's [1997] just culture). Notice that in a different organization and different place and time characterized by high trust and different political issues, a confidential reporting system might not be necessary and might even be counterproductive. Indeed, over time, the parties might be able to build sufficient trust that people would be willing to report openly. The point here is that we can only make our best guess about the necessary policies and procedures based on a careful analysis using all three lenses and then examine the results and make adjustments as needed.

Safety Management Through the Three Lenses

Over the past decades, attention has shifted from technological approaches to human error reduction to management and organizational issues, and will undoubtedly cycle through these repeatedly. Current "systems" approaches to safety draw primarily from the strategic design lens, whereas the growing influence of "safety culture" links to the cultural lens. Interestingly, stakeholder conflicts are usually seen as impediments to change, sand in the gears, as well as irrational and shameful, rather than being explicitly understood through the political lens.

Safety Management Systems (SMS) (also known as Safety and Environment Management Systems) establish goals and measures of both process and performance and define roles and responsibilities in the management structure. In the traditional form of safety management, requirements are written and compliance is enforced. Requirements often come from professional societies such as the American Society of Mechanical Engineers or regulatory authorities, including both functional specifications, such as the required material composition and thickness of pipes, and inspection routines to ensure compliance. In risk-informed approaches to safety management, organizations are given risk targets and have latitude to choose among the ways to reduce risk. The same organization may choose to control the risks associated with older pipes either by replacement or inspection or a combination (depending on the age of the pipes, their location, and/or the specific hazards associated with each pipe).

SMS essentially function by issuing and enforcing rules and organizing around rules. But it is extremely difficult to write all the necessary rules and to avoid any possibilities of rules being incomplete, ambiguous, confusing, in conflict, in error, or out of date. Do workers see the rules as a requirement, a resource, or an excuse for management to blame them if anything goes wrong? In many organizations, people circumvent or reinvent the rules in order to get the work done efficiently, or simply for their own convenience, creating informal rules about "how we work around here." Some people may be allowed to break rules (the experts?), whereas others must follow them. But which rules can be broken, when, and by whom?

Because organizations pursue multiple goals, such as production, profit, and safety, there are conflicts that must be resolved among those goals and between short-term and long-term goals. Different stakeholders tend to advocate for different priorities among those goals: The production department prioritizes production, whereas the safety department prioritizes safety. Hence, goal conflicts are translated into political conflicts among stakeholder groups. Of course, the organization does not have to group goals in this way: Safety could be a goal for production managers, with safety experts reporting to production managers, or safety experts could advise production managers while reporting to a safety department. If safety has its own department, experts can easily share information, develop competence, and stay on top of the latest professional information in their field and industry. Career paths are clear. However, it may become difficult for the professional experts to understand the operational issues on the shop floor, since they rarely get out of their offices or out from behind their computers, and operating managers find their advice difficult to understand or inflexible—out of touch with their needs. As a result, pressure develops to relocate the experts or reassign them to operating departments, thereby resulting in more flexibility and innovation that helps operations. But when that occurs, there is a tendency to lose focus on safety and to slowly erode specific safety expertise. At that point, pressure may develop to strengthen the central safety group in order to rebuild expertise and ensure that someone is "in charge of safety." Then every 10 years we reorganize again (Nickerson and Zenger 2002).

One of the newest and most systematic approaches to safety management is the System-Theoretic Accident Model and Processes (STAMP) (Leveson 2012, 2015). STAMP is based on the concept that safety is an emergent systems property rather than an aggregation of reliable components. Safety is ensured by maintaining control over hazards through control actions and information feedback, arranged in a hierarchical structure of control. Such control structures include both human and technological components. In the modern airline cockpit, for example, the pilot does not "fly" the plane but rather issues commands to computers that actuate the physical components of the plane. Instrument indicators and sensory cues return feedback about what the plane is actually doing. The electronic controls have embedded within them a model of how the plane is supposed to behave, including issuing warnings or overriding a pilot's command if it is deemed dangerous or impossible. Of course, this creates new failure modes, as pilots may no longer understand what the controls are doing in planes that have been designed to be flown by computer, not by humans.

But the pilot is only part of the control structure. The pilot in turn receives advisories and commands from airline operations management and air traffic control (ATC) and additional advisories from the electronic Traffic Alert and Collision Avoidance System (TCAS). These elements of the control structure are concerned not only with a single plane (the primary role of the pilot) but also with a system of planes and support structures. Operations management needs to move planes around to serve customers and also to minimize costs (airline fuel, etc.). ATC needs to ensure smooth and safe takeoffs and landings and transfer of control across geographical boundaries. Airline operations reports to the airline corporate structure, which itself receives requirements and delivers reports to shareholders, regulators, the public, financial markets, and so on. ATC itself receives direction from—and reports to—various governmental entities. TCAS receives information from the transponders on other aircraft in the vicinity and provides advisories to ensure safe distance with aircraft at the same altitude.

STAMP is a comprehensive and logical approach to creating structures that maintain control over safety. However, still buried within the STAMP control structure are the human and organizational elements that must function appropriately to maintain safety. Human "controllers" have their own mental models of safety functions, and those mental models may not be fully accurate or consistent across the entire system. There are still necessary human processes of planning and design, reporting of issues, interpretation and analysis, and redesign that engage multiple goals and multiple stakeholder interests. STAMP can help greatly in reducing the number of conflicts and clarifying the aspects that need to be resolved, thus making the system more controllable, but in any human system, there will be a need for human intervention and system improvement.

Interestingly, the "safety culture" movement has taken a very different approach to ensuring safety. The goal is to instill the value of safety as a high priority from the top of the organization to the shop floor, to ensure hazard awareness and vigilance that leads to a rapid reporting of issues, and to provide the necessary resources and expertise to support safety. After years of resisting any regulatory intrusions into management prerogatives, including "culture," almost every industry has industry groups and regulators that offer measures and suggestions, or even requirements, for culture (e.g., in nuclear power, the INPO 10 Traits [2012]). Accident investigations routinely identify weak safety culture as a cause of incidents, and corrective actions are designed around improving culture. Although this is a huge change, there is no accepted recipe for "improving culture." Part of my argument in this chapter is that a strategic design approach to culture change—with a project team, timeline, culture metrics, and incentives—is not likely to work without more specific attention to the other lenses; but neither will a cultural approach by itself create safety.

For example, high-reliability organizing could be considered a cultural approach to safety. High-reliability organizing (e.g., Weick and Sutcliffe 2001) exhorts everyone to pay attention, focus on the work, give weight to expertise, expect problems and learn from them, and never become complacent (e.g., NASA started referring to the space shuttle as a "bus," mislabeling its operations as simple, familiar, and routine). But high-reliability organizing principles have to be enacted, which involves not only individual behaviors but also organizational structures and processes designed around redundancy of function, slack resources, cross-training, mechanisms for event analysis and learning from operating experience, and so on. For example, although deference to expertise is partially cultural, illustrated by the difference in status accorded to craft workers in the United States and Germany, deference to expertise is also about power. In Germany, the master craftsman is revered as an expert, craft workers have powerful unions, and workers are represented on company boards of directors. In the United States, the chief operator in a nuclear power plant control room is officially (and legally) in charge during any emergency, and yet when an executive shows up and tries to give orders or even ask questions, it is difficult for the chief operator to ask the executive to leave the control room.

One danger of the high-reliability organizing approach is that it can be construed as placing responsibility on the lower ranks of workers to make decentralized decisions. Exhortations for workers to be vigilant about weak signals and to defer decentralized decisions to frontline workers who have detailed knowledge of the work can slip into blaming those workers when something goes wrong (for a failure to be vigilant). A basic engineering principle states that reliance on human attention is the weakest form of defense against accidents. Reliance on decentralized decisions and exhortations to be vigilant in a highly coupled system misses the opportunities to examine the larger system and make improvements in design and operations that help those decentralized decision-makers work better. As Rasmussen (1997) explained in his analysis of the Herald of Free Enterprise ferry disaster, each local actor could "not see the forest for the trees." Expecting a person to interpret and respond to a unique event in the moment is like blaming the goalie in soccer or ice hockey for every goal—reducing shots on goal is everyone's job in a team sport, whereas the goalie is the last (and sometimes desperate) line of defense.

The conceptualization of safety itself—a cultural concept that differs from place to place—affects the way safety is managed. For example, over the past 25 years, BP has had an impressive and measurable reduction in personal safety incidents, driven by an obsessive focus on hazards. The cultural belief was that if employees took care of these personal safety hazards, BP operations would be safe. Unfortunately, as revealed by the Texas City chemical plant explosion in 2005 and the Gulf oil spill in 2010, ensuring process safety or system safety involves a different set of skills and knowledge. Process safety hazards are often invisible and/or involve combinations of multiple pieces of equipment, materials in process, human actions, and computer software that cannot be understood just by looking at them. Nor will following the procedure manual necessarily help in avoiding accidents, since the procedures are sometimes missing, incomplete, confusing, or wrong. Operators at Three Mile Island were trained to do exactly the wrong thing: They believed they should keep the pressurizer from filling completely with water, since that would make the plant vulnerable to water hammer, which could break even very large pipes. Indeed, breaking a pipe on a submarine (which is where many of the operators received their first training in nuclear power operations) is an extreme hazard, whereas losing cooling water in a small reactor with very little nuclear fuel is not much of a problem. However, in a huge commercial nuclear power plant with a huge amount of nuclear fuel, letting the water boil off is a far greater hazard.

Determining risks is also a political act. Perrow's seminal *Normal Accidents* (1984) includes the insightful comment that different industries have different rates of accidents, not simply because of the inherent complexity and riskiness of their technologies but also because of who is at risk. In mining and fishing, two of the most dangerous industries, the miners and fishermen are lower-status workers whose lives and troubles are of little interest to most of society. Their injuries and deaths generate little attention or alarm outside their local communities, unless there is a union or investigative reporter to champion their cause. In contrast, the airline industry is extremely safe in part because the people at risk are elites. Political leaders, industry executives, and wealthy travelers are on board, and if a plane crashes there is enormous attention directed toward the causes of the accident. The Federal Aviation Administration and the National Transportation Safety Board receive far more generous funding than many other regulators because elites influence their representatives to ensure airplane safety.

The SUBSAFE program explicitly recognizes the potential conflict among goals and stakeholders and designed a system of checks and balances reminiscent of the tripartite structure in the US Constitution. Equal voice and weight are given to three key roles: (1) the platform program manager responsible for the design and operation of a particular sub design or "platform"; (2) the independent technical authority responsible for the technical expertise; and (3) the independent quality assurance and safety authority responsible for compliance with requirements. None of these actors can make a unilateral decision: For example, the platform program manager can only choose from among acceptable designs recommended by the independent technical authority; designs can move forward only if all three have agreed that their goals are satisfied.

Putting the Lenses Together: What's Next for Safety Management?

The three-lenses approach is not a theory of organizations or of safety management, but rather an approach to achieving more useful understanding. The lenses are not mutually exclusive, and dividing knowledge up by lens (as we have done sometimes in the above discussion) is only a checkpoint to make sure we are taking everything into consideration. Using all three lenses does not guarantee the right answer. Complex situations do not have a "right answer." Systems do not have root causes; they have causal relationships. In analyzing an event or an organization, the ideas from each lens are not so much added together as they are compared against each other and combined to achieve a more comprehensive analysis from multiple perspectives. Most importantly, a richer analysis suggests more ways to intervene to bring change, support change, overcome resistance, and achieve the desired outcomes.

Researchers and practitioners are increasingly forced to confront the tensions among multiple goals and approaches as systems become more complex and surprising accidents continue to occur. Strong frameworks help greatly with organizing our knowledge, providing ways to link across different domains, and raising new questions. But we should not fall into a certainty trap of believing that any framework is complete; we must maintain openness to new ideas and conversations that cut across areas of professional expertise.

References

Ancona, D., T. Kochan, M. Scully, J. Van Maanen, and D.E. Westney. 2004. *Managing for the future: Organizational behavior & processes.* Third ed. Boston: South-Western College Publishing.

Anderson, M.H. 2007. "Why are there so many theories?" A classroom exercise to help students appreciate the need for multiple theories of a management domain. *Journal of Management Education* 31: 757–776.

Beer, M., and N. Nohria, eds. 2000. *Breaking the code of change.* Boston: Harvard Business School Press.

Carroll, J.S. 1998. Organizational learning activities in high-hazard industries: The logics underlying self-analysis. *Journal of Management Studies* 35: 699–717.

Dekker, S. 2011. *Drift into failure: From hunting broken components to understanding complex systems.* Boca Raton, FL: CRC Press.

Duhigg, C. 2014. *The power of habit: Why we do what we do in life and business.* New York: Random House.

Edmondson, A. 1999. Psychological safety and learning behavior in work teams. *Administrative Science Quarterly* 44: 350–383.

Institute of Nuclear Power Operators (INPO). 2012. *Traits of a healthy nuclear safety culture.* Atlanta: INPO.

Leveson, N. 2012. *Engineering a safer world: Applying systems thinking to safety.* Cambridge, MA: MIT Press.

———. 2015. A systems approach to risk management through leading safety indicators. *Reliability Engineering and System Safety* 136: 17–34.

Nadler, D., and M. Tushman. 1997. *Competing by design: The power of organizational architecture.* New York: Oxford University Press.

Nickerson, J.A., and T.R. Zenger. 2002. Being efficiently fickle: A dynamic theory of organizational choice. *Organization Science* 13: 547–566.

Perrow, C. 1984. *Normal accidents*. New York: Basic Books.

Pfeffer, J. 2010. *Power: Why some people have it—and others don't*. New York: Harper Collins.

Rasmussen, J. 1990. Human error and the problem of causality in analysis of accidents. *Philosophical Transactions of the Royal Society of London B* 327: 449–462.

———. 1993. What can be learned from disasters in other endeavors? Perspectives on the concept of human error. Manuscript for invited contributions to the society for technology in anesthesia conference, New Orleans, 1993, and the First Danish conference on cognitive science research, Roskilde, Denmark, 1992.

———. 1997. Risk management in a dynamic society: A modeling problem. *Safety Science* 27 (2/3): 183–213.

Reason, J. 1990. *Human error*. New York: Cambridge University Press.

———. 1997. *Managing the risks of organizational accidents*. Brookfield: Ashgate.

Repenning, N., and J. Sterman. 2001. Nobody ever gets credit for fixing problems that never happened: Creating and sustaining process improvement. *California Management Review* 43 (4): 64–88.

Schein, E.H. 1996. The three cultures of management: Implications for organizational learning. *Sloan Management Review* 38: 9–20.

———. 2016. *Organizational culture and leadership*. 4th ed. San Francisco: Jossey-Bass.

Schwartz, B. 2011. Practical wisdom and organizations. *Research in Organizational Behavior* 31: 3–23.

Sullivan, P.E. 2003. Statement before the house science committee on the SUBSAFE program. http://www.navy.mil/navydata/testimony/safety/sullivan031029.txt

Tyre, M.J., and W.J. Orlikowski. 1994. Windows of opportunity: Temporal patterns of technological adaptation in organizations. *Organization Science* 5: 98–118.

Vaughan, D. 1996. *The Challenger launch decision*. Chicago: University of Chicago Press.

Weick, K.E. 1992. Agenda setting in organizational behavior: A theory-focused approach. *Journal of Management Inquiry* 1: 171–182.

Weick, K.E., and K.M. Sutcliffe. 2001. *Managing the unexpected: Assuring high performance in an age of complexity*. San Francisco: Jossey-Bass.

8

Errors and Error Management in Biomedical Research

Ulrich Dirnagl and René Bernard

The validity of biomedical research results has come under scrutiny that revolves around factors regarding the quality of these results. However, due to the complexity of the experiments involved, errors quite naturally occur frequently. They include quality-compromised devices, errors due to limitations of measurement, protocol deviations, reporting errors, and human errors caused by carelessness or moments of distraction during complex tasks. Additionally, there are errors of unknown cause, which makes it vital to communicate them and keep a record of them for further investigation.

A way of managing these errors is the "Laboratory Critical Incident and Error Reporting System" (LabCIRS), a software tool to record all incidents anonymously and to analyze, discuss, and communicate them. It has been adapted from the Critical Incident and Error Reporting System (CIRS), used in the clinical world to improve patient safety in complex, fast-paced, and often understaffed settings.

LabCIRS is a nonpunitive format devoid of emotional connotations, exclusively focused on how to avoid errors in the future. Errors are reported, viewed, and initially classified. Thereafter, a decision is made about the urgency of actions. After further discussion, measures to be taken in response are determined and entered into the system. They are presented to the research group in question. A

U. Dirnagl • R. Bernard
Berlin, Germany

© The Author(s) 2018   **149**
J. U. Hagen (ed.), *How Could This Happen?*, https://doi.org/10.1007/978-3-319-76403-0_8

newsletter, issued on a regular basis, summarizes both errors and actions that were taken. No personal information or computer IP is ever recorded, ensuring the confidentiality of the reporter.

LabCIRS could be considered an essential model for any community seeking a systematic error-management strategy to handle quality issues that have become a matter of concern.

Errare humanum est. (To err is human.) Biomedical research, a human enter-prise, is no exception in this regard. Ever more sophisticated methodologies probing how complex organisms function invite errors on all levels—from designing experiments and studies to the collection of data and the reporting of results. The stakes are high in terms of resources spent and professional rewards to be gained for individuals. Up to now, the public has held scien-tists—in particular those aiming to improve human health—in very high esteem. Nevertheless, the exposure of spectacular cases of fraudulent and irre-producible research (Cyranoski 2006; Obokata et al. 2014) and the realiza-tion that biomedical results appear to lack robustness as well as the rigor of the scientific process have recently begun to undermine some of that public trust (Carey 2015).

Even within the research community, there is growing concern that a con-siderable fraction of research is actually waste (Macleod et al. 2014), a notion that is reflected in the fact that a majority of scientists agree that we are expe-riencing a significant "reproducibility crisis" (Baker 2016a). The search for causes and potential remedies has led to introspection, and science has turned its scrutiny upon itself (Ioannidis et al. 2015).

Many factors have been singled out that may be invoked to explain the current concerns about the validity of biomedical research results. At the top of the list are exceedingly low statistical power (i.e., sample sizes are too small), as well as low levels of internal validity (Ioannidis 2005). Internal validity encompasses a number of quality factors, most of them being related to bias. Bias can be eliminated, or at least controlled, by such measures as randomization, blinding, or the pre-specification of inclusion and exclusion criteria.

Clearly, the discussion is revolving around factors that negatively impact the quality of research—and that may be remedied by structured measures to improve research quality (Baker 2016b). The potential contribution of errors to the disappointingly low level of reproducibility and predictiveness of bio-medical research, and how scientists deal with these errors, has not yet been considered. This is highly surprising, as error management plays a central role in any structured approach to safeguard quality. It is also safe to assume that, due to its multiple levels of complexity, errors must be quite frequent in bio-medical research. In the following, we explore the types of errors that might occur in biomedicine. We then propose and offer a simple tool to establish a mature error culture in biomedical research.

Systematic (Device) Errors

Such errors happen when a device fails in its precision to measure in the desired range or a complete device malfunction occurs. It is especially difficult to discover such failures if the device does not contain a self-check mechanism for proper operational range or an internal standard. A prominent example is measuring pipettes operating in the microliter range. In microbiology or cell biology experiments, faulty volume measurements result in serious mistakes and directly lead to false outcome measures that often go undetected.

Therefore, every research laboratory, however small or large, needs to inventory its devices and lab equipment, which will provide information regarding warranty status, maintenance cycles, routine checks, and possible calibration procedures. Corresponding event dates need to be listed showing when these tasks were last performed and when they are due. Setting up an automated reminder system can prove very helpful to prevent errors due to lack of calibration. In industry, contractors or service agents from device makers usually take over all these tasks for a fee. Academic biomedical research laboratories usually do not possess sufficient funds to outsource maintenance for all devices. Therefore, it is vital that they identify all critical devices in the experimental process and ensure that all of them function properly prior to the experiment. Only then can valid results be obtained. When noticing that an uncalibrated or otherwise quality-compromised device is being used in an experiment, every researcher needs to note this in their laboratory notebook along with results and protocols used. Only then can results be further evaluated and, by comparison, a decision made whether to keep or discard the experiment.

Errors Due to Limitation of Measurement

Many laboratory devices use changes in physical properties (light or ray emissions, chemical reactions) of the analyte as proxies for the parameter under study, simply because these are easily detectable and quantifiable. However, there are certain measurements that rely on human judgment, such as color-scale matching of pH paper. Another more common measure using human evaluation scales are behavioral scores for laboratory animals. Even though a common description exists, misjudgments or discrepancies in interpretation among lab personnel occur and contribute greatly to the large variances in behavioral experiments.

One counterstrategy is the replacement of these measurements with objective assays, for example, calibrated, electronic pH meters. Regarding scoring behavior, training, as well as easily understandable, detailed standard operating procedures are good starting points. Ideally, video examples representing specific scores can both help during training and offer better recall during actual scoring. Every training should be followed up by blinded tests to confirm the validity of the practice. In addition, multi-lab comparisons for test procedures can help identifying ambiguities in protocol and therefore ensure reproducibility.

Protocol Deviation

Protocol deviation is any noncompliance with an existing protocol, standard operating procedure, or work instruction. Another irregularity related to this category is known as "protocol drift," which happens when a protocol is executed without—or only limited—supervision or content checks. If this alteration does not result in immediate experimental failure or is otherwise noticeable, the practice becomes the norm and is most often only detected by accident, if at all.

To combat this error, several steps can be taken. The standard operating procedure can be accompanied by a mandatory checklist containing key elements of the protocol, arranged in a concise manner, that need to be checked, or accompanied by certain data that needs to be inserted. Another element concerns regular mandatory checks of the protocol content by a supervisor or other responsible persons. Every protocol should contain information regarding this validity check, that is, an expiration date. What are most effective against protocol deviations are internal reviews or method audits.

Reporting Errors

Reporting errors can be the result of insufficient or faulty documentation during an experiment. Post-experimental analytical errors, such as statistical errors, also belong to this group. Without access to the original data or the original documentation, it is hard to detect such errors, especially when the publications have already been peer-reviewed.

Various publication platforms have emerged, such as *F1000Research*, permitting public post-publication review, transparency of the entire review process, commenting tools, and the possibility of "versioning" a publication, for example, in response to a comment. They also require a public deposition of the underlying original data. Data platforms such as *FigShare*, *Dryad*, and *Mendeley Data* host any research data, including data underlying published reports, which then contain cross-references to the deposited data.

Consequently, the entire scientific community can scrutinize the validity of raw and summary measures and reuse this data for further analysis, data synthesis, and aggregation.

Another often underutilized tool to prevent reporting errors or unnecessary ambiguity are reporting guidelines. International scientific organizations have long recognized that, despite peer reviews, many publications lack vital information for data interpretation or definition of responsibilities in the research and publication process. Two prominent examples for established guidelines are the ARRIVE guidelines, which are intended to improve the reporting of research using animals, and the ICMJE guidelines to establish best practice and ethical standards in the conduct and reporting of research. Similar to protocols, these guidelines are often accompanied by checklists, which make it easier for authors to verify their concordance with these guidelines. Journals are partially to blame for errors on method reporting because often there are strict word limits on specific sections of the manuscript (including the method section), forcing authors to be less specific or use references to other sources that are often not accessible to all readers. Fortunately, an increasing number of journals encourage authors to provide links to the underlying raw data for each figure; some even make this step mandatory.

A retraction of a publication is necessary when an error contained in it cannot be clarified by a corrigendum or when important conclusions of the article are affected by the error. Other reasons for retraction may be plagiarism or duplicate/concurrent publishing, which will not be considered further here. In the past, retractions happened "quietly" and were therefore often not noted by the community. This changed in 2010, when an internet blog service called Retraction Watch appeared. This blog aims to cover all retractions of research papers and to report on the reasons or background of the retractions. Retraction Watch is widely read in the community and by journalists. Importantly, the editors of Retraction Watch also point out commendable retractions. As stated earlier, to err is human, and to stand by one's errors and to expose and correct them are important elements of the self-correcting quality of science. Hopefully, this will foster the development of an error culture in science.

Errors of Yet Unknown Cause

Laboratory protocols often contain experimental controls or checkpoints in which verification or comparisons with a known standard take place. Despite adherence to the protocol and verification of all used reagents, the obtained result may not measure up to the standard. We classify these errors here as "of yet unknown cause." It is important to communicate these errors and to keep a record of them. If such an error happens more than once, an underlying systematic error must be suspected, which requires further investigation until the source is identified and eliminated.

For instance, the cell survival rate in the preparation of a cell culture suspension from neonatal rodent brains is a standard procedure that delivers an anticipated yield of living neuronal cells in culture when the protocol is followed. However, occasionally, a large fraction of cells is dead. The causes are sometimes unknown, and an error must be suspected. If a second, similar incident occurs by another experimenter soon thereafter, a structured search for a potential error source is indicated. In our department, cell toxic impurity of one of the ingredients of the cell culture medium, accidently introduced by the manufacturer, had caused such an error. Only through swift and systematic investigation we were able to minimize the waste of resources, not only in our laboratories but also for other customers of the manufacturer of the cell culture medium.

Human Errors

In any work environment in which people are planning and executing tasks, so-called human errors are bound to happen. Main causes include carelessness or moments of distraction during complex tasks. Most often, human errors in the biomedical lab present themselves as mix-ups, for instance when a wrong reagent is used with a similar appearance, samples in identical containers get mixed up, or when a container receives a wrong label (Fig. 8.1). Examples of negligence include the failure to close the door of a lab freezer that contains important samples, or the introduction of thermolabile equipment into an autoclave. Despite the fact that many lab records are obtained electronically, human errors can occur when the electronic documentation of experiments is not saved or is accidentally overwritten.

Error Management

A number of specific measures can help to reduce the potential for error in biomedical research: Critical reagents that are prone to mix-ups should receive a distinctive color-coding. Critical work steps should be witnessed by another person (known as four-eye principle). Solutions that assist humans by autom-

Fig. 8.1 Illustration of an ideal process of error handling in the biomedical laboratory. A researcher mistook two faintly labeled reagents A and B, which ruined his experiment. Reporting: Entry of the incident into LabCIRS. Assessment: A group of experts (scientists and technicians) review the error, and take preventive action by color-labeling the reagents. Feedback: The error as well as the measures to prevent it in the future are communicated to the entire laboratory. (Source: Adapted from Dirnagl et al. 2016)

atizing repetitive workflow or involve alarms are particularly effective, such as freezers with an active alarm system or automatic centralized data backups that are concurrent with data generation. Most important, however, is that errors are recorded, evaluated, and communicated. In the clinical world, such error-discussion sessions are known as "Morbidity and Mortality" conferences: Medical doctors regularly present cases that involve human errors in order to come up with preventive measures and to help prevent others from making the same mistakes. Another structured approach to error communication and prevention is the anonymous reporting tool known as the CIRS. Up to now, such a stringent error-reporting practice has only taken place in highly regulated environments, such as healthcare, aviation, and power plants.

LabCIRS: A Simple and Free Error-Management Tool for Biomedicine

In our department, we have developed, implemented, and tested a free and simple error-management tool for biomedicine. The LabCIRS is an adaptation of the clinical CIRS model. Biomedical lab personnel are encouraged to report any laboratory practices, results, or situations that could negatively impact safety, animal welfare, and longevity of material and devices, in addition to observed protocol deviations or any other errors of yet unknown causes (Dirnagl et al. 2016). Even though this directive seems logical and reasonable, the reality of error-handling in biomedical laboratories today is different. Commonly, many errors go unnoticed or are not communicated at all because, currently, there is no mandatory error-management system for preclinical research laboratories. Errors have a negative connotation, and there is the fear of personal liability and humiliation, which may discourage biomedical lab personnel from reporting such incidents. With the introduction and free provision of LabCIRS, we hope that this will change, as CIRS has changed the error communication culture and has become a standard in the medical field.

A CIRS was first described by Flanagan (1954) in 1954, introduced in anesthesiology by 1978 (Cooper et al. 1978), and is today an established worldwide mechanism that improves patient safety in complex, fast-paced, and often understaffed clinical settings. What made it so attractive to adapt this system for the preclinical world was the fact that all incidents are recorded anonymously, analyzed, discussed, and communicated (Fig. 8.1). The reports possess a nonpunitive format devoid of any emotional connotations of the incident, entirely focusing on how to avoid the described error in the future.

As most communication and reporting procedures nowadays are electronic, we developed a freely available software package called LabCIRS. LabCIRS permits safe and anonymous lab-related error reporting via an intranet network environment. No personal information or computer IP is ever recorded, ensuring the confidentiality of the reporter. LabCIRS has common login credentials for every department member which not only allows error reporting—everyone can view the entire history of all errors. Within the first two years since the introduction of LabCIRS in the Department of Experimental Neurology at the Charité, 49 incidents have been entered in the system, of which, 4 were device errors, 18 protocol deviations, 18 human errors, and 6 errors of unknown cause. In addition, three injuries were reported. This is a testimonial that LabCIRS not only works as intended but is accepted by the lab members of the department.

After entries are made into LabCIRS, errors are viewed and initially classified by our quality management officer, and a decision is made about the urgency of actions. Most errors are then discussed among the quality representatives of all research groups. They decide if, and which, measures need to be taken in response. These measures are then also entered into LabCIRS. All newly reported LabCIRS errors are presented during a weekly lab meeting. A monthly newsletter to all department members summarizes all LabCIRS errors of the past weeks and the actions that were taken. Most reporters of incidents now reveal their identities, a further indication that the system has been accepted and that the reporting of errors has no ill consequences for employees. We sincerely hope that LabCIRS is adopted by many laboratories and departments of the academic research community and will contribute to the development of a much-needed open error culture in the preclinical research laboratory.

Outlook

As in any other scientific field, biomedical research is susceptible to various types of errors. Compared to the aviation industry, clinical medicine, or radiation safety, most errors in biomedicine do not have potentially life-threatening consequences. Therefore, governmental oversight in biomedical research is minimal and most commonly restricted to work with genetically modified organisms, animal welfare, occupational health-related safety, and environmental protection. Nevertheless, errors in biomedicine may cause a major waste of resources and potentially harm patients if clinical studies are based on erroneous or faulty results. Despite the existence of protocols and guidelines in biomedical laboratories, most errors simply "occur" and are not systematically followed up for future prevention. Policies, established procedures, or tools regarding error management are virtually nonexistent in this environment. We posit that the biomedical research community, which is currently undergoing a "reproducibility crisis" to which quality issues may contribute substantially, should develop and implement minimal standards for quality management, which includes systematic error-management strategies (Riedl and Dunn 2013; Davies 2013; Begley et al. 2015).

Acknowledgments The authors thank Sebastian Major, Ingo Przesdzing, and Claudia Kurreck for developing, implementing, and testing LabCIRS.

Funding Statement Ulrich Dirnagl acknowledges the financial support of the German Federal Ministry of Education and Research (BMBF 01 EO 08 01) and the Herman and Lilly Schilling Foundations. The funders had no role in the decision to publish or the preparation of the manuscript.

Competing Interests None of the authors have any competing interests to declare.

References

Baker, M. 2016a. 1,500 scientists lift the lid on reproducibility. *Nature* 533: 452–454.
———. 2016b. How quality control could save your science. *Nature* 529: 456–458.
Begley, C.G., A.M. Buchan, and U. Dirnagl. 2015. Robust research: Institutions must do their part for reproducibility. *Nature* 525: 25–27.
Carey, B. 2015. Science, now under scrutiny itself. *New York Times*, p. D1. http://www.nytimes.com/2015/06/16/science/retractions-coming-out-from-under-science-rug.html?_r=1
Cooper, J.B., R.S. Newbower, C.D. Long, and B. McPeek. 1978. Preventable anesthesia mishaps: A study of human factors. *Anesthesiology* 49: 399–406.
Cyranoski, D. 2006. Verdict: Hwang's human stem cells were all fakes. *Nature* 439: 122–123.
Davies, R. 2013. Good research practice: It is time to do what others think we do. *Quasar* (124): 21–23.
Dirnagl, U., I. Przesdzing, C. Kurreck, and S. Major. 2016. A laboratory critical incident and error reporting system for experimental biomedicine. *PLoS Biology*. https://doi.org/10.1371/journal.pbio.2000705.
Flanagan, J.C. 1954. The critical incident technique. *Psychology Bulletin* 51: 327–358.

Ioannidis, J.P.A. 2005. Why most published research findings are false. *PLoS Medicine* 2: e124.

Ioannidis, J.P.A., D. Fanelli, D.D. Dunne, and S.N. Goodman. 2015. Meta-research: Evaluation and improvement of research methods and practices. *PLoS Biology* 13: e1002264.

Macleod, M.R., et al. 2014. Biomedical research: Increasing value, reducing waste. *Lancet* 383: 101–104.

Obokata, H., et al. 2014. Retraction: Stimulus-triggered fate conversion of somatic cells into pluripotency. *Nature* 511: 112.

Riedl, D.H., and M.K. Dunn. 2013. Quality assurance mechanisms for the unregulated research environment. *Trends Biotechnology* 31: 552–554.

9

Empowerment

Jan Brommundt

In order to empower teams in medical practice, the train-the-trainer method has turned out to be a successful approach to sustainably implement open communication. Further steps include sign-out procedures at the end of every surgical procedure, in which technical details and problems as well as communication issues are discussed. Technical problems are to be resolved immediately. Communication problems and misunderstandings are to be tackled before they become chronic and impact the team climate. People who have not spoken up during sign-out are not supposed to complain and blame others behind their backs. If they do, listeners should inquire as to why they did not mention the given problem during sign-out.

Another way to communicate safety-related issues is to write incident reports. Through intranets, literally everybody in a hospital has the possibility to be heard if they perceive an incident and wish to report it. The idea behind these reports is not to blame anybody but to continuously improve processes. A multidisciplinary peer incident-report commission of empowered employees has to meet regularly every month to do additional research into the reported incidents and to formulate advice on how to progress over the following weeks. This way, new insights are perceived as being welcome, and people see that they are being listened to.

Yet, to empower others requires insight, courage, and leadership. The leadership needed has to move away from a command-and-control style toward a leadership that works with facilitating, coaching, and guiding and is open to feedback.

J. Brommundt
Groningen, The Netherlands

© The Author(s) 2018
J. U. Hagen (ed.), *How Could This Happen?*, https://doi.org/10.1007/978-3-319-76403-0_9

This chapter illustrates that any error-management system, its techniques, and its structures need to be embedded in a broader error-management culture. Non-innovative and overly hierarchical structures are incompatible with such a culture, and the empowerment of personnel traditionally in the lower echelons of hierarchical systems (nurses, air hostesses) is a necessary, efficient, and cost-effective precondition and cornerstone for such a system.

In accordance with the author's background, most examples and experiences described are from the medical field.

Definition

Although historically a masculine, individualistic construct, the contemporary meaning of empowerment as the promise of greater responsibility and participation toward the individual employee was developed as a management concept during the 1980s and 1990s. Its modern origins lie in American community psychology. In this chapter, I strictly adhere to its connotation in workplace management and company culture.

Error Without Empowerment: The Kegworth Air Disaster

On January 8, 1989, British Midland Flight 92 crashed onto the embankment of the M1 motorway near Kegworth, Leicestershire, the United Kingdom: 47 died and 74 suffered serious injuries. (The following information is taken from the Air Accidents Investigation Branch (AAIB) report 4/1990). The Boeing 737-400 took off from Heathrow Airport at 19:52 with 126 passengers on board. Captain Kevin Hunt (43) had around 13,200 hours of flight experience and had been with Midland since 1966. He was accompanied in the cockpit by First Officer David McClelland (39), who had around 3300 flight hours. McClelland had been with the company since the previous year. Between the two of them, they had close to 1000 flight hours in the Boeing 737 cockpit, of which 76 hours had been done on the new 737-400 series.

While still climbing toward an intended height of 35,000 feet, a blade detached from the fan of the left CFM International CFM56 engine. This engine type was first introduced in 1974 and used in commercial and military planes. Severe vibrations were felt throughout the plane, and smoke entered into the cabin through the ventilation system. Smoke and sparks coming from the left engine could be seen from the cabin. Even though Captain Hunt and First Officer McClelland were not able to see the left engine from the cockpit, they determined that the right engine was the problem. In pre-737-400 versions of this plane, the right air-conditioning pack fed from the right engine supplied air to the cabin. Unfortunately, in the design of the 737-400, there was a change, and the cabin was in some parts also ventilated from the left engine.

Captain Hunt had disengaged the autopilot. He asked his first officer which engine was the problem. McClelland answered: "It's the le... no, the right one." Hunt shut down the right (perfectly functioning) engine. The cabin crew did not get involved. They did not perceive it as being part of their role to inform the cockpit that smoke and flames were coming from the left engine. The cabin crew later stated that they did not hear the captain refer to the right engine in his cabin address.

During the final approach to East Midlands Airport, the left engine burst into flames. The plane's tail hit the ground next to the M1 motorway—just half a kilometer away from the runway—bounced back into the air and crashed on the other side of the motorway, breaking into three pieces. Thirty-nine passengers were killed at the scene; eight died of their injuries later. All eight crew members survived (Fig. 9.1).

Aftermath

In 1989, the safety and error cultures in aeronautics in the United Kingdom were very different from those in place today. However, had the crew of British Midland Flight 92 acted in an empowered way and overcome the typical hierarchical divisions between cockpit and cabin still prevalent at the time, this accident could have been prevented. It is worth looking at the exact wording in the AAIB report from 1990:

> There can thus be at these times a firm division between flight deck and cabin, and it is notable in this context that in this accident the flight service manager made no initial attempt to approach the flight deck until he was called. However, it must be stated that had some initiative been taken by one or more of the cabin crew who had seen the distress of the left engine, this accident could have been prevented. It must be emphasized, nonetheless, that present patterns of airline training do not provide specifically for the exercise of coordination between cabin and flight crew in such circumstances.

Fig. 9.1 Crash site of British Midland Flight 92, with the runway seen in the rear. (Source: Air Accidents Investigation Branch, Air Accidents Investigation Branch Report 4/1990 Boeing 737-400, G-OBME (January 8, 1990))

Today, assertive communication to determine which engine is dysfunctional would not be seen as "initiative" but rather as the embracing of shared responsibility by an empowered cabin crew. It is evident that well-designed and well-managed teams make positive contributions to safety.

Since then, a cultural change has been initiated in some industries, with aeronautics having taken the lead. Today, crews are trained in crew resource management (CRM), which includes soft skills, effective communication, and creating a culture of safety. A condition sine qua non for this is the degree of empowerment for teams.

To draw one more conclusion from this case study: A non-blaming or fair-blaming culture goes hand in hand with this development. It is worth noting that Captain Hunt and First Officer McClelland were dismissed due to the criticism of their actions in the AAIB report. We can only hope that retraining rather than dismissal would be the first choice today. It would offer the benefit of two experienced officers, baptized under fire, who would have learned just how necessary a culture of open communication and empowerment is.

Saving up to 28,000 Lives and $2.3 Billion Annually Through Empowered Nurses

P. Pronovost is an intensive care specialist at Johns Hopkins University. He teaches at its School of Medicine, at the Carey Business School, and at the Johns Hopkins Bloomberg School of Public Health. Pronovost works on patient safety and advises the World Health Organization. In 2006, his group published a groundbreaking work in the *New England Journal of Medicine* entitled "An Intervention to Decrease Catheter-Related Bloodstream Infections in the ICU" (Pronovost et al. 2006). In this paper they show that the careful, monitored, and sustained implementation of a five-point checklist for the placement and management of central venous catheters (CVCs) can save up to 28,000 lives and $2.3 billion annually.

Medical Background: Central Venous Catheters

CVCs are frequently placed in severely sick intensive care patients by a doctor while a nurse assists. They reach through the skin and either a neck, chest, or groin vein to within a few inches of the heart. CVCs are used to administer medications, obtain blood samples, and measure the central venous pressure. Some medications cannot safely be given any other way—some of which are lifesaving in the context of the individual intensive care patient (Fig. 9.2).

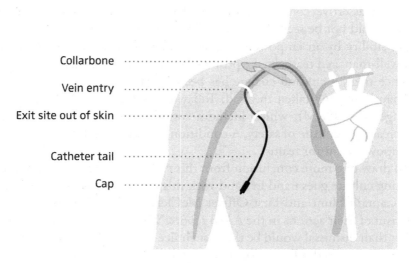

Collarbone

Vein entry

Exit site out of skin

Catheter tail

Cap

Fig. 9.2 A CVC line. (Source: Blausen Medical, Medical gallery of Blausen Medical (2014))

Even though these CVCs are vital for patients, they contain a potentially fatal risk, namely, catheter-related bloodstream infections. Pronovost et al. (2006) point out that "each year in the USA central venous catheters may cause an estimated 80,000 catheter-related bloodstream infections and 28,000 deaths." With the average cost of care at $45,000, these infections cost up to $2.3 billion.

The five-point-checklist protocol contained nothing a physician would not agree with or that had not already been included in their training, namely: Before putting in CVCs, doctors should:

- wash their hands with soap
- clean the patient's skin with chlorhexidine antiseptic
- put sterile drapes over the entire patient
- wear a sterile mask, hat, gown, and gloves
- put a sterile dressing over the catheter site

These are simple rules, and when they were strictly followed, the median rate of infections at a typical ICU decreased from 2.7 per 1000 patients to 0 within 3 months. The so-called Keystone Initiative published its results in the abovementioned article: 103 ICUs in Michigan had participated; in the first 18 months, the initiative showed that 1500 lives and $100 million had been saved. When calculated for the entire United States, the resulting numbers were staggering.

How is it possible that such a relatively simple five-point checklist can have such an effect? What are the obstacles that hinder institutions from adhering to these points, which should have been common medical practice for years? Gawande gave the answer in his article titled "The Checklist," published in *The New Yorker* in 2007. He described how Pronovost and his team had first empowered nurses to observe doctors for a month when putting in CVCs and recording how often they missed at least one of the five points. This was the case for more than one-third of all patients. The next step was to formally empower the nurses to stop doctors if they saw that they were not complying with the checklist. This was achieved by involving the hospital administration's management. As a consequence, the 10-day infection rate went from 11 percent to 0. Calculating the saved costs and lives during a follow-up, the simple checklist had saved eight lives and $2 million dollars.

However, it is not just the simple five-point-checklist protocol that brings about change. The truly innovative step involved the empowerment of nurses. Depending on the country and medical traditions, giving nurses power can create a revolution and—as shown above—makes sense.

Overcoming the Obstacles

So what are the obstacles? According to Csikszentmihalyi, intrinsic motivation correlates with being goal-directed, enjoying challenges, and an increase in over-all happiness. The optimal state of intrinsic motivation is reached when the challenging level of a task meets a person's highest skill level (Csikszentmihalyi 1990).

It is very rare to encounter resistance or obstacles from nurses or, in other industries, people on their level in the hierarchy. We are lucky that nurses are well-trained and do care about the outcome of their work, that is, the health of the patient. They enjoy their empowerment and see the challenges it entails as job enrichment and fulfillment of their mission.

Leading executives can be convinced by the evidence of numbers. The obstacles to empowerment are more likely to be encountered in the middle echelons of systems, where managers would have to redefine the ways in which they experience their power if those "below" them are empowered. Doctors are a good example.

Gawande (2007) quoted three obstacles when it came to introducing checklists monitored by nurses:

- the ego of physicians, who may feel insulted that professionals with their wisdom and experience should have to stoop to the level of being monitored by nurses and governed by a checklist;

- the feeling of being too busy, and an aversion to more tasks in a world that is already consumed with too much bureaucracy; and
- a medical research establishment that is almost entirely focused on "exciting" subjects and on finding therapies for treatment, often ignoring the more "mundane" tasks of measuring if their therapies are being effectively delivered to patients.

In reflecting on these findings for business, Goldsmith (2008) concluded: "If we can get over our own egos, admit that we need checklists to do what we know we should, and focus on the needs of others, we can all 'reduce infection' in our own ways, better serve our key stakeholders, and make our organizations more effective."

The problem of big, heroic, non-team-oriented egos has reached epidemic proportions, according to authors Twenge and Campbell (2013). It clearly takes a person with true sovereignty in their field and a dedication to best outcomes to accept being monitored by people further down in the hierarchy. That is why error management needs to be implemented in a sustainable way. The insights, for example, of doctors recognizing the benefits of such systems, need to be exercised in daily practice.

Pronovost et al. (2006) considered three months to be the time needed to implement an intervention process. At least one doctor and one nurse were assigned as team leaders of the implementation process. They received special training through conference calls twice per month, coaching by research staff, and conducted meetings in-person twice per year.

Error Management and Empowerment in Our Institution

We have used train-the-trainer approaches to sustainably implement open-communication structures and error-management tools. We implemented sign-out procedures at the end of every surgical procedure, in which technical details, problems, and communication problems are discussed. Technical problems are to be resolved immediately. Communication problems and misunderstandings are to be tackled before they become chronic and impact the team climate. We train our multidisciplinary teams to talk openly about communication problems during sign-out. We try to ensure that people who have not spoken up during sign-out do not complain and blame others behind their backs in the informal setting of the coffee room or the corridors of the hospital. If they do, listeners should inquire why they did not mention the given problem during sign-out.

If a severe communication or aggression problem is revealed during sign-out, every team member has the right to ask for a debriefing. For a debriefing, the operating room procedures are halted and the team with the problem receives the time and space to resolve their issue. If this cannot be achieved through peer communication, a debriefing supervisor can be dedicated to the team for this process. We see already that just the possibility of such a debriefing helps, and that nearly all communication problems can be resolved during the standard sign-out. We believe that only a well-functioning and openly communicating team can provide ideal care for our patients in the complex setup of an operating room.

Other processes we have in place to empower every team member are incident reports. Through our intranet, literally everybody has the possibility to be heard if they perceive an incident. An incident is a shortcoming in a process or material that can potentially lead to an accident, to a complication, and/or to a patient being harmed. This can be anything from an insufficient handover to the use of the wrong connection cable. The idea behind these incident reports is not to blame anybody but to continuously improve processes. A multidisciplinary peer incident-report commission of empowered employees meets twice per month to do additional research into the reported incidents and to formulate advice on how to improve processes based on the incident within six weeks. This way, new insights are perceived as welcome. People see that they are listened to and that their input may be acted upon. We foster and invite incident reports because nothing can be learned from unreported occurrences.

Ideally, these strategies lead to quality safety and continuous improvement. By empowering individuals, the trap of "groupthink," in which peer pressure inhibits people from expressing critical opinions, is overcome. If ideas and observations fall on deaf ears, a disengaged workforce results.

Empowerment and Leadership

To empower others requires insight, courage, and leadership. The leadership needed has to move away from a command-and-control style toward a leadership that works with facilitating, coaching, and guiding and is open to feedback.

The new leader who has overcome their own ego will be able to empower their employees, who will not only tolerate it but be grateful for it. They will be specific when saying "thank you": "Thank you for pointing out that my gloves became non-sterile when I accidentally touched the ventilator."

This new leader embraces their empowered team members as partners. They ask questions and invite answers to inspire their teams. It is interesting to check our own push/pull levels in this context. Our non-reflected push/pull ratio might be in the magnitude of 5–10:1, but we should strive for a rate of around 2:1. Mature communication on the same level is more efficient than condescension.

Part of the texture of the new leader is the insight that perfection does not exist. They will be able to say "I made a mistake."

When sufficient time and training have been offered to establish an open error management climate and new democratic leaders have been created, it might still be necessary to let those people go who are stuck in anachronistic, ego-driven, command-and-control communication structures. If the new system is not happy with them and they are not happy with the new system, they better find their fulfillment somewhere else.

The Future of Medicine: Error Culture and Empowerment

The publication of *To Err Is Human: Building a Safer Health System* by the Committee on Quality of Health Care in America and Institute of Medicine was a milestone in the field of medicine (Kohn et al. 2000). This report came to the conclusion that between 44,000 and 98,000 patients die each year because of preventable medical errors. The report inspired a new focus on patient safety and error management. It claimed that the tools to prevent errors were already known and that it was merely a question of implementing them wholeheartedly to reduce mortality. This is in line with the findings of Pronovost: Solutions and techniques are known; following them and implementing them is another matter.

The Patient Will See You Now

Among his other medical achievements, Topol has been at the forefront of wireless medicine. In his book *The Patient Will See You Now*, he envisions a development in medicine that will empower the patient through the use of smart phones and biosensors to monitor their own vital signs, get blood tests, and complete diagnostics through the use of artificial intelligence (Topol 2015). He sees medicine as being at a "Gutenberg moment"—the moment that made printed media, and thus knowledge, available to everybody. According to Topol, who believes that most of the medical establishment will resist these changes, the times of paternalistic medicine will soon be over and the patient will be empowered. With big data, new scientific ways of finding cures and individualizing strategies will be possible for them.

Conclusion

Although positive examples from the field of medicine are used for this chapter, it needs to be stated that medicine itself is one of the most conservative industries, and that changes embodying empowerment are met with resistance and a lack of vision in some parts.

Yet, it is my opinion that there is a huge potential revolutionizing healthcare as we know it, and industry-wide changes will take place. This development will probably be user-driven, that is, patient-driven. Medicine will become less expensive, leaner, and more accessible. The individual patient will not only be empowered and receive higher-quality medicine than before, they will also be more responsible for the choices they make concerning their health.

Healthcare encompasses multidisciplinary teams from different training backgrounds in a complex setting. Initially starting from lessons learned in aeronautics, error management in healthcare has developed considerably in recent years.

References

Air Accidents Investigation Branch. 1990. *Air accidents investigation branch report 4/1990 Boeing 737-400, G-OBME*, January 8. http://www.gov.uk/aaib-reports/4-1990-boeing-737-400-g-obme-8-january-1989

Blausen Medical. 2014. *Medical gallery of Blausen Medical 2014.* https://en.wikiversity.org/wiki/Blausen_gallery_2014

Csikszentmihalyi, M. 1990. *Flow: The psychology of optimal experience.* New York: Harper & Row.

Gawande, A. 2007. The checklist. *The New Yorker,* December 10.

Goldsmith, M. 2008. Preparing your professional checklist. *Business Week,* January 15.

Kohn, L.T., J.M. Corrigan, and M.S. Donaldson, eds. 2000. *To err is human: Building a safer health system.* Washington, DC: National Academy Press.

Pronovost, P., et al. 2006. An intervention to decrease catheter-related bloodstream infections in the ICU. *New England Journal of Medicine* 355: 2725–2732.

Topol, E. 2015. *The patient will see you now: The future of medicine is in your hands.* New York: Basic Books.

Twenge, J., and W.K. Campbell. 2013. *The narcissism epidemic: Living in the age of entitlement.* New York: Atari Paperback.

10

Open Error Communication in a High-Consequence Industry

Julianne Morath and Mallory Johnson

When dealing with error, the human tendency to focus on a single reason often appears during a root-cause analysis. To mitigate this tendency, some organizations have developed a two-step alternative process that is a variation of the root-cause analysis. The first step, a "sequence of events analysis," is conducted immediately after an accident or near miss to capture the timeline of decisions and activities leading up to and surrounding the accident or near miss. This data capture serves to inform the later, second analysis, called a "focused event analysis." The focused event analysis is a causal analysis study involving all key stakeholders for the purpose of seeking knowledge about the contributing variables and the steps that can be taken to eliminate system vulnerabilities and latent conditions that could realign to produce future accidents. Formal procedures and resources are used to guard against blame, attribution, and hindsight bias—all human tendencies that become magnified in the context of a devastating event. The prerequisite of both analyses is an environment that supports open and transparent communication.

Despite the many barriers to transparency, effective solutions have begun to emerge. Specially designed curricula and trainings have been shown to build providers' knowledge, skills, and attitudes surrounding the disclosure of errors. Preparatory training in a low-stress environment establishes routines and habits that providers are more likely to return to during trying events.

J. Morath • M. Johnson
Sacramento, USA

© The Author(s) 2018
J. U. Hagen (ed.), *How Could This Happen?*, https://doi.org/10.1007/978-3-319-76403-0_10

The Institute of Medicine (now the National Academy of Medicine) defines a medical error as "the failure of a planned action to be completed as intended or the use of a wrong plan to achieve an aim" (Kohn et al. 2000). The definition speaks to the many varied ways that medical treatment that is intended to heal can instead harm. The actions themselves may be unintended, as when a clinician accidentally confuses two medications with similar packaging but different indications. Likewise, the outcome of an intended action may be unexpected, as when a patient responds adversely to a correctly administered medication (Makary and Daniel 2016).

Errors of execution and errors of planning do not always result in patient harm; however, many do. Medical error is the third leading cause of death in the United States. Researchers estimate that mistakes lead to more than 250,000 deaths annually (Makary and Daniel 2016). In other Western countries, fatal medical errors remain under-recognized in death-record reporting and mortality statistics (Office for National Statistics' Death Certification Advisory Group 2010; Statistics Canada n.d.).

Medical errors are not only numerous but diverse in nature. Common errors include adverse drug events, wrong-site surgery, retained surgical items, patient falls, pressure ulcers, and hospital-associated infections. As the number and complexity of medical procedures increase, so do potential missteps. Sir Chantler of the King's Fund is famously quoted as saying, "Medicine used to be simple, ineffective, and relatively safe. Now it is complex, effective, and potentially dangerous" (Chantler 1999). The proliferation of treatment options undoubtedly improves outcomes for patients, but variation also increases the opportunity for errors.

Multiple landmark publications have focused the attention of the medical community and the public at large on the issue of medical errors (Donaldson 2002; Kohn et al. 2000). However, despite the growing awareness of the frequency and severity of errors, communication surrounding the issue remains muted.

Transparency, or Open Error Communication

Transparency, or open error communication, is defined as "the free, uninhibited flow of information that is open to the scrutiny of others" (Leape et al. 2009). In 2015, the National Patient Safety Foundation Lucian Leape Institute convened a roundtable of patient safety experts to explore the topic of transparency in depth. The report resulting from the proceedings, *Shining a Light: Safer Health Care Through Transparency*, outlined four fundamental reasons for open error communication (Lucian Leape Institute 2015):

- to promote accountability
- to catalyze improvements in quality and safety
- to promote trust and ethical behavior
- to facilitate patient choice

Accountability is perhaps the clearest rationale for transparency in healthcare. Policymakers desire patient safety data to provide protection to citizens and oversee the appropriate use of taxpayer dollars. Private payers such as insurers or health plans also rely on transparency to ensure that their members receive safe and appropriate care.

Transparency is also critical for creating organizations that acknowledge and learn from their mistakes. Although many system failures can be avoided by implementing best practices, some mistakes emerge in complex processes. In these cases, it is vital that organizations identify, assess, and correct system vulnerabilities (Edmondson 2011). An environment that supports open and transparent communication is vital to an organization's ability to learn from its mistakes and prevent recurrence. Without a safe space to make sense of tragedy, clinicians are robbed of the opportunity to glean actionable lessons for improving their practice (Morath and Turnbull 2005).

Transparency is also fundamental to encourage ethical conduct from providers, without which an honest and trusting relationship between patients and providers is impossible. Honesty is one of the most fundamental ethical principles for all human relationships, and patients expect the truth from their care providers, even when errors occur (Ghalandarpoorattar et al. 2012). Clinicians have an ethical obligation to respect patients' autonomy; therefore, providing patients with complete, truthful information about their care is a vital aspect. Professional agencies, patients' rights organizations, and accrediting bodies unanimously agree that clinicians have an ethical duty to disclose adverse events to patients (National Patient Safety Foundation 2009; Snyder 2012; The Joint Commission 2015).

Transparent information also facilitates choice in the healthcare marketplace. Consumers rely on complete information to make informed choices regarding where to receive their care. Asymmetric information in any marketplace is generally believed to create the opportunity for moral hazard (the tendency for an entity that is under-monitored to engage in undesirable behavior) and adverse selection (a misrepresented trade resultant from either the buyer or seller holding more information than the other party) (Mankiw 2007). Complete information allows patients to identify top-performing facilities and providers, thereby obtaining optimal utility in the healthcare marketplace. This process rewards top performers and allows others the opportunity to follow their practice.

Levels of Transparency

For transparency to be complete, it must enable the free flow of information through four domains: transparency between clinicians and patients; transparency among clinician colleagues; transparency between healthcare organizations; and transparency between healthcare organizations and the public.

Transparency Between Clinicians and Patients

Communication between clinicians and patients is the most basic and fundamental level of transparency in medical care. Transparency within this domain encompasses a wide range of communication, including informed consent, shared decision making, unobstructed communication during care, and openness when things go wrong.

Communication surrounding medical errors is most often referred to as disclosure. Complete disclosure involves four steps: (1) description of the event, (2) acknowledgment of responsibility, (3) apology, and (4) discussion of plans to prevent recurrences (Powell 2006). When errors occur in the process of patient care, patients expect their provider and healthcare team to *complete* all four elements (Manser and Staender 2005; Mazor et al. 2013). Patients value an apology or an expression of empathy and regret foremost (Mazor et al. 2013). However, patients and families also expect that clinicians and healthcare systems will use the experience to prevent recurrences. An apology without a commitment to learn and improve can feel hollow or perfunctory to the patient (Mazor et al. 2013). Yet, patients' expectations for an apology are frequently unmet, perhaps due to physicians' lack of awareness of patients' needs and expectations (Manser and Staender 2005; Mazor et al. 2013).

Patients expect to be informed, both immediately following the event and while a full investigation into the error is conducted. Disclosure is an ongoing process rather than a discrete event or single discussion. However, a gap persists between patients' expectations for ongoing information and current practices. Many patients report receiving partial disclosures or incomplete information. Furthermore, some clinicians may deflect patients' questions or use misleading statements (Fein et al. 2007). Patients typically want more information than is provided by physicians (Hingorani et al. 1999). An overwhelming majority of patients expect notifications regarding errors during the time of their care, even when the harm is minimal and low-risk. In 2004, the University of Washington Medical Center notified patients who had been impacted by an incomplete endoscope cleaning process. In surveys following the disclosure, patients strongly affirmed their right to all information related to their health and healthcare, regardless of risk and harm level (Prouty et al. 2013).

When transparency between clinicians and patients is not practiced, both parties suffer. Silence or incomplete information can be interpreted by patients and families as attempts to hide information, or worse, a lack of respect for the patient and family (Hickson et al. 1992). These divisive feelings ultimately damage the patient–clinician relationship (Gallagher and Levinson 2007). Limited transparency can lead to increased litigation—an action many physicians attempt to prevent by limiting their communication (Gallagher and Levinson 2007). Due to fears of legal action, uncommunicative clinicians may create a situation that is primed for litigation. Although providers are often concerned about their legal standing and reputations, the evidence to date indicates that disclosure appears to decrease the risk of malpractice litigation (Kachalia and Bates 2014).

Transparency Among Clinician Colleagues

Clinicians' attitudes about disclosure to patients are closely related to their attitudes about transparency between clinicians. Physicians who view disclosure to patients positively tend to be more open to discussing adverse events with their peers (Bell et al. 2015). Both sets of communication are vital to the health system's ability to respond to adverse events and prevent recurrences. Yet, clinicians often struggle to openly communicate their errors due to the strong emotions connected with disclosure.

Medical errors impacting patients often claim a second victim: the caregiver. In the wake of tragedy, providers are left holding the heavy weight of guilt and regret and the feeling that they have failed a patient and family. The burden further encumbers clinicians, as they hold the shame associated with the perception of failure (Morath and Turnbull 2005). Scholars have aptly described errors and their attendant hardships as being traumatic for clinicians.

Caregivers involved in disclosure frequently experience an intense emotional response, and this experience puts them at increased risk for depression, burnout, and post-traumatic stress disorder (Schwappach 2015).

Efforts to maintain perfection in image, if not in practice, begin during medical training, when residents are acculturated to the "hidden curriculum." The hidden curriculum transmits behavioral norms, professional values, and social beliefs to initiates via senior clinicians (Bosk 1979). This process extends to disclosure as well. Residents are frequently sanctioned, verbally humiliated, or abused by senior clinicians for acknowledging medical errors. Furthermore, many residents believe that they must compromise their values when addressing medical errors (Martinez and Lehmann 2013). Not surprisingly, residents frequently under-disclose medical errors to senior physicians, which results in strong negative emotions and a hesitancy to seek advice (Bari et al. 2016). However, exposure to positive role modeling of appropriate disclosure had positive effects on residents' attitudes toward transparency, whereas negative role modeling had the inverse effect (Martinez et al. 2014).

Transparency plays an integral role in the recovery process following an error. Communication itself between peers can have a protective effect from the damaging emotions that follow episodes of error and isolate communication (Schwappach 2015). Inversely, physicians who cope with errors in a positive manner are more likely to disclose errors, apologize to patients and family, discuss the errors openly, face their imperfections, and work to prevent recurrences (Plews-Ogan et al. 2016).

Transparency Between Healthcare Organizations

Just as open communication enables learning among clinicians, healthcare organizations also benefit from unimpeded exchanges regarding medical errors. These organizations include hospitals, payers, and vendors. Even though all these entities collect data on errors, data sharing between organizations is rife with obstacles. Organizational leadership may resist out of fear of litigation, detrimental financial impacts, or negative influences on their institution's reputation. Even among leaders who are supportive of transparency, open communication is difficult due to the technological and physical barriers to disclosure. Electronic medical records lack interoperability, making data sharing impractical or impossible. Separate governance structures and busy clinical schedules may obstruct efforts to relay information in more traditional venues, such as meetings and learning collaboratives.

A lack of transparency among healthcare organizations often has tragic results. One well-known example comes from Virginia Mason Medical Center in Seattle, Washington. On November 23, 2004, Mary L. McClinton died after receiving an injection of chlorhexidine, an antiseptic, instead of the intended contrast dye needed as part of a procedure to treat a brain aneurism. Not only was Mrs. McClinton's death preventable, it was later discovered that an identical error had occurred at a nearby facility just two years earlier. The Virginia Mason Medical Center realized that patients would continue to be at risk until a mechanism was created to share information across institutions. The hospital worked with state health regulators to survey area hospitals and implement changes to their procedure room and care processes as a result of Mrs. McClinton's tragic death (Virginia Mason Institute 2014).

Transparency Between Healthcare Organizations and the Public

The last domain of transparency involves the public reporting of patient safety data to state and federal agencies or private quality-improvement entities. The United States has employed multiple mechanisms to facilitate public reporting, including several mandatory state-based reporting systems (Editorial Board 2009) and voluntary national reporting organizations, such as the Leapfrog Group. Although these systems have increased transparency, public reporting has also had a polarizing effect.

The first goal of public reporting is to hold healthcare facilities accountable for faulty systems (Rosenthal 2007). However, public reporting can have unintended consequences. Efforts to score hospitals can discourage clinicians from taking complex cases or pursuing innovative treatments. For example, public reporting of surgical outcomes in the United States resulted in hospitals denying critically ill individuals access to lifesaving liver transplants, because these patients had increased risk for infection or mortality (Dolgin et al. 2016). A fall in rankings can also impact revenue and earnings for healthcare facilities and clinicians. Reputation may also be affected, creating a strong incentive to obscure information. Even though public involvement is necessary to support accountability, care must be taken to ensure that reporting does not penalize intrepid actions or encourage secrecy (Lucian Leape Institute 2015).

A second goal of public reporting is to facilitate improvement through the dissemination of best practices (Rosenthal 2007). This exchange requires a protected, safe, and supportive environment (Lucian Leape Institute 2015). Even among institutions that have successfully transitioned from a culture of blame and secrecy toward an environment of disclosure and learning, open exchange remains difficult. Complexities in collecting and reporting accurate and useful data abound. Data collection and validation are often laborious manual processes, which slow the pace of improvement and compound the issues of timeliness and completeness. One study of the National Health Service in the United Kingdom found that reporting of surgical Never Events varied between institutions, and few facilities sufficiently investigated or reported all vital details of the event (Wahid et al. 2016).

Errors of Omission

Often absent from the conversation about medical errors is the medical care that is never delivered, such as when a patient cannot access treatment or receives poor-quality care due to financial or geographic limitations. Too often, the surgery never undertaken proves as injurious as the surgery gone wrong. These errors of omission are often inflicted upon the world's most vulnerable and marginalized patients. For example, patients who are older (Libungan 2015), low-income (Fabreau et al. 2014), or belong to a racial or ethnic minority group (Lewey and Choudhry 2014) are less likely to receive evidence-based cardiac care in high-income countries. Even low-cost preventive medications for cardiac care are used at lower rates in low-income countries and rural areas compared to their more affluent counterparts (Yusuf et al. 2011). Geography and the relative regional wealth both impact healthcare treatment and outcome for patients with a wide variety of medical conditions (Ayanian 2003; Fang and Alderman 2003; Howard Mason 2009; McKinney 2012; Nunn et al. 2014; Periyakoil 2008; Ubel 2014). Inaction produces an invisible tragedy, and the results are often as deleterious to health as recognized medical errors. Transparency of variation in care is part of open error communication.

Why Open Error Communication Is So Difficult: A Case Study

An example of instituting open error communication as a value and practice in healthcare is discussed in the following case study of Children's Hospitals and Clinics of Minnesota, where the hospitals formally adopted the vision "To become the safest hospital in the world; and then become even safer."

This vision was met with considerable skepticism, both inside and outside of the organization. Transparency was identified as the primary vehicle to advance safety—including open error communication. The board of directors and senior leadership of Children's anchored its safety journey in disclosure and truth telling, especially in the face of errors that harmed or had the potential to harm a patient. This was not taken lightly, and a set of policies were developed.

* The first policy was "stop the line," or "if it looks wrong, it is wrong." This policy gives anyone who perceives a risk to safety the legitimate authority to stop a care process. This includes a patient and family members. All participants have the responsibility to identify the risk and stop the care process until the question of risk has been thoroughly examined and safety has been established. Fashioned after the "Andon Cord" policy in the manufacturing industry, this policy empowers all participants in the healthcare system to establish safety without regard to hierarchy or risk of retaliation (Morath and Turnbull 2005).
* The next policy was "disclosure and truth-telling." This policy provides guidance for working with patients and families in the face of adverse events, near misses, or medical accidents. It establishes and guides expectations for communication. Elements of disclosure include a prompt and compassionate explanation of what is understood about the event; information about the probable effects; information about what is being done to ensure safety; assurances that a full analysis will take place and that the findings of the analysis, as they are known, will be communicated; information about changes that are being made on the basis of the analytical findings to reduce the likelihood of a similar event happening to another patient; and an acknowledgment of accountability, including an apology (Morath and Turnbull 2005). Professionals need to develop communication skills regarding open error communication. The CEO has the responsibility for ensuring that the necessary resources for this training are made available.

The Test of Policy and Resolve: A Case Study[1]

This case study is a demonstration of how an organization enacted the policy of open error communication, even in the most difficult circumstances. A teenaged patient was diagnosed incorrectly. After initial improvement, he failed to respond to treatment, and his family and the managing physician began seeking new answers. They arranged for further diagnostic testing, evaluation, and an outside opinion. However, when the correct diagnosis was finally established, months of treatment had been lost, and the young man died of an elusive cancer.

Family members worked hard to learn from the organization how a misdiagnosis could have happened but were provided with little information. In a regulatory environment where errors are punished severely, and where courts can award settlements that have the potential to cripple an organization, the organization feared retribution and refused to respond to the family.

When family members threatened to tell their story to the media, the CEO agreed to meet with them, asking the hospital's risk manager and attorney to join him. The family members—the young man's parents and his siblings—arrived at the CEO's office and laid out a framed photo of their son and brother. They demanded to know who was at fault and what was being done to make sure this type of event would not happen again.

This was the first meeting the CEO had ever had with a family regarding a failure in care. Following the counsel from the hospital's attorney and risk manager, the CEO avoided disclosing any significant information. After the meeting, the attorney and the risk manager congratulated the CEO for his ability to demonstrate sympathy without disclosing any information. "It was the worst meeting of my career," the CEO said later. "We stonewalled this family."

The hospital was in the process of creating a policy of disclosure to families in cases of medical accidents, but progress was advancing slowly and with extreme caution. After the CEO's meeting with the family, leadership team members sat down to explore other ways the meeting could have unfolded. They asked each other, "How would we want to be responded to if we were the family faced with this situation?"

A second meeting was scheduled with the family. This time the chair of the board, the chair of the board quality committee, and a member of the executive leadership staff were present. Again, the family members brought pictures of their lost son and brother. There were no attorneys or risk managers present. It was agreed that the meeting would be held with full disclosure. The family was told the sequence of events in the young man's care and what was understood about the incorrect diagnosis. They were told what the organization had learned from the experience and the changes that had been made to prevent such an occurrence from happening again. In an emotional and tearful exchange, the officers of the organization apologized to the family and accepted responsibility for failures in the system of care.

The family asked that specific persons involved in the event be named and singled out for the sanction. Hospital leaders remained firm that the misdiagnosis had occurred due to the system, which had failed, and not because of careless or incompetent individuals.

The sorrow of failing a family inspired the organization to accelerate action around improving patient safety. Staff members and leaders discussed how an organization devoted to families could act this way in the face of a family's loss. They discussed the lessons learned from this family, including how to respond to tragedy and how to build a foundation of disclosure in the organization. A new commitment was forged to create a comprehensive culture of disclosure, truth-telling, and responsibility, built on a full partnership with families.

The staff caring for the patient and his family throughout the ordeal also required healing. Early reactions of blame, defensiveness, and criticism had damaged their trust in each other and in the organization. They felt isolated, guilty, and angry. Relationships had fractured, and staff members needed to find closure and move forward through their grief. Leaders met with the staff and providers who had been involved in the patient's care, apologizing for the organization's failure to respond to them as well as to the patient's family. Outside expert resources were offered and healing began.

Finally, the leaders fully accepted executive responsibility for patient safety. They made a commitment to design and operate safe systems. They promised patients' families and health professionals that the organization, as its first priority, would do no harm.

Open error communication established accountability for the Children's organization. A medical accident, especially when it harms a patient, is a defining moment for an organization. How such an event is managed both expresses and shapes the culture of the organization. When we mean to do well but harm results, we have failed the patient and the patient's family. An accident also affects the care providers at the sharp end—the point of care—where technical work is done. It is a devastating event. How the organization responds can reinforce a culture of secrecy and blame, or it can advance a culture of safety, which is characterized by open disclosure, analysis, learning, prevention, and face-to-face accountability.

In a safety culture, executive leaders stand shoulder to shoulder with family and caregivers. This means that families are involved in all aspects of the care process and are not left out when accidents occur. The concept of open error communication with families is a departure from the comfort zone of many executives and providers, but the greater risk lies in not communicating. Patients and their families are members of the care team and valuable partners in—and contributors to—creating safety. Participation in care is enhanced by information, truth-telling, and disclosure in the care process.

In the rare event of an accident or near miss, the family should be brought immediately into the process. This is a departure from the traditional response of risk managers and legal counsel, who have long followed procedures that distance caregivers, families, and organizational leaders. Through focus groups, families have identified the most essential elements of communication that are needed after an accident or near miss (Morath and Turnbull 2005). They want to be the first to know, they need to hear the story of what went wrong, they want to know what changes will be made to prevent the same thing from happening again, and they want to know that the healthcare providers are sorry.

Developing a Policy of Full Disclosure/Open Error Communication

Data from family focus groups, discussions among staff members, and professional literature were used to develop a disclosure policy at Children's Hospitals and Clinics of Minnesota. Its creation and content are summarized here. The board of directors endorsed a policy of full disclosure to families as part of the overall patient safety agenda. The policy states, "Children's Hospitals and Clinics works with its professional staff to achieve complete, prompt, and truthful disclosure of information and counseling to patients and their parents or legal guardians regarding situations in which a medical accident occurred (1) when there is clear or potential clinical significance or (2) when some unintended act or substance reaches the patient." The policy title was changed from "Sentinel Events" to "Medical Accidents and Disclosure, including Sentinel Events," reflecting the culture shift and an emphasis on patient safety, disclosure, and learning from near misses. The policy has the following purposes:

- to improve patient and staff safety by decreasing the system's vulnerability to future accidents
- to evaluate and improve the care provided to patients

- to predict and mitigate future events through reliable systems design
- to reduce the chances for morbidity and mortality
- to restore the confidence of patients, families, employees, providers, and the community that systems are in place to ensure that accidents are unlikely to recur
- to provide emotional, professional, and legal support to staff who have been involved in events
- to ensure the disclosure of accidents, near misses, and sentinel events to families, and
- to ensure continuous communication of system improvements to families and caregivers who have been involved in an accident

Event Analysis in the Disclosure Process

A full analysis of each accident and significant near miss is completed in the interest of understanding the multicausal components that produced the accident or near miss. The disclosure policy helps direct this analysis and sets in motion the processes and subsequent follow-ups that must take place.

The human tendency to focus on a single cause often appears during a root-cause analysis. To mitigate this tendency, some organizations have developed a two-step alternative process that is a variation of the root-cause analysis. The first step, a "sequence of events analysis," is conducted immediately after an accident or near miss to capture the timeline of decisions and activities leading up to and surrounding the accident or near miss. This data capture serves to inform the later, second analysis, called a "focused event analysis." The focused event analysis follows the sequence of events meeting. It is a causal analysis study involving all key stakeholders for the purpose of seeking knowledge about the contributing variables and the steps that can be taken to eliminate system vulnerabilities and latent conditions that could realign to produce future accidents. Formal procedures and resources are used to guard against blame, attribution, and hindsight bias—all human tendencies that become magnified in the context of a devastating event.

Confidentiality is maintained with respect to the patient and the providers who were involved, but a case study is created to inform others about the risks and lessons learned so that greater resilience can be introduced to prevent errors from happening again. Protocols are developed for explicit guidance of the notification process after a medical accident.

Disclosure and Truth-telling

In the disclosure process, a presumption of truth-telling guides all discussions. Generally, the managing physician should presume that all information that describes the specific event affecting a patient can and should be disclosed, with the exception of the identities of the specific staff members involved in the accident, if they are unknown to the family. The ultimate goal is to use a thoughtful, well-defined process that will reestablish confidence and maintain a therapeutic relationship. During initial and follow-up discussions, the following subjects are considered:

- the organization's and staff's regrets, with apologies, that an event has occurred
- the nature of the event
- the time, place, and circumstances of the event
- the proximal cause of the event, if known
- the known, definite consequences of the event for the patient, and potential or anticipated consequences
- actions taken to treat or ameliorate the consequences of the event
- information about who will manage the ongoing care of the patient
- planned analysis of the event
- information about who else knows about the event (in the hospitals, in external regulatory agencies, and so on)
- actions taken both to identify system issues that may have contributed to the event and to prevent the same or similar events from occurring again
- information about who will manage ongoing communication with the family
- the names and phone numbers of individuals in the hospital to whom family members may address complaints or concerns about the process surrounding the event
- the names and phone numbers of agencies with which the family can communicate about the event
- information about how to obtain support and counseling regarding the event and its consequences, both within and outside the organization
- removal from the patient's account of charges and expenses directly related to the event

This work by Children's was published in the July 2000 issue of *US News and World Report*. The feature article focused on Children's as an organization that declared an aim to achieve zero defects and be transparent in communication about safety and errors. The plan was called "radical" by the media. The old adage of "Physicians and hospitals don't make mistakes—they bury them" was still alive and well. Children's was called a trailblazer for its "do ask, do tell" approach to focus on systems and view caregivers as fallible human beings who bear a deep psychological burden when things go wrong. Elements of the strategy were a robust educational effort, reporting and feedback system, policy guidance, and personal engagement of leadership (Shapiro 2000).

The work at Children's suddenly gained attention. The major newspapers identified Children's as a "new player receiving recognition in healthcare" (Dornfeld 2000). Children's was heralded for its "daring efforts to take the mistakes out of medicine" and "blowing the lid off of medical errors, to learn from mistakes and improve care, rather than cast blame" (Editorial Department 2000).

An editorial titled "*Children's Hospitals—worthy effort to improve healthcare*" appeared in the lead state newspaper (Editorial Department 2000). The editorial cited segments from an episode of CBS' *60 Minutes* program that focused on secrecy, denial, and cover-ups in hospitals when mistakes are made and noted that "few hospitals are trying as hard as Children's to convert mistakes into learning experiences" (Editorial Department 2000).

US News and World Report stated that Children's will be a model for other hospitals facing the increasingly important issue of patient safety. Keeping families informed when accidents happen—and discussing the causes—has become a regular goal for Children's. That contrasts with the *60 Minutes* description of how hospital "risk managers" elsewhere often use concern and sympathy professed for families as tools to hide mistakes and avoid lawsuits (Shapiro 2000).

The work at Children's produced the intended outcomes—not perfect outcomes, yet better outcomes regarding safety, quality, staff engagement, as well as financial and market success. These were documented in a *Harvard Business Review* case study (Edmondson et al. 2001). Transparency and disclosure became something to value and were advanced as promises to patients and families.

Despite these accolades, other hospitals and health systems have been slow to undertake similar changes to their error-reporting systems. Further, the broader healthcare industry is still debating the acceptance of transparency, even with concerted agreement that transparency is an ethical imperative for moral practice. Gaps between expected standards and actual practice persist. What makes change so difficult? At a practical level, many barriers to open error communication exist within our institutions and by virtue of being humans. Transparency is difficult: culturally, technically, and personally. There are deep-seated cultural norms of blame, denial, and secrecy. In many cases, silence is the path of least resistance. But perhaps our foremost obstacle is ourselves. We are human, at once fallible and unforgiving of flaws.

Outlook: Potential Solutions for Promoting Transparency

Despite the many barriers to transparency, effective solutions have begun to emerge. Specially designed curricula and trainings have been shown to build providers' knowledge, skills, and attitudes surrounding the disclosure of errors (Stroud et al. 2013). Preparatory training in a low-stress environment establishes routines and habits that providers are more likely to return to during trying events (O'Toole and Bennis 2009). Some hospitals have deployed "readiness coaches" or "disclosure coaches" to assist uncertain providers (White and Gallagher 2013). These coaches should be part of a comprehensive disclosure support system that is available to all parties throughout the entire process (McLennan et al. 2016). Disclosure needs to be viewed as a highly professional intervention requiring training and skill.

These direct interventions work optimally when they are supported by a broad patient safety culture. A psychologically safe and nonpunitive organizational culture allows individuals to view errors as symptom of a larger system problem, which in turn facilitates course correction and prevents recurrences (Tsao and Browne 2015). Efforts to improve local culture have been bolstered in recent years by the Comprehensive Unit-based Safety Program, a toolkit that builds patient safety culture while growing caregivers' capacity to address patient safety hazards (Pronovost et al. 2006). The five-step program has been shown to improve safety climate, teamwork climate, and turnover rates for nurses (Timmel et al. 2010). The Agency for Healthcare Research and Quality has also released tools to support the development of patient safety culture. The Hospital Survey on Patient Safety Culture allows hospitals to survey staff and assess their progress toward transparency. The standardized tool also allows hospitals to compare their results against peer hospitals, facilitating the spread of best practices across institutions (Agency for Healthcare Research and Quality 2016). Inter-facility exchange is also encouraged through the Patient Safety Organization program, which provides health systems with a protected space to discuss patient safety issues. Information exchanges through a Patient Safety Organization program are privileged and confidential, so providers can have open, honest discussions without fear of litigation (Agency for Healthcare Research and Quality n.d.).

These efforts have made progress in promoting open and transparent communication about medical errors. Effective communication systems and supportive cultures can overcome the strong emotions, technical difficulties, and high risks associated with transparency. However, much work remains to be done if medicine is to achieve its most important goal, "First, do no harm."

Note

1. This case study was first published in *To Do No Harm* by Julianne Morath and Joanne Turnbull.

References

Agency for Healthcare Research and Quality. 2016. *Hospital survey on patient safety culture.* http://www.ahrq.gov/professionals/quality-patient-safety/patientsafetyculture/hospital/index.html

———. n.d. *About the PSO program: A brief history of the program.* https://pso.ahrq.gov/about

Ayanian, J.Z. 2003. Is geography destiny? Illuminating the survival advantage of elderly patients in New England after acute myocardial infarction. *American Heart Journal* 146 (2): 207–209. https://doi.org/10.1016/s0002-8703(03)00238-2.

Bari, A., R.A. Khan, and A.W. Rathore. 2016. Medical errors; causes, consequences, emotional response and resulting behavioral change. *Pakistan Journal of Medical Sciences* 32 (3): 523–528. https://doi.org/10.12669/pjms.323.9701.

Bell, S.K., A.A. White, J.C. Yi, J.P. Yi-Frazier, and T.H. Gallagher. 2015. Transparency when things go wrong: Physician attitudes about reporting medical errors to patients, peers, and institutions. *Journal of Patient Safety.* https://doi.org/10.1097/pts.0000000000000153.

Bosk, C. 1979. *Forgive and remember: Managing medical failure.* Chicago: University of Chicago Press.

Chantler, C. 1999. The role and education of doctors in the delivery of health care. *Lancet* 353 (9159): 1178–1181. https://doi.org/10.1016/s0140-6736(99)01075-2.

Dolgin, N.H., B. Movahedi, P.N. Martins, R. Goldberg, K.L. Lapane, F.A. Anderson, and A. Bozorgzadeh. 2016. Decade-long trends in liver transplant waitlist removal due to illness severity: The impact of centers for medicare and medicaid services policy. *Journal of the American College of Surgeons* 222 (6): 1054–1065. https://doi.org/10.1016/j.jamcollsurg.2016.03.021.

Donaldson, L. 2002. An organisation with a memory. *Clinical Medicine (London)* 2 (5): 452–457.

Dornfeld, S. 2000. Preventing medical errors. *Sint Paul Pioneer Press,* July 17, p. 8A.

Editorial Board. 2009. A national survey of medical error reporting laws. *Yale Journal of Health Policy, Law, and Ethics* 9 (1): 201–286.

Editorial Department. 2000. Children's hospitals: Worthy effort to improve health care. *Star Tribune,* p. A12.

Edmondson, A. 2011. Strategies for learning from failure. *Harvard Business Review* 89 (4): 48–55, 137.

Edmondson, A., M. Roberto, and A. Tucker. 2001. Children's hospital and clinics. *Harvard Business Review.* https://doi.org/PRODUCT#: 302050-PDF-ENG

Fabreau, G.E., A.A. Leung, D.A. Southern, M.L. Knudtson, J.M. McWilliams, J.Z. Ayanian, and W.A. Ghali. 2014. Sex, socioeconomic status, access to cardiac catheterization, and outcomes for acute coronary syndromes in the context of universal healthcare coverage. *Circulation Cardiovascular Quality and Outcomes* 7 (4): 540–549. https://doi.org/10.1161/circoutcomes.114.001021.

Fang, J., and M.H. Alderman. 2003. Is geography destiny for patients in New York with myocardial infarction? *American Journal of Medicine* 115 (6): 448–453.

Fein, S.P., et al. 2007. The many faces of error disclosure: A common set of elements and a definition. *Journal of General Internal Medicine* 22 (6): 755–761. https://doi.org/10.1007/s11606-007-0157-9.

Gallagher, T.H.S., and W. Levinson. 2007. Disclosing harmful medical errors to patients. *New England Journal of Medicine* 356 (26): 2713–2719.

Ghalandarpoorattar, S.M., A. Kaviani, and F. Asghari. 2012. Medical error disclosure: The gap between attitude and practice. *Postgrad Medical Journal* 88 (1037): 130–133. https://doi.org/10.1136/postgradmedj-2011-130118.

Hickson, G.B., E.W. Clayton, P.B. Githens, and F.A. Sloan. 1992. Factors that prompted families to file medical malpractice claims following perinatal injuries. *JAMA* 267 (10): 1359–1363.

Hingorani, M., T. Wong, and G. Vafidis. 1999. Patients' and doctors' attitudes to amount of information given after unintended injury during treatment: Cross sectional, questionnaire survey. *BMJ* 318 (7184): 640–641.

Howard Mason, P. 2009. The power of place: Geography, destiny, and globalization's rough landscape, by Harm de Blij. *Anthropology & Medicine* 16 (3): 333–336. https://doi.org/10.1080/13648470903295992.

Kachalia, A., and D.W. Bates. 2014. Disclosing medical errors: The view from the USA. *The Surgeon* 12 (2): 64–67. https://doi.org/10.1016/j.surge.2013.12.002.

Kohn, L.T., J. Corrigan, and M.S. Donaldson. 2000. *To err is human: Building a safer health system.* Washington, DC: The National Academies Press. https://doi.org/10.17226/9728.

Leape, L., et al. 2009. Transforming healthcare: A safety imperative. *Quality and Safety in Health Care* 18 (6): 424–428. https://doi.org/10.1136/qshc.2009.036954.

Lewey, J., and N.K. Choudhry. 2014. The current state of ethnic and racial disparities in cardiovascular care: Lessons from the past and opportunities for the future. *Current Cardiology Reports* 16 (10): 530. https://doi.org/10.1007/s11886-014-0530-3.

Libungan, B. 2015. *Acute coronary syndrome and cardiac arrest in the elderly.* Doctor of Philosophy (Medicine), University of Gothenburg. Sahlgrenska Academy, Gothenburg, Sweden. https://gupea.ub.gu.se/handle/2077/38347(978–91–628-9294-4)

Lucian Leape Institute. 2015. *Shining a light: Safer health care through transparency. A roundtable on transparency.* Boston: National Patient Safety Foundation. http://www.npsf.org/?shiningalight

Makary, M.A., and M. Daniel. 2016. Medical error-the third leading cause of death in the US. *BMJ* 353: i2139. https://doi.org/10.1136/bmj.i2139.

Mankiw, N.G. 2007. *Principles of microeconomics.* 4th ed. Mason: Thomson Higher Education.

Manser, T., and S. Staender. 2005. Aftermath of an adverse event: Supporting health care professionals to meet patient expectations through open disclosure. *Acta Anaesthesiologica Scandinavica* 49 (6): 728–734. https://doi.org/10.1111/j.1399-6576.2005.00746.x.

Martinez, W., and L.S. Lehmann. 2013. The "hidden curriculum" and residents' attitudes about medical error disclosure: Comparison of surgical and nonsurgical residents. *Journal of the American College of Surgeons* 217 (6): 1145–1150. https://doi.org/10.1016/j.jamcollsurg.2013.07.391.

Martinez, W., et al. 2014. Role-modeling and medical error disclosure: A national survey of trainees. *Academic Medicine* 89 (3): 482–489. https://doi.org/10.1097/acm.0000000000000156.

Mazor, K.M., et al. 2013. More than words: Patients' views on apology and disclosure when things go wrong in cancer care. *Patient Education and Counseling* 90 (3): 341–346. https://doi.org/10.1016/j.pec.2011.07.010.

McKinney, M. 2012. For better or worse. Report: Where you live affects the type of healthcare you're going to get. *Modern Healthcare* 42 (12): 6–7.

McLennan, S.R., M. Diebold, L.E. Rich, and B.S. Elger. 2016. Nurses' perspectives regarding the disclosure of errors to patients: A qualitative study. *International Journal of Nursing Studies* 54: 16–22. https://doi.org/10.1016/j.ijnurstu.2014.10.001.

Morath, J.M., and J.E. Turnbull. 2005. *To do no harm: Ensuring patient safety in health care organizations.* San Francisco: Jossey-Bass.

National Patient Safety Foundation. 2009. *The universal patient compact.* http://c.ymcdn.com/sites/www.npsf.org/resource/resmgr/PDF/UniversalPatientCompact.pdf

Nunn, A., A. Yolken, B. Cutler, S. Trooskin, P. Wilson, S. Little, and K. Mayer. 2014. Geography should not be destiny: Focusing HIV/AIDS implementation research and programs on microepidemics in US neighborhoods. *American Journal of Public Health* 104 (5): 775–780. https://doi.org/10.2105/ajph.2013.301864.

O'Toole, J., and W. Bennis. 2009. What's needed next: A culture of candor. *Harvard Business Review* 87 (6): 54–61.

Office for National Statistics' Death Certification Advisory Group. 2010. Guidance for doctors completing medical certificates of cause of death in England and Wales. http://www.gro.gov.uk/images/medcert_July_2010.pdf.

Periyakoil, V.S. 2008. Geography decides destiny. *Journal of Palliative Medicine* 11 (5): 694–695. https://doi.org/10.1089/jpm.2008.9905.

Plews-Ogan, M., N. May, J. Owens, M. Ardelt, J. Shapiro, and S.K. Bell. 2016. Wisdom in medicine: What helps physicians after a medical error? *Academic Medicine* 91 (2): 233–241. https://doi.org/10.1097/acm.0000000000000886.

Powell, S.K. 2006. When things go wrong: Responding to adverse events: A consensus statement of the Harvard hospitals. *Lippincotts Case Management* 11 (4): 193–194.

Pronovost, P.J., et al. 2006. A web-based tool for the Comprehensive Unit-based Safety Program (CUSP). *Joint Commission Journal on Quality and Patient Safety* 32 (3): 119–129.

Prouty, C.D., M.B. Foglia, and T.H. Gallagher. 2013. Patients' experiences with disclosure of a large-scale adverse event. *Journal of Clinical Ethics* 24 (4): 353–363.

Rosenthal, J. 2007. Advancing patient safety through state reporting systems. *Perspectives on safety.* https://psnet.ahrq.gov/perspectives/perspective/43/advancing-patient-safety-through-state-reporting-systems

Schwappach, D.L. 2015. In the aftermath of medical error: Caring for patients, family, and the healthcare workers involved. *Bundesgesundheitsblatt, Gesundheitsforschung, Gesundheitsschutz* 58 (1): 80–86. https://doi.org/10.1007/s00103-014-2083-4.

Shapiro, J. 2000. Taking the mistakes out of medicine. *US News and World Report* 129: 50–54.

Snyder, L. 2012. American college of physicians ethics manual. Sixth edition. *Annals of Internal Medicine* 156 (1 Pt 2): 73–104. https://doi.org/10.7326/0003-4819-156-1-201201031-00001.

Statistics Canada. n.d. *Canadian vital statistics, death database and population estimates.* http://www.statcan.gc.ca/tables-tableaux/sum-som/l01/cst01/hlth36a-eng.htm

Stroud, L., B.M. Wong, E. Hollenberg, and W. Levinson. 2013. Teaching medical error disclosure to physicians-in-training: A scoping review. *Academic Medicine* 88 (6): 884–892. https://doi.org/10.1097/ACM.0b013e31828f898f.

The Joint Commission. 2015. *Comprehensive accreditation manual. CAMH for hospitals: The official handbook.* http://www.jcrinc.com/2016-comprehensive-accreditation-manual-for-hospitals-camh-/

Timmel, J., P.S. Kent, C.G. Holzmueller, L. Paine, R.D. Schulick, and P.J. Pronovost. 2010. Impact of the comprehensive unit-based safety program (CUSP) on safety culture in a surgical inpatient unit. *Joint Commission Journal on Quality and Patient Safety* 36 (6): 252–260.

Tsao, K., and M. Browne. 2015. Culture of safety: A foundation for patient care. *Seminars in Pediatric Surgery* 24 (6): 283–287. https://doi.org/10.1053/j. sempedsurg.2015.08.005.

Ubel, P.A. 2014. Transplantation traffic – Geography as destiny for transplant candidates. *New England Journal of Medicine* 371 (26): 2450–2452. https://doi. org/10.1056/NEJMp1407639.

Virginia Mason Institute. 2014. *Terrible tragedy – And powerful legacy – of preventable death.* https://www.virginiamasoninstitute.org/2014/03/terrible-tragedy-and-powerful-legacy-of-preventable-death/

Wahid, N.N., S.H. Moppett, and I.K. Moppett. 2016. Quality of quality accounts: Transparency of public reporting of never events in England. A semi-quantitative and qualitative review. *Journal of the Royal Society of Medicine* 109 (5): 190–199. https://doi.org/10.1177/0141076816636367.

White, A.A., and T.H. Gallagher. 2013. Medical error and disclosure. *Handbook of Clinical Neurology* 118: 107–117. https://doi.org/10.1016/b978-0-444-53501-6.00008-1.

Yusuf, S., et al. 2011. Use of secondary prevention drugs for cardiovascular disease in the community in high-income, middle-income, and low-income countries (the PURE Study): A prospective epidemiological survey. *Lancet* 378 (9798): 1231–1243. https://doi.org/10.1016/s0140-6736(11)61215-4.

11

Confidence and Humility

Robert Schroeder

When analyzing the difficulties we have when we should speak up but do not, culture—with its strict system of values, norms, and rules—emerges as a major determinant. Culture regulates the way we feel, act, and judge, often superseding rational reasoning.

Belonging to a culture means profiting from its communal benefits. However, belonging requires conformity, whereas non-conformity means standing out and being judged according to the rules that are part and parcel of the system. Hence, violating these rules leads to stress, and sometimes existential fear, depending on how severe our transgression is.

Given a culture in which speaking up is not the norm, doing so means opposing the rules and standing out. It contains the possibility—and hence the fear—that, through our action, we isolate ourselves to such an extent that we are no longer part of the community, and thus lose the advantages it offers.

Therefore, if we want to encourage people to speak up, one way is to create the culture in which speaking up is part of its norms. In most cases, this will demand systemic changes, which can only happen if those who have the power to build the necessary culture have what it takes to lead the way.

R. Schroeder
Cologne, Germany

© The Author(s) 2018
J. U. Hagen (ed.), *How Could This Happen?*, https://doi.org/10.1007/978-3-319-76403-0_11

There seems to be the notion—especially given the enormous communicating and computing power nowadays—that we can control nearly everything, and that even the future may be controllable with the help of forecasts and the strategies we develop based on them. Sometimes it appears to me that we are close to believing that a world in which everything can be controlled will be a safer and better world. If that were true, I would be the exception: I would not want to live in such a world. In fact, I doubt that it would be a world suitable for any human being.

Still, I am a pilot, and pilots—as we know—need to have control, even to an extent that we may easily be called control freaks. However, to be a real control freak, you have to understand what is controllable and what is not and learn how to handle the difference.

It was supposedly Peter Drucker who quipped that culture eats strategy for breakfast. It is a clever observation, regardless of who said it. They could have added that culture then eats strategic control for a second helping, which is also to say that, when we deal with human behavior, culture belongs to one of the most powerful and overriding control systems we have.

Culture, with its system of values and norms, determines the way we feel, act, and judge. Therefore, if we want to change people, one way is to influence the culture that has formed them. If we intend to do this with the help of strategies and flowcharts, we will fail.

Here is a simple example of a cultural norm: Imagine that during a hot summer day you walk along one of Berlin's main shopping areas, a crowded Kurfürstendamm. The temperature is 38°C, so there is no physiological reason for anyone to be dressed. On the contrary, physiologically it would indeed be smarter not to wear anything at all, but imagine if you encountered a person wearing nothing. You would not think, "Hey, this is a good idea, I will strip as well." Rather, you would think, "Good gracious, this really isn't done." The underlying principle is that cultural norms can, and often will, supersede rational reasoning. Cultural norms also make us react instantaneously. We will see how this works in a moment.

Let us look at an airline accident that everybody from the aviation community will know about. It happened on March 27, 1977, and is the worst disaster in civil aviation history to date. On that day, two fully booked Boeing 747s collided on a runway in Tenerife. One was from KLM, the other from Pan Am. I will not relate the whole story but rather focus on one scene that illustrates the culture that informed the pilots' behavior that day.

On March 27, the runway in Tenerife was fog-shrouded, visibility was very much reduced, and the personnel in the tower could see neither the runway nor the two aircraft occupying it. The pilots of the two Boeings could not see the others: The KLM 747 could not see that the Pan Am was taxiing down their runway, and the Pan Am 747 could not see that the KLM was turning in their direction on the same runway.

Jacob van Zanten, the captain of KLM flight 4805, was under time pressure and had to meet a given time window for takeoff. If not, he would have to park his 747 on Tenerife airport, start a 10-hour crew rest period and find hotel accommodations for his passengers, with all the financial consequences involved.

At the time, van Zanten was the senior training captain for the Boeing 747 at KLM. *Senior training captain for the Boeing 747.* This has a ring to it. Somebody in this position is highly respected in the airline community. His copilot, Klaas Meurs, had been checked by him. On the day of the accident, Meurs had just 95 hours on the 747. So, the hierarchic gradient in that cockpit was steep.

Let us concentrate on the moment, when van Zanten turns his 747 around and the other jumbo is still on the runway. Van Zanten, despite seeing nothing but a gray wall of mist, advances the throttles. Meurs says, "Wait. We don't have clearance yet." Van Zanten gruffly answers, "No. I know that. Go ahead and ask!"

Let us freeze frame this situation and try to put ourselves either in the role of van Zanten or Meurs. I tried it and, as strange as it might sound, I can understand both of them. Imagine you were van Zanten, the senior training captain and a renowned pilot. Everybody looks up to you—you are a role model. Then comes a day when you are severely stressed, so that even you are going to commit the most careless and stupid mistake imaginable for a captain, namely, taking off without takeoff clearance. It does not help that your copilot—a man *you* trained and checked—interferes with your action by saying, "Wait! We don't have clearance yet."

We will never know what van Zanten felt in that moment. Given the enormity of his blunder, he may have seen himself wobble on his high pedestal. Maybe he imagined Meurs being back in Amsterdam and telling all his colleagues, "Hey listen, I just flew with van Zanten, and you can't imagine what that stupid guy did. I had to save his ass, as he actually wanted to take off without takeoff clearance." Or was van Zanten so sure of himself, so overconfident, that he felt nothing could happen to him and that his hasty action demanded no further thought. If that was the case, it would only be natural that he would simply wait for confirmation of his action.

Van Zanten says, "No. I know that. Go ahead and ask!" Meurs asks for clearance. The controller gives them departure clearance but not yet clearance to take off. But the word "clearance" was part of the message, and we all know how often we hear what we want to hear rather than what was said.

Van Zanten advances the thrust levers and says, "We gaan!" This time, Meurs does not interfere, but he may have had misgivings. To let the outside world know what his captain is doing, he takes the microphone and announces, "We are now at takeoff."

The Pan Am 747 hears the transmission. Their copilot says, "We are still on the runway." The tower answers, "Stand by for takeoff. I will call you." We know now that both transmissions crossed each other, and if two transmissions cross each other on very high-frequency communication, there is static and not a single word can be understood.

In the end, the two jumbos collided and nearly 600 people lost their lives. Why? Why did the copilot—facing his captain's mistake and aware of the inherent danger—not use his hands to decelerate the engines? What went through his mind? Why did he risk a fatal accident rather than speak up? The same goes for Willem Schreuder, the flight engineer, who seemed to have felt the danger and was concerned enough to ask, "Is he not off, the Pan American?" However, when van Zanten answered, "Oh, yes," Schreuder may either have thought this was correct or did not dare to contradict the captain.

What happened between these men? First of all, why was it impossible for van Zanten to say to Meurs, "Thanks. You just saved me and maybe everybody else on board. Let me buy you a beer when we get back to Amsterdam"? Why could he not say that? Why could his copilot not repeat his earlier warning?

The answer is that belonging to a culture requires conformity, and not conforming means standing out and being judged according to the rules. It is a notion that originates in the beginnings of our evolutionary process as humans. If people did not comply with standard behavior 40,000 years ago, they risked being expelled from their communities, which meant their certain death, since the individual was not able to survive alone. This may explain our stress symptoms, and sometimes even the existential fear we feel when our behavior is a transgression of social norms. Standing out, by definition, contains the possibility—and hence the fear—that we will be so far apart from the others, so different in our behavior, that we will attract unwelcome attention and may embarrass ourselves. This might already be the case when we decide to contradict those who are hierarchically higher up than we are. Accordingly, the cockpit crew of the KLM flight adhered to their hierarchically defined culture and no one "acted out." Van Zanten played his part of the all-knowing captain; Schreuder and Meurs played the parts of those who bow to his superior knowledge. Remember the unclothed person on the Kurfürstendamm and you know what I am saying. Some things are not done, be it assuming a role that is not yours or promenading along the Kurfürstendamm without clothes.

Fig. 11.1 Charles Lindbergh

Let me give you another example. For this, we have to go back to the 1930s, when aviation was still in its early stages. Imagine you were a passenger in an aircraft at that time. There are no turbine engines. There are unreliable piston engines that burn more oil than fuel. There is no weather radar. There is no ground-proximity warning system. Every so often an airplane crashes. So, what would your pilot have to look like in order for you to trust him with your life? Would you want to see a timid little guy with thick glasses, or would you want to see someone like him? (Fig. 11.1).

Does he not look like a fighter? If we focus on his eyes, do they not have the capacity to see into the far distances and realize things we fail to catch?

Of course you want to see a guy like Charles Lindbergh. You would not be the only one. Lindbergh became the role model for all the pilots to come. He oozed competence, was the first to cross the Atlantic in his *Spirit of Saint Louis*, and he founded Pan American with the entrepreneur and commercial aviation pioneer Juan Trippe. The questions are: What is it? What do we believe we see in him? What makes us admire and trust him?

In 1979, the American writer Tom Wolfe published his book *The Right Stuff*, a novel about an old brand of test pilots—personified by Chuck Yaeger and Scott Crossfield—and a new type, namely, the Project Mercury astronauts selected for the NASA space program. For Wolfe, the right stuff meant remaining cool under pressure, always knowing the score, having good reflexes, never showing weakness, and always looking good.

Fig. 11.2 Scott Crossfield

Let us take a look at Scott Crossfield (Fig. 11.2), test pilot of the X-15 and one of my childhood heroes. Boys especially often have a role model like him. Wolfe had a good term for this type of man as well: "single-combat warriors." I usually refer to the phenomenon as "single-handed competence." It is an image that we often strive to fulfill, one which has survived in the culture dating back from the mythical origins of Hercules. Consequently, the movie *The Right Stuff* by Philip Kaufman was a huge box office success, grossing more than $161 million worldwide. In it, Chuck Yaeger and Scott Crossfield are friendly rivals breaking each other's speed records.

These are the kinds of people we like to see. But if we look at this super-humanness of the right stuff, is it realistic? Of course not. We learn about how we really are when we read accident reports and try to reconstruct the actions and reactions of people such as van Zanten, Schreuder, and Meurs.

The problem, though, is that we oscillate between wanting to be cultural heroes and realizing our limits. We tell our pilots all the time in crew resource management training and in aviation safety culture, "This type of hero is not you. The hero is a mythical figure. Whereas, you are real and alive. You are a human being. You have natural limits. You make mistakes."

To come back to our question of control: Can we control human error to the extent that it will become extinct? No. Can we manage human error? Yes.

The acceptance of our capacity to err would be the first step. By discovering the source of our mistakes and attempting not to repeat them, we may eliminate a number of them. But rest assured: As long as we live in our highly complex world, in which so many interdependent chains of actions, moods, motives, concerns, fears, and desires are at work, we will always make new ones.

We will certainly not be able to manage our errors by watching movies and identifying with the hero or heroine. James Bond would be as unrealistic a role model as Ellen Ripley from the *Alien* series.

A real-life role model whom I favor is Chesley Sullenberger, who ditched his Airbus A230 on January 15, 2009, on the Hudson River and saved the lives of all 155 passengers and crew. I care about the attribute that they gave him after this feat, namely, "a cockpit leader with confident humility."

A Leader with Confident Humility   I want you to chew on that for a bit. If we try to position ourselves somewhere between James Bond and Mr. Bean, someone with "confident humility" may be a good compromise. It means, "Okay, I am neither James Bond nor Superman. I am not beyond making the most stupid mistakes. But I know how to do a thing or two. I can be confident. I can be confident that I am up to a lot of challenges that life will throw at me."

Will this be easy? No, it will not. One more thing about Sullenberger: When he was 50 feet above the water and about to ditch a passenger aircraft for the first time in his life, he was still able to realize that there was a resource sitting next to him that he could tap. So he asked his copilot, Jeffrey Skiles, "Any ideas?" Skiles answered in the tone of an equal and said, "Actually not."

In general, our role models in aviation are the check airmen. In fact, their influence cannot be overestimated. What the check airman does will be copied by his trainees—not only his flying techniques but also his behavior. I remember when I was a young copilot on a 737 in line training, the check captain sitting on my left looked at me and said, "Robert, I make mistakes. You better watch over me." I looked back at him and thought, "Good grievance, what is with this guy? He makes mistakes?" Today, I say the same to my copilots.

Actually, the behavior and attitudes of your check and training personnel have an immense power in building and forming the culture you want to establish in your work environment. From their level, it will trickle down through the organization.

Another formative element—it has nothing to do with flying—means putting facts above one's ego. Chet Baker and Gerry Mulligan played jazz in the 1950s. They laid the foundation for West Coast Jazz with the Gerry Mulligan

Quartet—and they hated each other's guts. However, one day after a particularly well-played set, they overcame their antipathy and embraced before leaving the stage. Their art ranked higher than their egos.

You might ask, "How can we shape a culture in which leaders are confident and have humility and in which people pay attention to facts rather than nourishing their egos?" First of all, you must want it. You must be convinced that this is the right way to succeed in a world that is infinitely more complex than it was 40,000 years ago. You must have the desire for it. Otherwise, it will not work. Or, in the sense of Saint Exupery in *Citadelle*, it is not the allocation of jobs or tasks that builds a ship. You have to put the yearning for the vast and endless sea in the heart of the men.

12

Just Culture

Helmut Kunz

Eurocontrol—the European Organisation for the Safety of Air Navigation—defines "just culture" as a culture in which frontline operators and others are not punished for actions, omissions, or decisions taken by them that are commensurate with their experience and training, but rather a culture in which gross negligence, willful violations, and destructive acts are not tolerated.

However, establishing a just culture is a management task governed by the most important element of a just-culture philosophy, but also the hardest one to gain—namely, trust. This requires management to walk the talk and communicate its dedication to a fair process in an open and transparent way. Other stakeholders have to be involved in formulating a clear and concise just-culture policy that leaves no doubt as to where the line will be drawn between blameless, unsafe acts and unacceptable, dangerous behaviors.

In case of an error, management will have to evaluate behavioral choices and its current system design. Processes and procedures will have to be reviewed, which may be followed by their redesign as well as the retraining of the individual.

Management must make sure that there are no inherent incentives for risk behavior and instead should create incentives for safe behavior. Furthermore, they must ensure that the individuals selected to manage the just-culture processes are of the highest moral integrity, respected and trusted by management and employees alike, and thoroughly trained in applying fair treatment.

H. Kunz
Essen, Germany

© The Author(s) 2018
J. U. Hagen (ed.), *How Could This Happen?*, https://doi.org/10.1007/978-3-319-76403-0_12

An investigation group—usually comprising members of the safety department or members from other operational departments—has to collect the facts of an event and gather all relevant information. They need to draft a report with findings of the investigation based solely on facts, without assigning blame or liability. The reporting system itself must be easily accessible, and reports must be followed up expeditiously to address error-producing conditions. These have to be dealt with, even if they require changes that affect organizational processes and the corporate culture itself.

The aviation industry has a formidable accident record, which has consistently improved with the development of new technology, more and better training of the people involved (flight crews, air traffic controllers, maintenance professionals, and airport operators), and continuous striving toward improving safety reporting systems. As such, commercial aviation remains the safest form of transportation: It requires the strictest standards in certifying new equipment, qualifying future personnel, and maintaining existing equipment and infrastructure.

One of the most important pillars of aviation safety management comprises its voluntary and mandatory reporting systems, which are based on a no-blame or nonpunitive/nonreprisal philosophy and help to develop a just culture.

Historical Development

Aviation started with trial and error to improve the performance of early designs. Many inventors and early aviators lost their lives getting too close to the edge in trying to improve upon previous versions.

"Aviation in itself is not inherently dangerous. But to an even greater degree than the sea, it is terribly unforgiving of any carelessness, incapacity, or neglect," wrote Captain A.G. Lamplugh of the British Aviation Insurance Group in the early 1930s.

After aviation developed into an accepted mode of transportation, public pressure and expectations were put upon lawmakers for them to continuously improve safety records as more paying customers took to the air. Technology improved, the training of the crews became more rigorous, and legislation became more comprehensive. At the same time, people understood that systems would never be perfect, nor would the humans operating them. But in the aftermath of accidents, investigators found that extremely useful and insightful information went missing because people were reluctant to pass this information on due to fear of punishment and retribution.

Progress was made when the culture changed from a blame culture—trying to identify and punish the individual who had committed an error or mistake—to a no-blame approach, in which the reporting individual is protected by anonymity and people no longer have to fear sanctions. This no-blame culture improved the information flow by generating more reports, which then helped in identifying crucial system failures and deficient designs of standard operating procedures.

However, an anonymous reporting system can also lend itself to abuse by individuals who knowingly and intentionally violate safety rules. That is when the introduction of a just culture comes into play.

Definitions

To understand the foundations that a just culture is based on, we need to look at the behavioral definitions that are used.

J. Reason estimates that around 10 percent of actions contributing to incidents can be judged as culpable. This means that the rest—the large majority—of unsafe acts are not and can be reported without fear of sanction. Reason categorizes these as "honest errors," the kinds of lapses and mistakes that even the best people can make (Reason 1991). When we deal with deliberate violations, though, we have to know where to draw the line. One airline's safety manual contains the following typical definitions:

Error is an action that does not go according to plan. Three basic error types may be distinguished:

(1) skill-based error (e.g., breakdown in visual scan pattern, task fixation, poor airmanship, distraction, failure to see and avoid, negative habit, task overload, lack of system knowledge, etc.);
(2) decision error (inappropriate maneuver/procedure, wrong response to challenge); and
(3) perceptional error (due to visual illusion or disorientation/vertigo or misjudged distance, altitude, airspeed, or clearance).

A *mistake* is an action that goes according to plan, but the plan is inadequate to achieve the desired outcome. Known as a "cognitive error," a mistake occurs when an individual does what they planned to do but should really have done something else to achieve their goal.

Misconduct is improper behavior.

Recklessness is a lack of regard for danger or consequences. The person committing the violation did not think or care about the consequences. Although there is no intent to do harm to others, recklessness implies that an individual knowingly ignored the potential consequences of their actions.

An *unintended violation* is a rule or procedure that is violated because people were not aware of the rule or did not understand it.

A *situational violation* is a violation where the rules are broken due to pressure to complete the task, or because it is difficult to comply with the rule in the circumstances. A job cannot be done if the rules are followed. Instead of stopping, the job is done anyway and the rule is deliberately violated.

An *exceptional violation* means to deliberately not follow the rules in unforeseen or undefined situations. It is a violation created when something goes wrong and the individual believes that the only solution is to break the rules even though it could be seen as taking a risk.

A *routine violation* is a willful disregard of rules that, through custom and practice, has become the norm. Routine violations tend to be habitual. Violators will say, "I always do it this way" or "Everybody does it like that."

Substandard application of company procedures is a *possible reckless violation*.

Sabotage means to deliberately destroy or damage something. To constitute sabotage, there needs to be intent for both the action and the consequences to cause damage, disrupt operations, or incite fear.

Violation for organizational gain means to deliberately not follow the rules with the aim of benefiting the organization. The person committing the violation thought it was better for the company to do it that way. They acted to improve the performance of the organization or to please their superiors.

Violation for personal gain means to deliberately not follow the rules with the aim of benefiting the individual.

A typical example of a situational violation is an optimizing violation, in which flight crews will disregard a rule to stay on time or avoid a burdensome diversion. Most airlines specify a maximum speed that their crews are allowed to fly at low altitudes. This serves two purposes: first, to reduce the possibility of an unstabilized approach and to avoid the risk of severe damage to the airframe in case of a bird strike. Many crews will violate this rule when they are faced with the dilemma of arriving on time or trying to beat a curfew that would otherwise have them wind up at a diversion airport, with all the ensuing discomforts for the passengers.

Such a situational violation can also lead to an unintended violation, as a "hot and high" approach will often lead to an unstabilized approach in which the aircraft is not in landing configuration at a predetermined distance from—or stipulated altitude above—the touchdown zone. Unstabilized approaches can lead to hard landings, causing substantial damage to the airframe or to runway overruns, with severe consequences.

When analyzing these violations, management must look at the rules that were broken as well as the circumstances that led to their breach. In the above example, one root cause could be the schedule of the airline itself. If the airline does not allow enough buffer time for delays in between rotations, crews will be tempted to meet curfew times, as they are the ones that have to bear unpleasant passenger reactions due to these undesirable diversions.

Also, management may arrive at the conclusion that some well-meant rules that were thought out in the boardroom fail the reality test, meaning their implementation is so impractical that crews are hampered from doing their jobs effectively, which will increasingly result in disobedience. Therefore, three different aspects need to be taken into account to determine appropriate corrective measures that are designed to prevent the reoccurrence of an undesirable event.

The substitution test: Would another ordinary person with the same competence behave in the same way under the same circumstances? It is an assessment of whether another individual sharing the same knowledge, experience, and perceptions; special skills; education and training; physical characteristics; and mental capacity might have reasonably followed the same course of action, given the same circumstances. If the answer is YES, then it is inappropriate to punish the individual, since it is most likely a system problem.

The routine test: Has this event happened before to either the individual or the organization? This is designed to ascertain whether:

(1) the actions of the individual are in fact normative, that is, that they are a reflection of the normal way of working (this should align with the findings of the substitution test);
(2) the individual has been involved in similar occurrences previously;
(3) the organization has experienced similar occurrences previously but remedial actions failed to prevent a recurrence.

Determining whether behaviors are routine or whether an event has happened previously will have a direct influence upon determining an appropriate intervention. Possible managerial implications and/or procedural errors need to be considered.

The proportionality test: What safety valve would a possible punishment have? This test is designed to determine the appropriate extent of any administrative or disciplinary action in terms of its contribution to safety learning and improvement (Dekker 2009).

The overriding goal of any corrective action must be to ensure and enhance the company's safety culture.

Implementation

The most important element of a just-culture philosophy, but also the hardest one to gain, is trust. Management must walk the talk and communicate its dedication to a fair process in dealing with errors in an open and transparent way. Unions and employee councils have to be involved in formulating a clear and concise just-culture policy that leaves no doubt as to where the line will be drawn between blameless, unsafe acts and unacceptable, dangerous behaviors. This includes a matrix of remedial actions to be taken once agreement has been reached about the severity of the violation (Havinga 2014).

In case of an error, management will have to focus on behavioral choices and on its current system design. Processes and procedures will have to be reviewed, and this will be followed by a redesign as well as the retraining of the individual. Environmental conditions that may have played a contributing factor must also be reviewed.

Risk behavior involves a conscious choice of the individual because the risk is deemed to be insignificant or perceived to be justified. Management must make sure that there are no inherent incentives for risk behavior and create incentives for safe behavior instead. This can be achieved by coaching individuals to increase their sensitivity regarding the situation and the consequences of their actions.

Reckless behavior, on the other hand, constitutes a conscious disregard of substantial and unjustifiable risk and needs to be punished as well as accompanied by remedial actions.

Apart from clearly stating a just-culture policy by displaying it in the workplace and putting it as the foreword in every employee manual, a company must ensure that the individuals selected to manage the just-culture processes are of the highest moral integrity, respected and trusted by management and employees alike, and thoroughly trained in applying fair treatment.

An investigation group, usually comprising members of the safety department or members from other operational departments, will collect the facts of an event and gather all other relevant information. They will draft a report with findings of the investigation based solely on fact without assigning blame or liability.

In the next step, an event review group will determine the accountability of the individual. A flowchart is used to determine the behavioral classification of the event; it also serves to assess the relative level of culpability or accountability. The verdict of the event review group is final and cannot be overturned by the heads of other departments in the organization. All decisions must be unanimous. In case of split opinions, a mediator is called in to foster mutual agreement.

In addition, there must be a monitoring process that detects system flaws, which may lead to the (wrong) punishment of errors or inadvertently excuse violations that would undermine the just culture.

The reporting system itself must be easily accessible, and reports must be followed up expeditiously to address error-producing conditions. These can affect management decisions, organizational processes, and the corporate culture itself.

Conclusion

Whenever there is fear of punishment or prosecution, people and organizations will be afraid to report their mistakes, errors, or other safety breaches, rendering a learning-organization approach impossible. Fear of retribution will deter people with inside knowledge of an incident or accident from coming forward and sharing this information so that a reoccurrence of a potentially fatal incident or accident can be prevented in the future.

A just culture needs to be strongly supported by employees and management alike and be part of an organization's DNA. There must be clear definitions of what constitutes acceptable and inacceptable behavior. Sanctions for inacceptable behavior have to be documented and rigorously applied.

The just-culture policy of an organization must be clearly communicated, and reporting systems must be easily accessible. The follow-up of reports must be prompt. Error-producing conditions have to be addressed with remedial actions. Most important, however, is the fair treatment of people who committed honest mistakes, to leave no one alone with the consequences of their actions, and to provide appropriate remedial training or counseling.

The just culture has to be meticulously monitored so that deliberate violations will not be excused and unintentional errors will not be punished.

References

Dekker, S.W.A. 2009. Just culture: Who gets to draw the line? *Cognition, Technology & Work* 11 (3): 177–185.

Havinga, J. 2014. Just culture: Reporting the line and accountability. *Journal of Aviation Safety Management,* March: 51–55.

Reason, J. 1991. Human error: Models and management. *British Medical Journal* 320 (7237): 768–770.

13

Error Management in the German Armed Forces' Military Aviation

Peter Klement

Selected personnel trained to operate in high-reliability organizations (HROs) must be able to hold their own in the face of high levels of activity and the density of information in critical situations. They are exposed to these situations constantly and develop routines or automation techniques to be able to cope with periods of high stress.

In order to be able to create a mental model of a given situation, it is necessary to perceive the elements in the environment within a volume of time and space, comprehend their meaning, and project their status in the near future. However, our attention-related capabilities and working memory make this situational awareness a limited resource. We must decide between what is most significant and what is less so, and compensate for the lack of information with experience.

Reaching, and sometimes even exceeding, the limits of human capacity plays an increasingly crucial role in incidents involving modern and highly complex weapons systems. As a result, examples are on the rise in which people draw the wrong conclusions by assessing the information available and supplementing it with their own experiential background. The statement that specially qualified personnel can or must prevail in all critical situations may hence prove to be wrong.

Crew resource management (CRM) has been established for air personnel to use the exchange of information regarding the facts of a given situation to create a mutually reinforcing and correct picture of reality, and to correct any deviations before they can lead to an accident or incident.

P. Klement
Cologne, Germany

© The Author(s) 2018
J. U. Hagen (ed.), *How Could This Happen?*, https://doi.org/10.1007/978-3-319-76403-0_13

However, the effective transfer of the CRM principles requires rethinking the processes that affect the classical roles of crew members. What was formerly an individualist in the cockpit has—and must increasingly—become a communicative team player. This requires not only that soft as well as hard skills have to be continuously trained and evaluated, but also that a complete CRM assessment becomes an integral part of all practical trainings.

According to the European Aviation Safety Agency's 2014 annual report (European Aviation Safety Agency 2015), the year 2013 was one of the safest years for civil aviation worldwide. The statistics collected by the International Air Transportation Association in 2016 claim that there were only four aircraft accidents with fatalities in 2015 (International Air Transport Association 2016). In June 2016, the German Armed Forces set a new all-time record for its military aviation with two accident-free years in manned military flight operations.

In 1965, the year that marked the peak of the F-104 Starfighter crisis, the German Air Force lost 27 Starfighters: 21 due to technical malfunctions such as engine failures. By comparison, the average loss rate of the German Armed Forces' military aviation over the past 10 years is around one aircraft accident annually. The progress achieved over the years in terms of aviation safety has been more than remarkable (Fig. 13.1).

Major progress has been made with system reliability in particular. The reliability criteria for the likelihood of failure of a component that could lead to the loss of the aircraft cannot exceed one to one billion (10^{-9}). These are dimensions that quickly test the limits of human imagination.

The Human Factor

However, comparable advances in human reliability have not been realized over the years. For humans, effective design and organizational changes are not nearly as easy to implement. Even the considerable progress that has been made in further developing selection processes and training has not led to people becoming safer to the same degree as such improvements have been seen in technology.

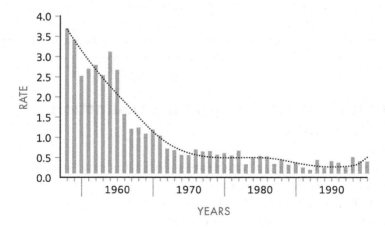

Fig. 13.1 Federal German Armed Forces accident rate 1958–2013 per 10,000 flight hours

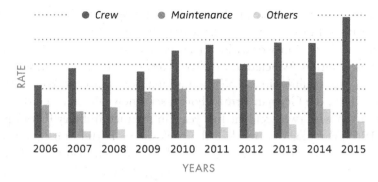

Fig. 13.2 Human factor in German Armed Forces incidents. (Source: Authors)

Human error is now the most frequent cause of aviation accidents: Incidents with human error as the causal factor have doubled over the past 10 years.

Consequently, we cannot ignore the fact that—despite all the progress that has been made in screening, education, and training, as well as through the introduction of CRM[1] and innovative technical subsystems to assist operators—the rate of human error remains one of the major challenges in accident prevention (Fig. 13.2).

This is just as true for aviation as it is for nearly any other organization in which wide-ranging decisions are made in a complex environment under time pressures (see HROs; Waller and Roberts 2003).

This is a topic that has been vividly addressed over the past two decades, in terms of both research and public interest. Yet, it is also a topic that raises numerous questions, some of which are still unanswered, and one that is characterized by ambiguity.

For preventive work, that is, avoiding incidents and accidents, it is of fundamental importance to identify and understand the true causes of mistakes. In order to avoid repeating mistakes, we can only succeed in addressing the right issues if we correctly identify the original sources of mistakes.

Definition of an Error and the Distinction from a Violation

At first glance, defining an error seems to be a fairly easy task, but it turns out not to be easy at all. Perusing the literature on the subject reveals that there is no generally accepted scientific definition for "error," since the research on the topic takes different approaches with a range of interests.

According to Zapf et al. (1999), errors must satisfy three conditions in order to qualify as such:

(1) they are actions (or omissions) that occur during a goal-oriented behavior;
(2) their result is the failure to achieve an objective or sub-objective; and
(3) they are potentially avoidable.

Although this core definition comprises the essential features of an action or omission leading to an unintended result, it fails to take into account a crucial aspect: the motivations of the person who has committed the error and, therefore, the question of whether the incorrect action was consciously or unknowingly carried out.

The motivation may be a crucial criterion in differentiating between an unconscious action or omission and a violation committed deliberately.

If someone makes a mistake and believes that they have made their best effort, the same action in a situation involving a conscious wrongdoing may be considered a punishable violation. For example, if—despite a system malfunction—a pilot chooses to return to the departure airport instead of carrying out the immediate landing required at a diversion airport for the sole purpose of being able to spend their evening with family and friends, it would be considered a violation. On the other hand, if the pilot simply interprets the warning indicator incorrectly, it could be considered an error.

This means the motivation behind an action is actually a key criterion, at least with respect to the German Armed Forces' military flight operations.

Therefore, in the context of the German Armed Forces' military aviation, the definition by Zapf et al. (1999) needs to be expanded by the aspect of motivation. Accordingly, to qualify as an error:

(4) it must be committed unknowingly.

In order to be able to effectively and purposefully deal with errors, the target group must understand the difference between an unintentional deviation and a violation. A corporate philosophy that is considered fair (a "Just Culture") can only be put into practice if we make the rules of conduct and their categorization transparent, specify that they are universally applicable, and communicate them in a way that everyone can understand.

Why Do Humans Commit Errors and How Can They Be Reliably Avoided?

Errare humanum est: Humans being prone to error has always been proverbial, even in ancient Rome. The history of modern research on error dates back to the early nineteenth century, when the focus was on studying perceptual errors, optical illusions, and mistakes in listening, writing, and printing (see Carl Friedrich Gauss in 1823 and Louis Albert Necker in 1832).

In Sigmund Freud's *Psychopathology of Everyday Life*, published in 1901, Freud concluded that misspeaking and mishearing could be a manifestation of unconscious motives, and that errors (in thought) were not simply random occurrences but were, in fact, based on principles of information processing and motivation. Freud had therefore already highlighted the interaction between motivation, information processing, and mistakes that we are still dealing with today.

In the years following World War II, the study of decreased levels of human output in military aviation became more important than ever before, not least due to the sheer number of aircraft accidents. A group of German Armed Forces experts began investigating every aircraft accident and summarizing their findings in case accident reports. The practical knowledge gleaned from these reports helped mitigate potential danger areas.

However, the reports' psychological findings, which focused on the field of cause and error research, remained purely within the realm of science at that time. Hence, the primary focus of the psychologists was improving the selection process and not—as part of the aircraft accident research team—necessarily finding the sources of errors. The common belief was that, by selecting suitable personnel and training them intensively, every effort had been exhausted to reduce decreased levels of human performance—including the infamous "pilot error"—to an unavoidable minimum.

This is how pilot error mutated into an undifferentiated collective term for the causal human factor in numerous aircraft accident investigation reports, without researching and addressing the underlying causes. A critical view of early investigations into aircraft accidents involving the German Armed Forces in the 1950s and 1960s illustrates that effective preventive work was only completed to a limited extent. Commonly, only the surface-level causes of accidents were identified and the symptoms addressed, even though these symptoms were merely an outward expression of a deeper problem.

The shift toward cognitive theories, which began in the 1970s and 1980s with the works of Zapf and Reason (1994), Rasmussen (1982), and others, triggered a change of mindset in accident research. Errors were now considered to be more than purely behavioral incompatibilities between stimulus and response. Science determined that errors are almost inevitable and that the likelihood of occurrence increases exponentially as levels of complexity and time pressures rise (Baxter et al. 2007).

Three Levels of Causes of Human Error

The analysis of accident investigations allowed for the conclusion to be made that "individual knowledge, skills, and abilities" (Level 1) only represent one of three levels of potential causes of human error. Selection processes and training are primarily limited to this first level.

The other two levels we attribute to a person, as potential sources of error, comprise physiological/biological factors (Level 2) and information processing and motivation regulation (Level 3) (Badke-Schaub et al. 2008).

The insights gained from Levels 2 and 3 continue to rise in importance for effective preventive work, particularly with regard to complex weapons systems, which are a challenge to comprehend in their entirety (Fig. 13.3).

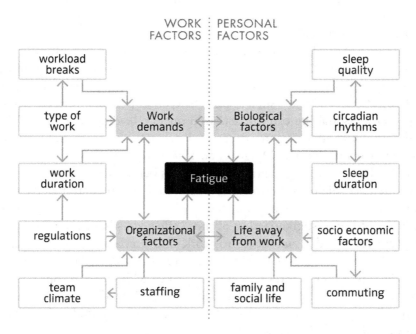

Fig. 13.3 Error factors. (Source: Hobbs et al. 2011. Adapted from the Australian National Transport Commission (2004))

Effects of Biological and Physiological Factors (Level 2)

To varying degrees, biological and physiological factors and the resulting characteristics are relevant to every task and every profession. The increasing significance of this subject area in preventing accidents is less obvious, however. In fact, it is deeply hidden. Psychological and medical selection processes can be used to determine the candidates best suited to the job from the perspective of physical and cognitive characteristics. This ensures that they will have a high probability of meeting the requirements of the respective job. Among other things, this increases the prospects of successful completion of this cost-intensive training.

Fatigue

Nevertheless, we are only able to control many of the factors contributing to aircraft accidents that are attributable to the physiological/biological level to a limited extent through the selection process. *Fatigue* is one of these factors and cannot, unfortunately, be combated solely by complying with rest periods and a balanced diet. Fatigue refers to a physiological state of reduced mental or physical capability. This is often attributed to sleep deprivation, being awake too long, disruptions to the circadian rhythm, or being physically or mentally overworked.

Fatigue negatively impacts attentiveness, the ability to process information, and responsiveness. It also leads to problems in decision making and communication skills as well as to the acceptance of excessive levels of risk (Millar 2012). Additional factors such as task structure, a person's work environment, and even personal life can impact sleep quality, leading to a state of fatigue and thus limiting a person's capacity. Error rates increase exponentially as fatigue increases linearly (Dinges et al. 1997) (Fig. 13.4).

Reliably determining the triggering factors behind this requires a trustworthy and open dialogue between those affected and their respective supervision; after all, the cooperation of those affected is vital to identifying fatigue early. In addition, stigmatization of those affected—that is, the assertion that they are less capable or unable to work under pressure—must be avoided among their colleagues and friends. Any kind of ostracism would be a fatal mistake and a counterproductive signal, since willingness to open up about problems is generally up to each individual. Only if the indicators of an impending problem are recognized early can goal-oriented preventive measures be effectively implemented.

Compared to commercial aviation, personal contact between members of a military squadron is much more intense, with all of the associated advantages

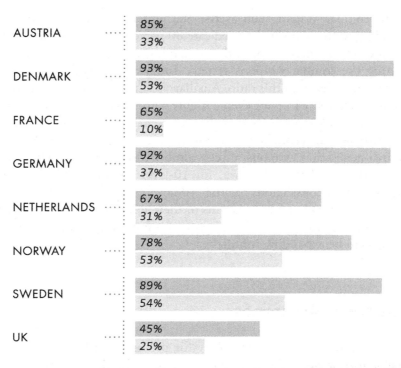

Fig. 13.4 Percentage of pilots experiencing fatigue (dark grey) and dozing off and/or experiencing micro-sleeps (light grey) in the cockpit. (Source: European Cockpit Association, *Pilot Fatigue Barometer* (N.p., 2012))

and disadvantages. The advantages are clear: People know each other and can recognize changes in demeanor or personality. Ideally, people are so familiar with one another that they are able to address any problems with others, and the person they address is then willing to discuss any issues they may be having.

The disadvantages of such a close community are a tendency toward a herd instinct and hastily seeking consensus. Heavy professional burdens may be carried in team spirit, even if this leads to overextending individuals.

Information Processing and Motivation Regulation (Level 3)

Selected personnel trained to operate in HROs must be able to hold their own in the face of high levels of activity and the density of information in critical situations. They are exposed to these kinds of situations constantly during their training, and they develop routines or automation techniques to be able to cope with periods of high stress under all circumstances.

With combat aircraft such as the Starfighter, which is aerodynamically demanding to fly, pilots had to dedicate 80 percent of their attention span to manually fly the aircraft; only the remaining 20 percent was available for operating the combat weapons system. Today's ultra-modern weapons systems have now reversed this ratio. Auxiliary technical systems and subsystems make it much easier to pilot even a highly aerodynamically unstable aircraft, such as the Eurofighter, as long as all systems are functioning as designed.

An experienced technician is able to understand the system dependencies in fourth-generation weapons systems almost effortlessly through circuit diagrams and flow charts. However, for 10-layer circuit boards with 600 tie points and cross-connections to other 10-layer circuit boards, that same technician would quickly reach the limits of their abilities. What is required with respect to the ability to absorb and process information is steadily increasing and seems to be expanding infinitely.

Situational Awareness

There are limits to humans' capacity for processing information. Endsley's *Situational Awareness Theory* (1995) states that situational awareness itself is part of information processing; awareness, attention, and memory are equal components when processing information. In order to be able to create a mental model of the prevailing reality or situation, subjectively speaking, we have to successfully carry out three consecutive steps:

* the perception of the elements in the environment within a volume of time and space,
* the comprehension of their meaning, and
* the projection of their status in the near future.

However, our attention-related capabilities and working memory make situational awareness a limited resource. People rely on experiences stored as part of their long-term memory, especially in situations in which the density of information exceeds our mental capacity to take this information in, or where the information is insufficient to achieve an acceptable level of situational awareness. In the first case, we must decide between what is most significant and what is less so; in the second, we must compensate for the lack of information with experience. In both cases, we rely on our long-term memory.

These processes, which partially occur below our perception threshold, allow us to make predictions, make decisions, and remain capable of taking action, even when we are relying on information with significant gaps or information that is questionable (Badke-Schaub et al. 2008).

Intuitive and Rational Decisions

D. Kahneman primarily attributes this capability to two different judgment and decision-making processes: intuitive and rational decision-making processes. Here, intuitive thinking is a process that is carried out constantly and almost unconsciously, taking place at high speeds with low levels of mental effort. Intuitive decision-making processes generate a sense of security, since they rely on reference values taken from long-term memory that may have led to successful outcomes in similar situations in the past. Information is compared to knowledge stored in a person's long-term memory and assembled into a subjectively plausible representation of the situation. Decisions are taken, and further courses of action are determined on this basis.

A study of firefighters' decision making in critical situations has shown that, based on a person's perception and individual experiential background, the process is not that multiple options for action are developed. It is always the case that only one course of action is chosen and implemented, based on the perceptions and experiences available (Kahneman 2011).

Compared to intuitive decision making, rational thinking requires concentration, conscious effort, and a deliberate decision. However, even rational thinking, and therefore our initial assessment of a situation, is based on the suggestions and assessments of our intuition.

Should it be necessary to review and correct this initial evaluation of a situation, rational thinking processes must be deliberately and willfully activated, which in turn requires renewed effort to be made. This means that the decisions that are the result of a rational, and therefore structured, decision-making process are, in fact, based on a conscious thought process carried out in combination with a process of self-regulation. This reduces our ability to engage in parallel decision-making processes.

Our tendencies, education, and training primarily enable us to quickly engage in intuitive judgment and decision-making processes involving specific subjects or tasks while at the same time enabling us to take action with high chances of achieving a successful outcome. Challenging a recreational chess player with complicated moves during a walk may influence their pace. A professional chess player may solve the same challenge without any reduction in pace. Hence, a recreational chess player must dedicate significantly more attention to the challenge than the professional, which may even have influence on basic functions such as the walking pace (Kahneman 2011).

Incidents Involving Highly Complex Weapons Systems

Reaching—and sometimes even exceeding—the limits of human capacity increasingly plays a crucial role, especially in incidents involving modern and highly complex weapons systems. Examples are on the rise in which people draw the wrong conclusions by assessing the information available and supplementing it with their own experiential background. Above all, it appears that behavioral patterns internalized over a period of years that have proven themselves in older and much less complex (weapons) systems promote incorrect conclusions in a highly complex system configuration.

For example, if a display instrument fails in an older weapons system, it is highly likely that the pilot will be able to analyze the resulting limitations and draw correct conclusions based on experience and system knowledge. By contrast, the complexity of digital systems can overwhelm a pilot's analytical expertise and lead to an incorrect response. Examples such as the Air France 447 crash, which resulted from a loss of control when the speed indicator failed (Bureau d'Enquêtes et d'Analyses pour la Sécurité de l'Aviation Civile 2012), as well as numerous findings from incidents that occurred as part of the German Armed Forces' military aviation emphatically demonstrate this.

The resulting implications for practice and for dealing with errors are diverse. The more complex the situation, the greater the likelihood that the gaps in a person's knowledge pertaining to reference values retrieved from their long-term memory are only filled in incompletely, or are filled in with incorrect information. This means that the likelihood of the wrong decision being made is almost directly proportional to the complexity of the situation or task. When faced with such conditions, a person's capacity for perception and their ability to make sound judgments rapidly reach their natural limits, even if that person has been handpicked or specially trained for that task.

Based on a study of 143 aircraft accidents, 78 percent of accidents are attributable to Level 1 errors (Jones and Ensley 1996). This means that mistakes in gathering and processing information are a significant source of human error. Therefore, the statement that specially qualified personnel can or must prevail in all critical situations may prove wrong based on the above deduction.

Applied Strategies to Prevent and Compensate for Errors

Early Detection of Potential for Mistakes

This survival maxim was still widespread in the 1980s, even among crew members in military as well as in civil aviation. As a rule, errors were considered something negative and were frequently associated with a lack of professionalism.

The questions are therefore: How many mistakes or mistakes per unit of time are acceptable? Where to draw the line between professionalism and a lack of competence? Can we be confident in the decisions of someone who admits they make mistakes? Can I trust their decisions in critical situations? (Fig. 13.5).

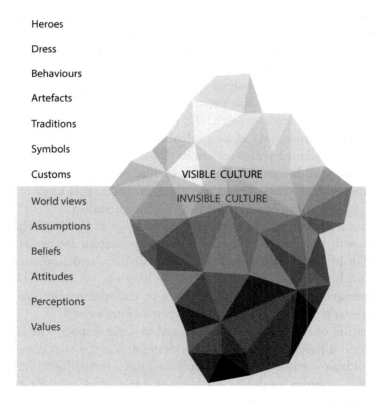

Fig. 13.5 Iceberg model of organizational cultures. (Source: E. Schein, *The corporate culture survival guide: Sense and nonsense about cultural change (1990)*)

Evolution has taught us that only the strong survive. We often consider making and acknowledging mistakes to be a sign of weakness. This led to tactical content dominating the debriefings that were held immediately following flights. Still arguably plagued by a bad conscience, those involved in these debriefings tended to forego any detailed discussion of mistakes in favor of "team spirit." They did not want to place their hierarchical ranking in jeopardy. This was accompanied by the idea that if I do not mention the mistakes of others today, I can potentially assume that my own mistakes will not be discussed tomorrow.

It is the author's belief that the reversal of this attitude is not fixed to a specific event or date. It was a gradual, positive process, which was facilitated by the development of capable inflight recording systems. Although flight data and flight maneuvers were already being recorded on board the F-104 Starfighter, these were not available for flight debriefings, except for blurry shots through the windshield. The memories of the crew and their handwritten notes were therefore the only basis for debriefing the sequence of events and the lessons learned of a mission.

The options for analyzing mistakes have taken a quantum leap with the recording devices available in military aircraft today. Today, high-quality video of the entire front sector is immediately available; all other relevant flight data is recorded with GPS references and provided three-dimensionally for flight debriefings using modern analysis software.

However, this shift was also promoted by continuously disseminating the findings of modern error research. We now recognize that mistakes are both part of human nature and can be a valuable part of the learning process.

The aviation sector has also revised its thinking with respect to the relationship between mistakes and competence. Instead of questioning and discussing the competence of those who admit their mistakes, this kind of analytical thinking is now considered an attribute of professionalism.

This has replaced the idea that you cannot make an omelet without breaking eggs with the maxim of recognizing the potentials for errors early and learning from the mistakes of others. Unfortunately, as demonstrated by the analysis of the rise in aviation incidents, we have not yet achieved our aim of comprehensively implementing a "fully open and transparent error culture." To acknowledge this is part of an open error culture as well.

The nature of mistakes has also changed in some respect. The last of Zapf et al. (1999) differentiation characteristics in particular—that error be potentially avoidable—requires us to reconsider things in a differentiated way. If "avoidable" is correspondingly qualified to mean that an error could have been avoided through greater certainty of action and greater system expertise, we must ask ourselves if this goal can truly be considered realistic, given the exponentially increasing levels of complexity of these systems.

Strategies for Early Recognition

Error-Reporting System and Flight Operations Questionnaire

As already mentioned, an open error culture depends on a personal willingness to openly discuss mistakes and potentials for errors. However, there are still sociocultural barriers that limit people's willingness to engage in open dialogue. The German Armed Forces introduced an error-reporting system in 2012 to make even concealed information about mistakes accessible. Under that system, any member of the German Armed Forces is now able to report issues in writing, by phone, SMS, or text to designated members of the Flight Safety Department using a confidential reporting system, and even to do so anonymously. The person reporting the issue and the personnel in charge of evaluating their report engage in a dialogue on how to handle the information provided. If specific actions are required, reports are generally acted upon and pursued further. Reported errors remain unsanctioned, unless it involves a violation. Violations are always pursued as part of the Just Culture of the German Armed Forces and passed on to the authorities responsible for issuing any penalization.

Another avenue of early detection is gathering information on the unembellished atmosphere of flight operations. Members of flying units regularly complete a questionnaire on a voluntary and anonymous basis. This questionnaire is used to determine the underlying climate in the unit and to assess this information with respect to indicators such as workload, staffing situation, motivation, and leadership behavior. Those in positions of responsibility within the unit receive the results for their reflection. The findings are also compared across several years to analyze trends in order to detect potential shifts as early as possible. The findings are addressed with the unit leadership, and options for possible actions to be taken are discussed to promptly counteract any escalation of the situation.

Compensatory Strategies

As stated previously, mistakes made at the level of implementation are often the result of incomplete or erroneous perceptions. According to Baxter et al. (2007), the likelihood of erroneous interpretations increases with the level of complexity.

CRM is probably the most widely used strategy for compensating for decreased individual performance using a team approach. The German Armed Forces introduced this concept in a policy paper published in 2006. The main

226   P. Klement

objectives are as follows: "The aim of CRM is to minimize or exclude the impact of mistakes made by individuals and groups in the German Armed Forces' flight operations. It is therefore crucial to identify and name those conditions found in basic and deployed operations that may lead to errors during military flight operations" (Bundeswehr 2006).

The active principle associated with CRM is simple, logical, and straightforward to implement, at least superficially speaking. Put simply, the idea behind the CRM principle is to use the exchange of information regarding the facts of a given situation to create a mutually reinforcing and correct picture of reality, and to correct any deviations from the target before they lead to an accident or incident.

The German Armed Forces periodically trains all staff involved in military aviation on CRM. The three pillars of this concept are:

- the knowledge and acceptance that human error is always present;
- a communication strategy that takes this knowledge into account; and
- the realization that it is necessary to critically assess one's own intentions when taking action and allowing criticism of the same.

The last two points, in particular, lead to challenges in implementation that we have yet to fully overcome.

Based on Reason's (2000) "Swiss cheese model," we are linking a chain of events that could lead to an accident or incident with the notion of a linear sequence of events and opportunities to intervene (Fig. 13.6). This suggests

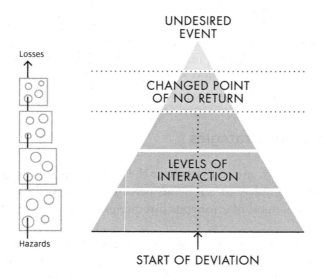

Fig. 13.6 Reason's modified Swiss cheese model. (Source: Authors)

that the same probability of success exists to interrupt or correct the course of action being taken at every point along the chain of events. In the author's view, however, complex systems are in need of a long-term rethink in this regard, since this complexity has a serious impact on decision-making processes, communication requirements, and possible courses of action.

Crew Resource Management/Human Factor

Communicative Behavior or Diffusion of Responsibility?

Every HRO has established hierarchical structures that are generally based on expertise and/or responsibility. The personnel with the skills necessary to be given positions of responsibility earned those positions with above-average performance levels and a willingness to assume responsibility.

The term "responsibility" is widely considered to mean the transfer of an obligation to a person or group of people acting in relation to another person or group of people based on a normative requirement. Depending on the relevant social practices and value system according to which those in positions of responsibility live, their actions—or lack thereof—and the implications of this may lead to consequences such as praise, blame, rewards, punishments, or claims for compensation (Sumerauer 2016).

This is a potentially delicate and difficult facet of CRM for many organizations, especially for a military organization such as the German Armed Forces, which traditionally functions under hierarchical structures. Those to whom responsibility for a task is given have both the power to enforce their instructions and the liability for any consequences of their actions or instructions.

In light of human error, CRM requires a calibration of the relevant actors in potentially ambiguous situations in order to identify any deviations early enough, to generate a common level of understanding, and to agree on the actions that must be taken. However, investigating flight accidents makes clear that the guiding principles behind CRM often fail in such critical situations. Firsthand accounts of those directly involved show that, despite a potentially dangerous situation that is familiar, often no verbal or direct intervention is undertaken. The logs provide us with sentences such as "I identified the discrepancy, but had endless confidence that the person in charge had the skills to rectify the situation in a timely manner."

Yet, why do people not intervene, despite the continuously evolving and potentially dangerous situations, and despite the knowledge that people are prone to error? The answer to this comprises a number of different aspects but primarily involves the diffusion of responsibility. The quiet acceptance that those in positions of responsibility hold the same mental images as you and others do—and, in addition, that they have previously experienced similar critical situations and corrected them in time—means that people expect a positive outcome in this case as well.

Additionally, personal experiences mostly demonstrate that deviations from the ideal have little to no impact on the outcome of a critical situation and are automatically corrected by those in charge before they escalate. For example, the pilot in command has completed hundreds of landings in bad weather: "Why wouldn't it work this time?" one may think during a critical situation. "Why should I place any strain on this cooperation by prematurely interfering or criticizing?" So we keep quiet and leave responsibility to the pilot, who is officially in charge, without examining whether they actually have the same image in mind as we do ourselves. Group members do not take action or only do so reluctantly, because they do not consider themselves obliged to take action (Darley and Latané 1968). People leave it up to those officially in charge to take action in order to avoid having to take responsibility for their own actions and the resulting consequences.

Thus, an effective transfer of the CRM principles onto complex systems requires rethinking the processes that affect both the understanding of the individual role and the training methods. What was formerly an individualist in the cockpit has—and must increasingly become—a communicative team player, without limiting the decision-making capabilities of the person responsible and the crew. This requires not only that soft and hard skills are continuously trained and evaluated using modern synthetic training devices, but that a complete CRM assessment becomes an integral part of all practical trainings.

Conclusion

How does Nietzsche put it in *Beyond Good and Evil*? "'I have done that,' says my memory. 'I cannot have done that,' says my pride, and remains adamant. At last, memory yields." There is no better way of describing the challenges that any serious error-prevention work must address.

However, prevention is a delicate structure, the balance of which is based on numerous intercommunicating pillars. These include knowledge of the human susceptibility to err as well as the conditions that promote incorrect decisions. Add to this the fact that we are dealing with error rates both individually and collectively and are establishing a transparent value system. Mistakes are distinct from violations in this value system.

I have done that, says my memory. This insight is important but not sufficient for managing errors. The aim is not solely to identify and analyze improper action but to identify and analyze the circumstances that led to this action. The "obvious" error is often just a symptom of a deeper problem. With complex systems in particular, the following question crops up increasingly often: Can the system operator still possess the necessary certainty of action, especially when time-sensitive decisions are involved in unfamiliar situations?

Were the original causes of the Air France 447 crash in 2009 or the Deepwater Horizon blowout in 2010 technical malfunctions, erroneous interpretations made by system operators, insufficient certainty of actions due to a lack of training/practice, insufficient definitions of the human-machine interface, incorrect or insufficient uses of CRM, or some combination of these factors?

Changing perspectives and the sheer depth of understanding we have mean that these and similar cases are evaluated differently every time. That is why each person involved must explore each and every source of available information and analyze the resulting information in order to identify the deviations that led to the mistake.

I cannot have done that, says my pride. In hierarchically structured companies in particular, in which people hold responsibility and decision-making skills, it is not always easy for members of the organization to accept that humans are susceptible to err. Expressing criticism without questioning the competence of the person in charge is a Herculean task in terms of communication. The association between discussing mistakes, criticism, and calling competence into question is deeply rooted in our consciousness.

The trust necessary to establish and maintain an open error and communication culture but also to expose ourselves to that same culture takes time and is only capable of growing slowly. Taking this into consideration and setting an example is one particular challenge faced by a company's executive management. The evaluation of the questionnaires completed by the German Armed Forces' flying units indicates that there is a strong interdependency between how leadership identifies with CRM principles and the perceived value of CRM within the organization.

At last, memory yields and pride triumphs over reason. The "correct" way to handle mistakes is the linchpin of effective preventive work. This includes a foundation of trust that allows us to discuss errors professionally and to learn from our own mistakes and those of others. In a credible Just Culture, errors and violations are neither denied nor forgiven on principle. It is inevitable that the issue of competence is occasionally the result of analyzing (repetitive) errors. A healthy Just Culture is not free of punishment per se, but it is just and comprehensible.

Over the past 15 years, the German Armed Forces has invested much effort to recalibrate its position on human error and has been taking major steps toward a healthy corporate philosophy in terms of communicating and managing mistakes in military aviation. However, it will need a similar period to complete this process because there is a need to go beyond changing regulations and procedures; human nature itself and established social-cultural conventions must be addressed. Only with the support of the knowledge gained from scientific research and the use of high-fidelity simulators in training will this process gain and maintain the required momentum to overcome traditional behavioral patterns. Even if the associated investments seem high, the costs of an accident are usually much higher and not limited to financial losses.

Note

1. Crew, Maintenance, and Team Resource Management are all referred to as CRM in the text.

References

Australian National Transport Commission. 2004. *Fatigue management within the rail industry: Review of regulatory approach*. Melbourne: Australian National Transport Commission.

Badke-Schaub, P., G. Hofinger, and C. Lauche. 2008. Human factors, Psychologie sicheren Handelns in Risikobranchen. N.p.

Baxter, G., D. Besnard, and Captain D. Riley. 2007. Cognitive mismatches in the cockpit: Will they ever be a thing of the past? N.p.

Bundeswehr. 2006. CRM Konzept – Deutsche Luftwaffe. N.p.

Bureau d'Enquêtes et d'Analyses pour la Sécurité de l'Aviation Civile. 2012. *Final report Flight AF 447*, July. N.p.

Darley, J.M., and B. Latané. 1968. Bystander intervention in emergencies. *Journal of Personality and Social Psychology* 8 (4): 377–383.

Dinges, D.F., F. Pack, K. Williams, K.A. Gillen, J.W. Powell, G.E. Ott, C. Aptowicz, and A.I. Pack. 1997. Cumulative sleepiness, mood disturbance, and psychomotor vigilance performance decrements during a week of sleep restricted to 4-5 hours per night. *Sleep* 20 (4): 267–277.

Endsley. 1995. Torward a theory of situation awareness in dynamic systems. *Human Factor* 37 (1): 32–64.

European Aviation Safety Agency. 2015. *Annual safety review 2014.* N.p.

European Cockpit Association. 2012. *Pilot fatigue barometer.* N.p.

Freud, S. 1901. *Zur Psychopathologie des Alltagslebens.* Reprint 1948. Frankfurt a.M.: Fischer.

Gauss, C.F. 1823. Theoria combinationis observationum erroribus minimis obnoxiae. Commentations societ. reg. Scient. Götting. rec. Vol. V. hrsg. 1880 von der Königlichen Gesellschaft der Wissenschaft. Leibzig: Teubner.

Hobbs, A., K.B. Avers, and J.J. Hiles. 2011. *Fatigue risk management in aviation maintenance: Current best practices and potential future countermeasures.* Technical report No. DOT/FAA/AM-11/10, Federal Aviation Administration.

International Air Transport Association. 2016, February 5. International Air Transport Association releases 2015 safety performance. N.p.

Jones, D.G., and M.R. Ensley. 1996. Sources of situation awareness errors in aviation. *Aviation, Space, and Environmental Medicine* 67 (6): 507–512.

Kahneman, D. 2011. *Thinking, fast and slow.* New York: Farrar, Straus and Giroux.

Millar, M. 2012. Technical officer (human performance), ICAO. Measuring fatigue Asia-Pacific FRMS Seminar. Bangkok.

Necker, I.A. 1832. Ueber einige merkwürdige optische Phänomene. *Annalen der Physik* 103 (3): 497–504.

Rasmussen, J. 1982. Human errors: A taxonomy for describing human malfunction in industrial installations. *Journal of Occupational Accidents* 4 (2–4): 311–333.

Reason, J. 2000. Human error: Models and management. *BMJ: British Medical Journal* 320 (7237): 768.

Sumerauer, A. 2016. Was bedeutet Verantwortlichkeit. *Sachverständige* Heft 1.

Waller M.J., and K.H. Roberts. 2003. High reliability and organizational behavior: finally the twain must meet. *Journal of Organizational Behavior* 24 (7): 813–903.

Zapf, D., and J.T. Reason. 1994. Human errors and error handling. An introduction. *Applied Psychology: An International Review* 43: 427–433.

Zapf, D., M. Frese., and F.C. Brodbeck. 1999. *Fehler und Fehlermanagement.* N.p.

14

Crew Resource Management Revisited

Jan U. Hagen

Crew resource management (CRM) is a concept that involves the entire crew working as a team throughout the flight. It was conceived due to the fact that controlling a modern-day aircraft was beyond the skills of a single person. Therefore, the rest of the crew had to be liberated from their roles as subordinates and become actively integrated into the workflows and decision-making processes. This made it necessary to reduce the established hierarchy gradient on the flight deck and learn a new behavioral scheme. Communication was accorded a special role in this process. The aim was to achieve open, factual exchanges of information and thought processes in order to ensure the safe operation of flights.

But what priority does CRM take now, 35 years after its conception? Despite the much-cited benefits of CRM, initial results from an ongoing research study have shown that its status represented a recurring issue. Most of the interviewed pilots portrayed CRM as not being a fixed, integrated part of their procedures for increasing safety and reducing the rate of errors on the flight deck. Most interviewees seemed to consider it rather as an add-on that ranked below carrying out their mission, safety, and standard operating procedures (SOPs). Especially the nonhierarchical communication envisaged in CRM does not occur.

J. U. Hagen
Berlin, Germany

© The Author(s) 2018
J. U. Hagen (ed.), *How Could This Happen?*, https://doi.org/10.1007/978-3-319-76403-0_14

On November 4, 2010, engine number 2 of the Airbus A380 on Qantas Flight 32 exploded shortly after takeoff from Changi Airport in Singapore (Australian Transport Safety Bureau 2013). On board were 440 passengers, 24 cabin crew, and 5 on the flight deck (3 captains and 2 copilots). The debris from the exploded engine tore through the left wing of the enormous aircraft, destroying numerous electric and hydraulic cables. This wiped out the main control systems. Despite this, the crew maintained control of the aircraft and landed safely back in Singapore two hours later. During that time, the pilots flew in holding patterns while they performed a complex series of emergency procedures and expended fuel to get down to the required weight to ensure a safe landing.

The investigation report compiled by the Australian Transport Safety Bureau (ATSB) revealed the difficulties faced by the pilots and the professionalism displayed by the entire crew in response to this emergency. To cite just one example, during the critical phase immediately after the engine exploded, the crew received 36 warnings from the Electronic Centralized Aircraft Monitor System (ECAM) in the space of 20 seconds.[1] However, the ATSB was unequivocal that the key to the safe recovery from the incident lay in the effective teamwork of the flight deck crew.

The emphasis is placed on *collaborative effort*, because in complex emergency situations, pilots must continuously keep each other informed, analyze facts, evaluate options, make decisions, and check each and every related outcome. No one can manage this on their own. Thus, it is not "the captain" who ensures a safe flight but rather the crew working together as a team.

Crew Resource Management

However, captains had long been responsible for setting the tone. In the past, the hierarchical gradient between them and the other crew members had been so distinct that genuine teamwork on the flight deck seemed inconceivable. It was only when the first NASA report revealed, in the 1980s, that a large number of air accidents were attributable to the captain and his decisions that things slowly began to change (Helmreich et al. 1999; National Transportation Safety Board 1994). The term "crew resource management" (CRM) was coined, and a concept was developed under this name that involves the entire crew working as a team throughout the flight. This does not mean that the initiators of CRM were questioning the captains' abilities. They simply recognized the fact that controlling a modern-day aircraft was beyond the skills of a single person. Hence, the rest of the crew had to be liberated from their roles as subordinates and become actively integrated into the workflows and decision-making processes. This made it necessary to reduce the established hierarchical gradient on the flight deck and learn a new behavioral scheme. Communication was accorded a special role in this process. The aim was to achieve open, factual exchanges of information and thought processes.

CRM now forms a part of civil pilots' compulsory annual training. The key principle of CRM is to ensure the safe operation of flights.

How Effective Is This Teamwork in Practice?

Today, teamwork on the flight deck can be observed during simulator training. Commercial aircraft pilots complete these training sessions every six months. They cover command of an aircraft's systems, standard procedures, and effective collaboration between the crew in difficult and dynamic emergency situations.

From February 2010 to May 2013, my colleague Zhike Lei and I observed crews during simulator training in a study of how teams collaborate and communicate (Lei et al. 2016). Among other things, pilots were required to handle emergencies such as the failure of speed sensors or an unexpected drop in cabin pressure. They had to solve the associated problems and complete the flight safely. Each task called for teamwork among those involved.

We established that the teams worked well together to solve acute emergency problems. However, we observed varying performance levels as the flights continued. Without exception, this was linked to the captain's communicational behavior. Crews performed best when the captain involved the copilot in the decision-making process by asking questions such as: "How do you evaluate the situation?" "What options do you have in mind?" "What do you suggest?"

In a second study, which Zhike Lei, Avner Shahal, and I conducted in 2016 and 2017, we wanted to ascertain whether crews knew what the method of "leading with questions" actually meant. At the same time, we expected the answers to provide us with an overview of the successes of CRM. In this case, we interviewed military aircraft pilots from the German and Israeli air forces—all of them experienced commanders, copilots, weapon systems officers, and technical loadmasters.

CRM: A Lot Has Been Achieved

The German commanders in our study reported that, before CRM, the copilot was a marginal figure on the flight deck. Commanders would let them carry out their work while observing and assessing them. Some commanders made copilots look foolish, but a repeatedly humiliated copilot could take revenge—in which case, he might wait for a good opportunity to let the commander trip himself up. However, our interviews showed that pilots are well aware of the CRM code of conduct by now. "Things are much better these days than they were," said one of the interviewees. "Communications are better. This enables the other person to contribute to the best of their ability." The reported improvements stem partly from CRM training itself and partly from the workload in increasingly complex aircraft—which racks up immensely in high-pressure military situations. All of this is no longer manageable by one pilot alone.

The demands that pilots have to meet—above and beyond the regular task of flying—are described in the British Civil Aviation Authority's *Flight-Crew Human Factors Handbook* (Civil Aviation Authority—Safety Regulation Group 2006) as follows:

> These might include concentrating, paying attention, calculating, trying to remember something, being careful, maintaining awareness, doing an unfamiliar or novel task, doing a challenging task, making a decision, assessing evidence, reviewing a situation, looking for something, listening to something or someone.

If additional external factors (i.e., stressful or emergency situations) then require pilots to carry out the abovementioned steps simultaneously or in rapid succession, anyone expecting to accomplish this on their own is destined for failure. Let us reconsider the above case of Qantas Flight 32. There were 36 warning messages that occurred within the 20 seconds following the shock of the exploded engine. In a situation like this, even the most experienced pilot will overlook something, act too hastily, or lose their focus. Our brains can only process a limited number of stimuli at one time, and as soon as we focus on one thing, we lose sight of the other. A number of commanders we interviewed concurred with this observation. One of them said: "A team functions better than a single person. If I have a crew member who supports me, I will complete my mission better. Or when he pulls me out of a place I got myself into unintentionally, or when he suggests something I hadn't thought of."

Others were keen to point out that their teamwork commences during the briefing, where the aim is to bring everyone involved in the mission "on board." We repeatedly heard how crews have to be cooperative and work as a team. They must also complement, listen to, and respect one another. In addition, each member of the crew has to count on the other to interpret—and thus respond to—a situation in the same way.

Therefore, communication is the key to CRM. If you do not inform the other person of your take on a situation but rather assume—in silence, and all too often incorrectly—that they see things the same way, this can lead to misunderstandings. The atmosphere on the flight deck must therefore not discourage either pilot from asking the other how they interpret a situation and encourage them to inquire rather than simply assume.

One of the commanders we interviewed summed things up well with the following words. At the same time, he addressed the risk that arises if one of the pilots feels excluded. "If he [the copilot] thinks differently and does not tell me because I did not ask him, then I may not have done the right thing; it could be that he doesn't feel comfortable and won't be with me 100 percent."

A "good commander"—whose characteristics are among the factors we wanted to identify—asks questions. "He inquires: 'How would you tackle this?' without it sounding as if they are testing the copilot. This calls for sensitivity. They may add: 'This is the solution I have in mind.'" A good commander must also "not be afraid to admit if there is something they don't know." We will come back to this point later on, as "not knowing something" would be held against a commander in a different scenario.

What Comes First?

But what priority does CRM take? Despite the much-cited benefits of CRM, we found that its lack of prominence among crew members has proven to be an ongoing issue. Most of the statements portrayed CRM as not being a fixed, integrated part of pilots' procedures for increasing safety and reducing the rate of errors on the flight deck. Our interviewees seemed to consider it rather as an add-on that ranked below carrying out their mission, safety, and SOPs. The following statement from a commander, or "pilot in command" (PIC), is representative of these kinds of responses:

My responsibility is to see that things get carried out the way they should and the way I think is right, which is, first of all, the mission, followed by safety. If it simply happens and not much needs to be done because the copilot pushes ahead, then it's easy and comfortable, which is also good for teamwork. But I am careful with the way I speak to the copilot. In the end, the atmosphere in the crew is also somewhat the PIC's responsibility.

The communication between the commander and the copilot—which we consider to be instrumental in the success of the "mission," according to our interpretation of CRM—crops up as an afterthought. It "somehow" falls under the remit of the PIC. Teamwork is deemed to have functioned properly if the "mission" is completed without difficulties and the copilot does what the commander wants. Basically, all actions fall under the responsibility and decision-making power of the commander. This state of affairs bears little relation to CRM.

"Copilots are being involved at an earlier stage nowadays," said one of the commanders, who spoke in favor of CRM. However, if he and his coworkers had completely adopted CRM, there would be no earlier or later, nor anyone deciding when the subordinate is involved, but rather a crew working together from the start.

Even in the examples that sound almost ideal, the teamwork was reliant on the goodwill of the commander. "The idea is to empower the copilot as much as possible, to give him a feeling that we are together." The fact is that, under CRM, the other crew members should not be given the "feeling" of inclusion, but rather they should be involved as a matter of course. However, our interviews painted the picture that even CRM-conscious commanders were unable to consider the second man as their equal:

> When to ask questions, I see two options. One is to say what you think is the right thing to do and then ask him [the copilot] for his opinion. The second is to give him a moment to say what he thinks and then speak. In the beginning I started by asking and then making the decision. That can make the copilot uncomfortable if he said something else. That's why I hint as to what I think is the right direction. I don't have a problem changing my decision if the copilot convinces me of his opinion. If they don't, I'll say, "Okay, I understand, but I think we should do x." So I think it is better at least to hint.

These are not the words of an old-style commander who ignores the copilot as someone way down in the ranks, but rather those of a new model of commander who sees himself more as a father figure. In this constellation, the opinions of copilots do not carry equal weight, and they must make a special effort to make themselves heard. They must be able to convince a commander of their opinions. If they do not succeed, they discover that—although the commander can follow their train of thought—their opinions are not taken on board. We generally perceive this kind of reaction as belittling and insulting. The same applies if the commander suggests the "correct" opinion before the copilot even speaks.

It also seems to be the copilots' task to edit their own thought processes in advance and distinguish between important and superfluous inputs. We were only seldom able to identify the same with regard to the commanders, as if their statements were bound to be correct:

> I expect my copilot to provide what he was asked to do and not offer everything he thought of. A good captain will say, "Aside from everything we mentioned just now, is there anything else important that you thought of?"

Although one or two of the commanders recognized the abovementioned potential for unwittingly insulting the second man, this does not in any way change the view that they themselves set the tone. The nonhierarchical communication envisaged in CRM does not occur. This paternalistic relationship is also fundamentally entrenched in the following quotation:

> I just let things get done and interfere if I see that it isn't done the way I think it should be done. I give some kind of guidance, something general, with the hope that I won't have to comment too much. If I give a lot of comments to someone, it ends up hurting him.

The following statement comes closest to the CRM mindset, but even then the relationship is not ideal. The rules of both military and civil aviation state that the captain/commander has the say in cases where there are any doubts; the copilot will not question this. Having said that, this does not mean the two cannot make joint decisions. In this respect, the father figure is lurking again, clearly setting the boundaries. The copilot can speak when invited to, but the commander retains the right to inform him that his comments will go unheeded:

> I invite his opinion. I say, "Monitor me, notice if I miss anything." If something is unsafe, I expect him to intervene and I will listen. I tell the copilot that the most that can happen to him is that I tell him that we are not going to deal with what he said at the moment.

Ranks Are a Problem

The examples presented above are just a small selection, but they are representative of the broader picture. On the left sits the man with all the say. On the right sits his subordinate, who has to choose his words carefully.

Of course, this problem is inherent in all hierarchies and begins with the allocation of titles and the different roles associated with the commander, the PIC, the pilot flying the plane, the monitoring pilot, and the copilot. This does not blend well with CRM principles. CRM refers to crews, by which it means units. This unit envisages an almost flat hierarchy. In other words, in cases of doubt, it means that the decision-making power lies with the captain/commander. In all other cases, both pilots complete their tasks as *colleagues*, in accordance with CRM. Indeed, military forces would undoubtedly benefit from a more "collegial" concept being emphasized in the cockpit. As long as the ranks and the associated steep hierarchy remain embedded in people's minds, the aforementioned attitudes that run contrary to CRM will remain part of this system.

Changing these kinds of attitudes is difficult, but not impossible, as we have seen in civil aviation. Such a change would not only redress the hierarchical perception of roles, but it would also put an end to behavior that sometimes reaches bizarre role-playing heights. "When I am flying," one pilot said, "I try to be more authoritative. When I am monitoring, then I try to be as attentive as possible." Why, an outside observer has to ask, are both crew members not equally "attentive"?

"My role as a PIC," another said, "is to ensure that the mission is carried out as safely as possible." No, the outsider thinks, that is the role of both people—the role of the crew.

Hierarchy Comes Before Safety

Authors Vincent Giolito and Paul Verdin have identified the unspoken precedence of "hierarchy first" over "safety first" in their chapter in this publication. Most of the crews we observed also seemed to uphold this priority, whether consciously or not. If this is really the case, it suggests that the "safety first" or "mission first" rule constantly cited by our interviewees serves, among other things, to cover up a concealed need for authority and to shield anyone who hides behind this mantra from criticism.

The "hierarchy first" rule means that the copilot completes the tasks and is generally permitted to speak only when invited to do so by the commander—as outlined above. However, this dismantles the CRM approach and reinstates the former image of the all-knowing commander. It also resurrects the problem that originally prompted the development of CRM: the fact that copilots retreat inwardly and subordinate themselves to the commander's decisions. At its extreme, this leads to a situation that one of the commanders we interviewed described thus: "… that the copilots can neglect to think for themselves. They rely on the commander." This attitude presents a danger in a nonnormal situation or an emergency.

The Role of the Commander

The strict hierarchy in the cockpit, the tone-setting or paternalistic role of the commander, the unequal weighting of input to communications—all this does not stem solely from the commander. Copilots frequently share this view and sometimes go as far as to magnify the commander's role even further, insisting that there needs to be someone in the cockpit who can do every-thing. From the copilot's point of view, the other person is not a colleague, either.

Almost all the copilots interviewed said they expect the following charac-teristics from their commanders: "Someone who knows where this thing is headed. Someone who is calling the shots." The commander must be capable of making decisions and remaining calm under pressure. They must be able to assert themselves and must be solid as a rock in a crisis. They must always command respect. They must also be able to assert themselves with their supe-riors. Apart from this, they must be able to summarize situations and justify their decisions in the cockpit. They must also be able to feed the copilot with the information they require and ensure that "everyone is on board." They must not ride roughshod over others or make them look foolish, but they must ensure that "the crew members feel comfortable so that they say what they think." They must not take others' comments personally. They have to know how to get the best out of their copilot, no matter what their capabili-ties. They have to make the copilot part of all decisions and keep them informed about what is happening during the flight. They must ask the copi-lot for their opinion, listen to them, and ask, "Do we want to do it this way?" They must not be an alpha male. They should never act alone, for a poor commander "feels in control and does not communicate with the copilot."

This scenario complements the previous one because it represents a child-like definition of a benevolent father figure who knows everything, can do everything, is also loving, and takes the child's stage of development into con-sideration. We see the same kind of thing in supervisory roles in industry, by the way; this defect is not unique to military forces.

Decision Making

So far, we have determined that the decision-making authority in the cockpit remains with the commander, even if they listen to and involve their copilot. None of the interviewees gave us the impression that decisions are based on proper discussions. As previously stated, this partly stems from both sides placing the commander figure on a pedestal. The commander believes in their own ability to make the right decision, and the copilot, despite also being a trained pilot, shares this view.

CRM offers a different approach to the decision-making process and emphasizes that, when it comes to major and complex decisions, we are not capable of considering all the necessary criteria by ourselves.

With reference to the conclusions drawn by Tversky and Kahneman from their cognitive-psychological research, the CRM handbook states (Civil Aviation Authority—Safety Regulation Group 2006): "When assessing information and making decisions, high workload can lead to complex decisions being taken more rapidly than normal, possibly without considering some factors, options, and complexities."

Based on the research mentioned above, the CRM approach also offers solutions for the cognitive traps that can crop up during the decision-making process. One example is the way freshly absorbed information disproportionately influences our decisions. This can lead us to forget or ignore equally important information received beforehand. It is also possible for us to base our decisions on explanations that seem plausible without necessarily being correct. Often we are satisfied with partial information, yet we persuade ourselves that we know all the necessary facts. The well-known "confirmation bias" (i.e., our tendency to select information that supports our hypothesis of a situation and to reject any contradictory evidence outright) is also referred to in CRM. It is just as mistaken to rely on past experiences. Of course, it is tempting to say, "The last time I was in this situation, I did this and that and it worked, so I will do just the same again." However, when decisions need to be made quickly, we do not have the time to check whether the criteria really are the same as before or if some difference means that what we learned from the previous experience is useless or requires modification.

Tools such as FORDEC[2] exist that lay down the decision-making process and subdivide this into an analysis of facts, options for action, and the identification of the risks and benefits of each option before the decision is made, implemented, and put to the test. However, stressful situations do not grant the time it takes to use tools of this kind. It therefore makes sense, as a principle, to go through the steps in pairs, to compare the two different viewpoints, and to ensure that the combined expertise goes into reaching, carrying out, and checking the best possible decision.

A vital element of this approach is for both pilots to consider themselves as colleagues who continuously share information with one another—without one of them thinking alone, suggesting what the other should think, or considering the other's opinion as being subordinate or a nuisance CRM obligation.

Our interviewees are a long way off from an equal exchange of opinions. "Decisions need to be carried out quickly, you tell the copilot what to do," explained one commander. The copilots see things exactly the same way. "You can try as much as you can to help during a flight, but eventually he makes the decisions and you carry them out." Or: "I share my opinion, but in the end, the PIC is the one who decides. Or I wait until he asks me."

Emergencies

It is interesting to note that commanders and copilots agree that they work well together, even in accordance with CRM guidelines. They believe that exceptions only arise in emergency situations, during which the copilot usually withdraws from the decision-making process as a matter of course and leaves this to the commander.

Let us refer once again to what the aforementioned *Flight-Crew Human Factors Handbook* (Civil Aviation Authority—Safety Regulation Group 2006) has to say about this subject: "The combination of circumstances and options (often accompanied by an emergency) are unlikely to be the same as previously practiced due to situational complexity. Hence, although expertise can be factored into such circumstances, large elements are effectively new and unpracticed on every occasion. [...] this means a process close to rational decision making." Rational decision making, as we have seen above, means that someone can overlook "factors, options, and complexities." The same applies to the commander.

Furthermore, the CRM strategy indicates quite explicitly that a stressful situation—which an emergency situation undoubtedly represents—can exceed the capabilities of a single person: "[I]f excessive demands are placed on an individual, it is possible to exceed the individual's capacity to meet them. This results in the deterioration of the individual's ability to cope with the situation."

Apart from that, CRM authors are conscious of potentially extreme reactions to stressful situations—our "fight or flight" mechanism or "freezing"—and warn about them. "Hypothetically and anecdotally, during flight or fight pilots can get mentally stuck within a situation (unable to interpret or resolve a situation, and unable to move on, even if that situation would present no problems under normal circumstances)." ... "The ultimate response to extreme levels of stress is to give up or freeze."

For the other crew member, the CRM instruction for situations like these is very clear: "Speak up when you see situational awareness (SA) breaking down." The one who is literally "paralyzed" with shock must be snapped out of a stupor, and this can only be achieved by talking to them in order to restore collaboration and consider the options for action.

Some of our interviewees had adopted the rules of CRM for emergency situations. "In situations like these," one said, "each keeps an eye on the other. The ball is passed back and forth. [...] The commander must be able to delegate."

Elsewhere, the point was made that "the commander should exude calm and security and not become hectic. If anyone freezes, the others have to intervene." Whereas other stated: "The commander ensures calm and collection. Nonetheless, *both* must also work through the problem and be aware of what the other is doing."

Otherwise, the behavior corresponds with the way roles are generally perceived, as outlined above: "I, as the captain, will present the alternatives and say what the advantages and disadvantages of each option are. I ask the copilot's opinion so that I don't make a decision without taking something into account. If he thinks differently, I check myself and explain to him why we are going to do x." If the correct CRM procedures were being followed, the commander would have said: "We, as the crew, discuss the alternatives...."

However, it is a fact that most commanders and copilots completely abandon CRM in emergency situations. "I as a PIC begin by calming the other person, give him the right perspective, show him that it is an abnormal situation and bring it to a normal situation."

Elsewhere, again, the point was made that "[t]he hierarchy only emerges when something happens, when decisions need to be made. Then it is clear that there is someone who provides information and there is someone making decisions." That distorted image of task sharing appears again here, as it is not both who compare information and make a decision together, but rather that one "supplies" and the other decides.

Or, as one copilot said: "During an emergency you need to have tact, because there are things that are urgent and your opinion doesn't always matter." It is interesting to learn that, although copilots do not wish to be "ridden over roughshod," they can do precisely this to themselves in an emergency. This is also reminiscent of the father-child scenario, in which the father "must not be disturbed" because he is working or has something else "important" to do. However, as we have seen above in relation to extracts concerning CRM approaches, it is precisely in emergency situations that it is vital for both crew members to work on reaching a solution, with one being able to assist the other, if necessary.

This means avoiding the following attitude: "The situation in the cockpit has to be calm. When there is a loaded and complex situation, the setting for introducing a differing opinion is more dangerous."

The following statements from interviewees also point in the same perilous direction: "In an abnormal situation, you will be busy with SOP. Things need to be done quickly and you don't have time to express your opinion." "If it is urgent I do what the captain says, there is no time for debates. You do what the captain says."

If you did not know any better, you would really believe that a child were sitting in the copilot's seat and not a trained pilot.

In comparison, let us look at the conversation between the pilots of the famous United Airlines Flight 811 in 1989 (National Transportation Safety Board 1992). The flight from Honolulu to Sydney was fully booked. Seventeen minutes after takeoff, the right cargo hatch flew open. This caused an explosive decompression that ripped off the door, parts of the fuselage on the right side of the plane, and sections of the cabin. Some of the debris entered both of the engines on the right, causing them to fail very rapidly. Even in these circumstances, the crew managed to keep the heavily laden plane under control and make it back to the airport in Honolulu. The crew attributed much of this extraordinary achievement to CRM. Below, we see how the conversation between the captain and copilot differs from the approach that the commanders and copilots we interviewed believe is correct in emergency situations. The names of the captain, copilot, and flight engineer on United Airlines Flight 811 were Slader, Cronin, and Thomas. Their dialog never reveals who was wearing which hat, as the three of them were genuinely, to quote the popular saying, "in the same boat." These are excerpts from the cockpit voice recorder transcript:

Slader:	"United eight eleven heavy, we're doing an emergency descent."
Slader [to Cronin]:	"Put your mask on, Dave."
Slader [to Thomas]:	"Go through the procedure for number three [engine]. I think we blew a door or something."
Cronin [to Thomas]:	"Tell the PA [public address] to get prepared for an evacuation. We don't have any fire indications?"
Thomas:	"No, I don't have anything."
Slader:	"Watch your heading, watch your heading. You want to go direct to Honolulu."
Cronin:	"Yeah."
Slader:	"You got a fire out there."

Cronin:	"There's a fire out there?"
Slader:	"Yeah, it looks like it's engine number four."
Cronin:	"Go through the procedure shut down the engine."
Slader:	"We're not gonna be able to hold this altitude on two [engines]."
Honolulu Center:	"United eight eleven heavy, pilot's discretion descend to four thousand."
Cronin:	"Okay. Four thousand. We got a fire on the right side. We're on two engines now."
Thomas (returning from a cabin inspection):	"The whole right side – the right side is gone. From about the one right back it's just open. You're just looking outside."
Cronin:	"Okay, it looks like we got a bomb that went off on the right side. All the right side is gone."
Thomas:	"Some people are probably gone. I don't know."
Cronin:	"We got a real problem here."
Cronin:	"What's the longest runway?"
Slader:	"Eight right, I believe it is."
Cronin:	"What? Ask him what the…"
Slader:	"Watch your altitude."
Cronin:	"Yeah. We're going to four thousand, right?"
Slader:	"Watch your airspeed."
Cronin:	"I got max [power] here. I don't know if we're gonna make this. I can't hold altitude."
Thomas:	"You're gonna make this!"
Cronin:	"Huh?"
Thomas:	"You're gonna make this!"
Slader:	"Make sure we don't hit any fuckin' hills on the way."
Cronin:	"I need a long final [approach]. Tell him I need a long final."
Thomas:	"Do not go below two ten [knots] though. Are you gonna try to evacuate the airport?"
Cronin:	"You bet."
Slader:	"You got the airport?"
Cronin:	"No."
Thomas:	"It's right over there to your right."
Cronin to Thomas:	"How are you doing?"
Thomas:	"I'm fine. I'm trying to catch up."
Cronin:	"Okay. Final check."
Thomas:	"Thirty (feet above the runway) – ten – zero."
Slader:	"We're on."

On board the even more famous United Airlines Flight 232 from Chicago to Denver in 1989 (National Transportation Safety Board 1990), it was the cooperation and continuous communication between four people on the flight deck that saved the day during the dramatic emergency landing of a stricken aircraft.

Captain Al Haynes said the following in the wake of the incident (Haynes 1991):

> But the preparation that paid off for the crew was something that United started in 1980 called Cockpit Resource Management [the predecessor of CRM]. Up until 1980, we kind of worked on the concept that the captain was THE authority on the aircraft. What he says, goes. We lost a few airplanes because of that. We would listen to him and do what he said and we wouldn't know what he's talking about. [...] So if I hadn't used CRM, if we had not let everybody put their input in, it's a cinch we wouldn't have made it. [...] The days of the captain being the ultimate authority are gone.

Aviation Culture

As already addressed above, hierarchical role allocation alone hinders collegial collaboration on the flight deck. Another problem lies in the elevated status of the captain or commander, which still incorporates elements of the solitary hero, as Robert Schroeder points out in his chapter in this publication, "Confidence and Humility." The authors of the CRM handbook also address this: "It is common for an individual to believe that admitting to suffering from pressure is an admission of failure of ability to meet the demands of the job. It has long been an accepted culture in aviation that flight crews and others should be able to cope with any pressure of any situation."

We spoke above about the workload and numerous interlocking steps that have to be performed in the cockpit. We have pointed out that one person alone cannot handle the complexities of the tasks and technologies involved, least of all in critical situations. The image of the heroic, all-knowing lone fighter was never the reality but rather a myth from the very beginning that someone should have consigned to history by now—something both commander and copilot should welcome.

One of the copilots explained that in emergency situations, the commander is not allowed to say "Oh God," to which I would like to respond: Actually, it is high time they should be able to say that. It is also high time for copilots to not just metaphorically wrinkle their noses at commanders in situations like these, but—in the vein of flight engineer Randal Thomas on United Airlines Flight 811—to respond, "You're gonna make this!" Or even better, "We're gonna make this."

The Collegial and Creative Problem-Solver

Overall, we had the impression that the interviewees often pay lip service to CRM. Yet, although people are aware of its advantages, they do not know exactly how to apply CRM in their behavior and communications. We repeatedly heard the same statement from commanders and copilots alike that they should be—and wanted to be—"on board the same boat," that the commander should ask the copilot's opinion, and that the copilot, in turn, should indicate anything they feel is not right. There was also talk of the "assertiveness" that the copilots needed to develop. This prompted those commanders who wanted to integrate the copilots to consider whether they should first ask their opinion so as not to influence them. They then considered whether it would offend the copilot if they went on to enforce their own opinion and that it would therefore be better to state their opinion to start with, or whether this would then deter the copilot from offering a different opinion.

Apart from the abovementioned hierarchical gradient and its negative effects on CRM, we also came across helplessness in handling CRM. After all, how are you supposed to implement CRM without an adequate understanding of the behavioral psychological aspects (Edmondson 1999) of working together in both small and larger teams? How can you if you do not know which behavior has a damaging effect? How can you if there is insufficient training in what we now call "emotional" and "social" intelligence? How can you if you do not know the effect of your body language, facial expressions, and words, and you cannot read the signals sent out by someone else? How can you if you are not aware of your own prejudices and do not know how these affect your behavior toward others? How can you if you have not learned how to talk to and negotiate with others in a situation of conflict?

The interviews showed that, despite extensive CRM training in civil and military aviation, the focus remains on the commander. Thus, it would make sense for captains and commanders to change their behavior first. This means involving the second man as an equal partner in tasks by asking him questions—a form of leadership that Ed Schein terms "humble inquiry" (Schein 2013). It also means that the lead person does not ask questions for the sake of it (i.e., not the kind that require only yes/no answers) but rather gathers information, opinions, and proposals for action, which are subsequently discussed.

This approach taps into the other person's expertise, calls up information, and reveals new perspectives and options. In the study we conducted during simulator training, we observed commanders who, in critical circumstances and under intense time pressure, still asked their copilots for their take on a problem and received a constructive answer. Crews with this type of commander performed consistently better than those with commanders who gave orders and who, at best, asked the copilot, "Do you agree?" or "Or do you see things differently?" These questions always resulted in the copilot backing up the commander's opinion.

A culture of open communication provides the copilot with the chance to not only get involved in tasks, but also volunteer questions and query a commander's or captain's decision without worrying how they will react.

There is one thing that captains, commanders, and other leaders do not need to worry about: Questions do not mean a loss of authority. In her book *Thinking Through Crisis*, Amy L. Fraher (2011) outlines the types of leaders our times require. She calls them "creative problem-solvers." We would go one step further and describe them as "collegial and creative problem-solvers." However, Fraher also makes it clear that the corresponding skills are not simply lying in wait, but must always be trained:

Today's leaders need: cultural awareness; an understanding of authority issues and how both overt and covert group processes can impede team performance, often in fatal ways; comprehension of the impact of technology on the pace and complexity of team operations; and sophisticated sense-making skills in order to manage team learning, evolve operations and incorporate new information as it emerges. To support these developments, even technical and professional fields, such as aviation, firefighters, law enforcement, maritime, medicine, military, nuclear power, offshore oil rigs, and railroads, must become more flexible and collaborative than ever before. And the leadership and teambuilding training programs for groups operating in these high-risk environments must follow suit, developing the creative problem-solvers our complex, evolving systems require.

It has been 35 years since CRM was developed as a means of improving aviation safety (Boeing Commercial Airplanes 2016). That initial attention to the necessity of communications between captain and copilot already improved upon prevailing conditions. The same can be said about incorporating the findings of modern-day cognitive psychology into CRM guidelines. However, as long as this is only being written on paper and not constantly being taught and practiced, CRM will not be properly implemented and remain merely a pleasant embellishment.

It is therefore high time for a change of perspective for creating the first framework that gets the most out of others by engaging them with the "leading with questions" approach. Despite having become an established cliché, leaders do not have to be heroes and know everything—even though we sometimes wish that.

Notes

1. The ECAM system on board an Airbus keeps the pilots up-to-date on the status of their aircraft's systems. First and foremost, it displays faults, checklists, and procedures.
2. FORDEC is an acronym for decision making. It is the model used to structure a problem according to the following steps: F—Facts (what is the problem); O—Options (hold, divert, immediate landing etc.); R—Risks/benefits (what is the downside of each option, what is the upside); D—Decide (which option); E—Execute (carry out selected option); C—Check (did everything work/go according to plan, what else needs to be done).

References

Australian Transport Safety Bureau. 2013. *ATSB transport safety report, aviation occurrence investigation – AO-2010-089, final investigation – In-flight uncontained engine failure overhead Batam Island, Indonesia, 4 November 2010, VH-OQA, Airbus A380-84*. Canberra: Australian Transport Safety Bureau.

Boeing Commercial Airplanes. 2016. *Statistical summary of commercial jet airplane accidents worldwide operations – 1959–2015*. N.p.

Civil Aviation Authority—Safety Regulation Group. 2006. *CAP 737, Flight-crew human factors handbook*. December. N.p.

Edmondson, A. 1999. Psychological safety and learning behavior in work teams. *Administrative Science Quarterly* 44 (2): 350–383.

Fraher, A.L. 2011. *Thinking through crisis: Improving teamwork and leadership in high-risk fields*. New York: Cambridge University Press.

Haynes, A.C. 1991. *The crash of United Flight 232*. Edwards: Dryden Flight Research Facility, NASA Ames Research Center. http://yarchive.net/air/airliners/dc10_sioux_city.html

Helmreich, R.L., A.C. Merritt, and J.A. Wilhelm. 1999. The evolution of Crew Resource Management training in commercial aviation. *International Journal of Aviation Psychology* 9 (1): 19–32.

Lei, Z., M.J. Waller, J. Hagen, and S. Kaplan. 2016. Team adaptiveness in dynamic contexts: Contextualizing the roles of interaction patterns and in-process planning. *Group & Organization Management* 41 (4): 491–525.

National Transportation Safety Board. 1990. *Aircraft accident report. United Airlines Flight 232, McDonnell-Douglas DC-10–10, Sioux City, Iowa, July 19, 1989.* NTSB/AAR-90/06. Washington, DC: NTSB.

———. 1992. *Aircraft accident report. Explosive decompression – Loss of cargo door in flight, United Airlines Flight 811, Boeing 747–122, N4713U, February 24, 1989.* NTSB/AAR-92/02. Washington, DC: NTSB.

———. 1994. *A review of flightcrew-involved, major accidents of U.S. air carriers, 1978 through 1990, safety study. NTSB SS-94/01.* Washington, DC: NTSB.

Schein, E.H. 2013. *Humble inquiry: The gentle art of asking instead of telling.* San Francisco: Berrett-Koehler Publishers.

15

Error Reporting and Crew Resource Management in the Israeli Air Force

Since the introduction of crew resource management (CRM) by NASA in the 1980s, flight crews around the world have implemented techniques in order to improve teamwork with the aim of reducing mistakes in flight and increasing flight safety. Though implemented in air forces around the world, few insights into the use of CRM techniques in military aviation units other than those in the US Armed Forces have been published.

However, there are several features of military aviation CRM that make it different in nature from civil aviation CRM. Primarily missions have higher priority in military aviation than in civil aviation, allowing for more risks to be taken. When transporting passengers from point A to point B in a civil flight, the pilots' first and foremost mission is to tend to the safety of the passengers. Therefore, if a malfunction occurs, the pilots will first consider how to best land the aircraft. Risks are avoided, as safety outweighs the mission of landing at point B. During a military flight mission, though, it is expected that the crew will first account for the completion of the mission, and hence take risks. The more important the mission, the more risk the crew is expected to take.

An adaptation of the tools and language of CRM is therefore essential in order to tend to the different needs not only of military aviation, but of each squadron. Rather than a one-size-fits-all approach to CRM, which might be appropriate for civil aviation, a custom-fit approach needs to be taken for the military, whereby the unique characteristics of the military setting in general are taken into consideration.

A. Shahal
Berlin, Germany

© The Author(s) 2018   **253**
J. U. Hagen (ed.), *How Could This Happen?*, https://doi.org/10.1007/978-3-319-76403-0_15

In the 1980s, three F-4 Phantoms of the Israeli Air Force (IAF) performed air-to-air training over the Mediterranean Sea against two F-16 Falcons. Leading both formations were the squadron commanders, well aware that they were competing against each other in this dogfight. The navigator of the leading F-4—one of the more senior reserve officers in the F-4 squadron—flew often with his squadron commander. Early in the dogfight, the leading F-4 was "shot down" by one of the F-16s. Being shot down by an F-16 was not unusual, but, as the pilot of the F-4 recalls, he was furious: because he was shot down so early in the exercise, but also on account of his navigator, who, in his opinion, informed him too late about the incoming F-16. He told his navigator: "[You warned me] too late … too late!" According to the game rules, the F-4 then left the maneuver to rejoin it at a later stage.

The pilot of the F-4 wanted to return to the action as soon as possible and not a second later. Upon waiting the required time before rejoining the dogfight, the navigator of the F-4 gave the pilot directions to one of the F-16s. The pilot acknowledged the information and, although being the lower-flying aircraft, said he saw the F-16 "below." The pilot recalls believing he was above the other aircraft and wanted to gain more altitude before commencing the interception from above. This was due to the pilot's disorientation in the vertical axis—a situation that can occur when flying in fast and maneuverable aircraft, especially when outside cues, such as the color contrast between land and sky, are unavailable (as it was in this case while flying over the sea). The navigator did not pay attention to the fact that the pilot claimed he saw the F-16 below them, even though the F-16 was actually above them. At that moment, the pilot rolled the F-4 and began—as he believed—climbing. In reality, the F-4 was inverted and commenced a dive from 12,000 feet toward the Mediterranean Sea. A little later, the navigator quietly said to the pilot, "Pay attention to the altitude." Thinking they were climbing, the pilot wondered what his navigator was talking about. He took a look at the altimeter and suddenly realized that they were diving. Instinctively, he further rolled the aircraft and pulled on his controls. This is a reaction to level out an upright-flying aircraft and put it into a climb. Unfortunately, because the aircraft was inverted, instead of climbing, the pilot's actions aggravated the situation, bringing the aircraft to an almost vertical dive into the sea. At this stage, both pilot and navigator understood what was happening and pulled at both their sticks with all their strength, escaping near death at a very low altitude only by considerably exceeding the aircraft's acceleration limitations (also known as g-force). Immediately after reaching a safe altitude, the pilot said to his navigator, "Forgive me, hey?" The exercise was cancelled and the crew flew silently back to the base. After landing and upon opening the canopies, the pilot said: "You saved me." The navigator replied: "I saved us."

What can we learn from this example in regard to crew communication? Could this near-death incident have been avoided? Can tools of CRM, which have been widely implemented in civil aviation around the world over the past decades, also be of relevance for the military setting, with its unique characteristics?

Since Israel's declaration of independence seven decades ago, the IAF has been employing highly sophisticated airborne machines in a unique geopolitical arena. Today, the IAF is an advanced and combat-proven military organization, accommodating state-of-the-art platforms. Unlike the US Armed Forces, in which the Army, Navy, Marine Corps, and Air Force all apply and control their own aircraft, the IAF is essentially the only part of the Israeli Defense Forces that employs airborne machines. These include fixed- and rotary-wing fighter and transport platforms, as well as "unmanned airborne vehicles." The extraordinary environments in which the IAF is required to work have given birth to rapid technological advances and skill acquirement rates, in which almost no time passes between the development of new technology and tactical methods and their implementation in training and on the combat field. However, these have not been the only areas where there have been significant rates of development during the past decades. Mission briefings and debriefings, simulators, and other training methods have also become crucial for the IAF to improve both efficiency and, more importantly, the safety of crews and missions alike.

Since the introduction of CRM by NASA in the 1980s, flight crews around the world have implemented techniques in order to improve teamwork with the aim of reducing mistakes in flight and increasing flight safety. Although CRM was generated in civil aviation, it has proliferated into other related fields such as military aviation, where different priorities have led to new points of focus. Though implemented in air forces around the world, few insights into the use of CRM techniques in military aviation units other than those in the US Armed Forces have been published.

The goal of this chapter is to shed light on the process of implementing reporting and CRM in the unique military context of the IAF. Where does implementation encounter difficulties, where is it especially efficient, and what lessons can be drawn from this process? These are the questions that will be discussed. The point of view is that of a transport pilot and a researcher of CRM and human factors.

Israeli Aircrews

In order to be able to discuss CRM in the IAF, we have to first become acquainted with the characteristics of Israeli aircrews.[1] All Israeli aircrews (pilots of fixed- and rotary-wing aircraft, navigators, and flight engineers) enlist with the Israeli Air Force Flight Academy, usually at the age of 18. In this setting, both ground and flight training are performed. As of 2002, a bachelor's degree is obtained upon graduation. The duration of the flight academy course nowadays is three years. Upon graduating, a new Israeli aircrew is sent for further operational training in the various squadrons. The course of service usually consists of two-year stations, in which one serves either in a squadron or in headquarters. In total, an aircrew stays for a term of approximately eight to nine years in the IAF before deciding upon a further career in the air force or being discharged. Even after being discharged, an Israeli aircrew member is expected to stay in reserve service, flying on average one day per week.

Looking at the aircrew's job from a social perspective, gaining a position in an aircrew is highly sought after. Starting with a campaign to increase enlistment to the IAF, the term "the best for the air force" was coined in the 1960s. Although it has received its share of criticism over the years, this term has prevailed.

The flight academy screening is among the first screenings that every soldier-to-be goes through, starting at the age of 16. The flight academy has its first pick of future soldiers. Only a small percentage of the soldiers found eligible for the flight academy ever finish the course. There are many screening steps—leading to high dropout rates—that start from the initial screening and end shortly before the completion of the course. The difficulty of becoming one of the selected few to graduate from the Israeli Air Force Flight Academy also raises the prestige of being a graduate and belonging to the IAF. Generally speaking, being an Israeli aircrew member means gaining high social status.

Error Reporting in the Israeli Air Force

In order to manage errors, one has to know which errors have been made, and why. To this extent, the IAF has achieved a reporting culture that relies on four behavioral forces: personal identification with the IAF, obedience when it comes to its rules, a code of honor that regulates conduct in the IAF, and solidarity with other members of the IAF in general, and specifically with members of the squadron to which one belongs.

During the long time spent in training in the Israeli Air Force Flight Academy, the future Israeli pilot learns about error reporting before ever taking to the sky. The rule is that the same norms that apply to flight also apply to the simplest everyday activities, such as camp rules. These have to be internalized well before a cadet ignites an aircraft's engine.

Therefore, pilots learn to run, crawl, navigate, and use a rifle long before they learn to fly. Parallel to the physical training, they are taught a new set of norms that define the rules of conduct for the cadets in their upcoming training and lives as Israeli airmen and airwomen. If they want to be a part of the few dozen who graduate from the flight academy, they are well advised to adhere to these norms—no exceptions allowed.

From the first day of training, and well before air force cadets receive their rifles, they are taught to report any rule-breaking that they advertently—or inadvertently—perform. These actions could relate to being late to an exercise, not completing the daily physical training that each one needs to perform on their own, or even inadvertently leaving their rifles unwatched for a few minutes. As many rules are new to the cadets, they constantly—and unwittingly—break them. Although they are not necessarily being observed by fellow cadets or their commanders, they are expected to report any abnormal activities that they perform and await sentencing from the commander, usually with the direct implication of losing leave hours or having to perform extra assignments, most of which are physical in nature. If a certain deviation from the rules is discovered without it being reported by the cadet who performed it, there is harsh punishment, which could even lead to expulsion from the flight academy. Most often, cadets lose precious weekend leave time for being late to certain activities or for not having cleaned their rifles to the satisfaction of their commanders. In other cases, cadets who try to cheat during ground navigation training are expelled from the course immediately. No exceptions regarding reporting or the adherence to the norms of the flight academy are accepted. The fact that personal responsibility outweighs possible repercussions is at the foundation of the IAF's understanding of incident reporting and is part of the resocialization process that every cadet undergoes during training.

However, the nature of mistakes is that they are unwanted and that negative consequences usually ensue. It is to this end that IAF cadets and pilots try to avoid making them. A significant point to take into consideration when analyzing error reporting in the IAF is that the IAF did not adopt the anonymity policy that NASA and the Federal Aviation Administration (FAA) endorsed early on during the implementation of CRM. Instead, when reporting an error during active duty as a pilot, the Israeli aircrew member can expect to see their name both on the squadron's safety board and in a published incident in the IAF safety program. This program is a platform that enables the aircrew to search for, see details of, and learn from each safety issue reported. The details of each incident include, among other relevant information, the names of the people involved. Although the intent is to facilitate learning from mistakes and share information in order to prevent them from being repeated by other crews, it is clear that, in these circumstances, reporting an error is not always the easiest thing to do, whether it is a grave error or just a minor one.

Given this aversive nature of error reporting, how can the consistent, ongoing, and high frequency of reporting errors in the IAF over the last decades be explained? It is surely partly due to the obedience ingrained into cadets early on during flight academy training. However, at its basis are two other aspects, namely the honor code, which Israeli airmen and airwomen share, and the solidarity among members of the IAF.

Setting an Example

Coinciding with the high social status Israeli aircrew members enjoy, it is expected that they set an example for proper conduct, both on the bases and within the units in which they serve. Each and every flight cadet hears about the requirement of setting a gold standard for conduct in their environments. The message is: If not the flight cadets (and later on, pilots), who then? For instance, since the field of work of pilots involves operating machines that they do not maintain themselves, pilots have to trust their fellow technicians that the airplanes are properly prepared for flight and that every deviation from normal maintenance standards is reported. So, if pilots do not report safety-relevant issues, they cannot expect fellow technicians to do the same. This rule of conduct—or honor code—motivates them on the occasions when they may hesitate before reporting the exceedance of a limit or other safety-related issues.

A further aspect of reporting in the IAF has to do with solidarity. While flying, one often encounters situations in which no outsider would know if an error was made. Let us take the example of accidentally exceeding engine parameters for a minute during the climb after takeoff. Although it does not necessarily affect the specific flight, such an instance of engine parameter exceedance could drastically affect engine operation in the long run, if it is not dealt with properly. Errors that have not been reported could lead to critical events, such as engine failure, during successive flights. If no one sees the error, and reporting it will lead to unwelcome attention and a fine, it may be tempting to not report it. However, in the IAF, pilots know most of their colleagues in a specific squadron and fly with them on a regular basis. They feel responsible for each other and, thus, report their own mistakes so that they will not be repeated and possibly endanger others. This act of solidarity may sound selfless in the short run, as one takes the blame in order to prevent the suffering of others. However, it can also be viewed as self-preservation in the long run, given that all aircrews act accordingly.

As mentioned above, reporting is not anonymous in the IAF. Pilots who report a mistake may be ashamed to see their names on the squadron's safety board and, thus, want to avoid reporting. It is nevertheless the case with the IAF that, oftentimes, fellow pilots come to learn from the mistakes of others, knowing that it could happen to them as well. This way—and counter to the line taken by NASA and the FAA in incident reporting in civil aviation—nonanonymous reporting serves as a form of support and a motivating force for most aircrews, which is a lesson that may be of relevance for organizations implementing error reporting.

Crew Resource Management in Military Aviation

Originating in the early 1980s from civil aviation, CRM has infiltrated the lines of many military squadrons around the world. However, there are several unique features of military aviation CRM that make it different in nature from civil aviation CRM.

Missions generally have higher priority in military aviation than in civil aviation, allowing for more risks to be taken. In order to elucidate this point, let us take two prototypical missions: one from the realm of civil flight and the other from military flight. In a civil flight flying passengers from point A to point B, the pilots' first and foremost mission is to tend to the safety of the flight's passengers. Therefore, if a malfunction occurs, the pilots will first consider how to best land the aircraft. Safety outweighs the mission of landing at point B.

Let us take air-to-air refueling as an example of a military flight mission. In this case, both tanker and tanked aircraft navigate to the point of interception, maneuver into position, fly dangerously close to each other for long periods of time, and advertently make contact to transfer fuel. If a problem occurs during the mission—be it on the way to the refueling or during the act itself—it is expected that the crew will account for the completion of the mission in their risk-taking. The more important the mission, the more risk the crew is expected to take. Thus, performing the mission in bad weather, at low flight, or even with defective systems is not only allowed but expected, as the risk-taking coincides with the mission priority. Although certain military missions require taking such risks, this would never be the case in civil flight, where safety comes first.

In addition, military missions are generally more heterogeneous in scope than civil flight and execute a broad array of missions. Whereas civil flight mainly transports passengers or cargo from point A to B, a military pilot is required to be able to perform a variety of missions, such as the air-to-air combat mentioned at the beginning of this chapter, air-to-air refueling, and air-to-ground missions, to name only a few.

Furthermore, whereas civil flight nowadays involves mainly two-seater passenger and cargo aircraft, military flight utilizes different fighters, helicopters, and transport aircraft. These different flight platforms involved in military aviation account for a plurality of factors, such as speed, flight altitude, crew seating, acting acceleration forces due to performed maneuvers, and so on, all of which make military flight more complex than civil flight.

Crew composition is a further factor in which military flight significantly differs from civil flight. Whereas civil flight is nowadays usually performed in two-man cockpits, military flight can involve a variety of crew constellations, from a single pilot aircraft (such as fighters and small transport aircraft), to two-seaters (fighters, helicopters, medium transport aircraft), and even multiple-crew cockpits, such as those found in large helicopters and transport aircraft.

Specifically concerning the IAF, after serving an average of eight years as a pilot, many of the Israeli pilots, navigators, and flight engineers retire to civilian life and fly in reserve. As a consequence, a high percentage of flight crews are mixed: Some of the crew members are enlisted pilots, who fly frequently, whereas others are reserve pilots, who fly on an irregular basis of one flight every one to two weeks.

An example from interviews held with IAF service members: Young first officers fly once or twice a day for several years of their enlisted service. They have more knowledge of procedures and regulations than most of the reserve captains with whom they often fly. This leads to a unique team situation in the cockpit: Some captains rely on the first officer to perform the flight, invite them to share their knowledge, and are open to their input; others mix knowledge with authority and hierarchy in an attempt to show their superiority, sometimes by discarding the first officer's good inputs.

However, after retiring from the IAF and starting to fly as reservists, the same abovementioned first officers, who have meanwhile become captains, realize the difficulty of the captain-in-reserve position. Flying once a week or every other week has drawbacks: The reserve captains are not immersed in the decisions and experiences discussed in the squadron on a daily basis. Therefore, they have to become informed prior to each flight in order to stay up to date with new procedures, safety incidents, and so on. Information is always available, but it requires extra time to retrieve it and learn it. Additionally, flight in the IAF is no longer their main occupation. Because they are also studying and working in other fields, it is difficult for them to focus and immerse themselves in the details of the flight at hand. They therefore depend on their first officers in order to receive the required information—during the briefing and throughout the flight.

The scenario of a captain in reserve flying with a young first officer may sound problematic, but it can actually be quite advantageous. Managed correctly, the reserve captain can offer advice and bring experience that the first officer has not yet acquired, whereas the first officer can complement the captain's experience with relevant, up-to-date knowledge. Because mixed teams are common practice in the IAF, it is obvious that improving the ability of such teams to work together is essential.

In a recent study of an Israeli transport squadron, my colleagues and I were able to observe the abovementioned unique aspects of crew composition concerning the differences between enlisted and reserve pilots. We interviewed 10 first officers and 11 captains regarding crew communication. In the interviews, which were held with each pilot separately, we focused on the ability of first officers to express themselves when they had suggestions to complement captains' decisions or when they disagreed with them. This ability, which is commonly referred to as "speaking up," was addressed both in normal flight situations and during emergencies. In order to complement the insights regarding speaking up that were acquired through the interviews with the first officers, we focused on the captains and their willingness to ask the opinions of first officers and encourage their participation in the process of taking decisions in normal and emergency situations. The latter aspect was referred to as "inquiry." As the training of Israeli transport pilots leads to practically all pilots acquiring the status of captain before retiring with reserve flight status, all the first officers we interviewed were young enlisted officers, whereas seven of our captains were reserve pilots.

The results of our study show that reserve captains regard inquiry to be a crucial aspect of their crew communication, owing to the fact that the first officer is more up to date on recent events, mission characteristics, and squadron procedures. Although captains often showed awareness of the benefits of actively encouraging the opinions of first officers and letting them voice their thoughts, many captains also mentioned difficulties in implementing the inquiry process. There were questions, for example, concerning when a captain should ask the first officer for an opinion—before the captain has shared thoughts on an issue (with the possibility that the first officer's opinion would then be overruled), or after the captain has shared thoughts (with the danger that the first officer would then be influenced by the captain and not be able to add their own unadulterated thoughts). Alongside the abovementioned captains who showed interest in the inquiry process and shared their hesitations regarding the timing of involving the first officers, there were also a minority of captains who showed little interest in CRM in general and in the inquiry process in particular.

The analysis of the interviews with the first officers shows that, although they were aware that they could voice their concerns and suggestions during a flight, most would refrain from doing so, unless they judged it to be crucial to the situation at hand. First officers tended to let the captain manage the flight in a certain envelope, as long as they did not exceed limitations or their decisions did not have serious negative consequences. First officers were generally more willing to speak up if the captain with whom they were flying was a reservist.

It is obvious, given the abovementioned findings, that, although IAF culture has made profound progress in error reporting, it might not be as effective in addressing communication issues. Experiences with CRM in civil aviation suggest that procedures for speaking up and inquiry could be successfully implemented in crew communication and thus improve both flight efficiency and safety.

Implementing Crew Resource Management in the Military Context

In the past 30 years, CRM methods have proven essential regarding the safety of civil flights. Although these have been widely adopted in civil aviation, they cannot be merely copied into the military setting. We have seen that mission goals, aircraft heterogeneity, and crew composition are all crucial factors that set civil and military aviation apart. An adaptation of the tools and language of CRM is therefore essential in order to tend to the different needs of each squadron. Rather than a one-size-fits-all approach to CRM, which might fit civil aviation, a custom-fit approach needs to be taken for the military, whereby the unique characteristics of the military setting in general—and each unit in particular—are taken into consideration.

The only way to adapt CRM techniques to the requirements demanded of each squadron is to do so together with the squadron. Much like the process of user-centered design, in which the end user participates from early on in the development process, CRM experts have to involve the aircrew in the specific squadron in which CRM is to be implemented. By doing so, the general CRM tools, which have been validated globally through more than 30 years of implementation in the civil context, can be adapted to meet the needs of the pilots, navigators, and flight engineers in the designated squadron.

As to the IAF, the characteristics of Israeli aircrews have to be taken into account. Relying on the abovementioned research, it has become clear that CRM tools need to be developed that will enable captains to inquire and receive helpful information from the first officers; enable reservists to receive the support they need in the crew; and motivate young first officers to speak up, not only in the event of an emergency but also during normal operations.

In the case of the F-4 mentioned at the beginning of this chapter, well-implemented CRM could have helped the crew escape the situation much earlier, and more safely, than they did—and maybe even help avoid the danger of diving into the sea in the first place. Although a dogfight is a fast and furious event, in which civil CRM has almost no chance of being implemented, techniques that have been adapted to the military context in general—and the specific squadron and mission characteristics in particular—could have enabled the reservist navigator to speak up earlier and question the captain's decision to dive, or intervene earlier during the dive in order to avoid the near-death situation.

The abovementioned example is but one of many—including also fatal accidents, sadly—in which adapted CRM tools could have helped crews avoid and overcome difficult situations in flight. The challenges encountered during the development of such CRM methods can be overcome if they are implemented from within the units. Only then will they be optimally customized and adapted to the norms, needs, and language of the organizations in which they are supposed to function.

Note

1. It might as well be argued that, in order to talk about CRM, ground crews such as air traffic controllers should also be introduced. Though this approach is beneficial in understanding the big picture, I focus on the cockpit team for the sake of this chapter.

16

Lessons from a Nuclear Submarine Mishap

L. David Marquet

An organizational structure in which a senior executive is directing processes and operational movements is fundamentally fragile and susceptible to error propagation. It is a system of command and control where the demands of the leading person are followed and their actions are neither commented upon nor openly questioned.

Even when those lower in the hierarchy are invited to speak up, the fundamental structure of the hierarchy remains the same, with senior personnel making decisions based upon the information they interpret directly from instruments or are provided by staff. The basic model means to "push information to authority."

A more resilient approach is to empower teams and crews so that their leaders do not have to give orders but can rely on the capabilities of those working with them. The challenge is to build a sufficiently trained set of people who do not require micromanagement but instead make decisions and operate based on the knowledge and skills they have, understand the intent of the organization, and state their intentions back to the senior executive, if required. In this scenario, the senior executive acts as a final safety monitor, perhaps asking questions, maybe even stopping the action, but resisting the pull to step in, give orders, and make things happen. They access information when necessary. This model means that authority is pushed to information instead of the other way around.

L. D. Marquet
Laurel, USA

© The Author(s) 2018
J. U. Hagen (ed.), *How Could This Happen?*, https://doi.org/10.1007/978-3-319-76403-0_16

On February 9, 2001, the US nuclear-powered submarine USS *Greeneville* collided with a surface ship, the *Ehime Maru*, while conducting a routine emergency blow demonstration off the coast of Hawaii. The *Ehime Maru* sank and nine lives were lost.[1]

The USS *Greeneville* accident highlights issues of situational awareness, communication, and psychological safety. However, this chapter focuses on the hierarchical model of "pushing information to authority" and provides an alternative script, one in which the same hierarchical relationships are maintained but used in such a way as to "push authority to information."

One of the problems that safety programs such as crew resource management are designed to overcome is the reluctance of junior personnel to speak up when they sense that things are not right. Additionally, these programs encourage senior personnel to invite junior people to speak up. Yet, the fundamental structure of the hierarchy remains the same, with senior personnel making decisions based upon the information they interpret directly from sensors or are provided by junior personnel. The basic model is to "push information to authority."

Whereas existing programs have made great progress in reducing the power gradient in hierarchies, this case demonstrates a fundamentally different approach, one that solves the problem structurally by inviting the junior person to be the decision maker and reducing the senior person's role to that of an observer and approver of decisions.

One difference between cockpit teams and bridge teams is that, whereas the captain of an aircraft personally operates the controls of the aircraft, seagoing captains do not typically operate any controls. Instead, they operate through directions in order to watch officers and crew.

Greeneville Embarks Civilians for the Day

The *Greeneville* was scheduled to conduct one day of routine peacetime training operations off the coast of Hawaii. Embarked for the day were 16 civilian "VIPs," who were riding the submarine as part of a public relations program. The last activity of the day was an emergency blow demonstration. Even though much has been made of the presence of civilian personnel onboard the submarine as being a contributing factor to the accident, the cause of the accident was the manner in which the crew of the *Greeneville* communicated—in an exclusively top-down, hierarchical way.

The emergency blow system is designed to save the submarine in the event of flooding. When triggered, an emergency blow rapidly releases a large volume of high-pressure compressed air into the ballast tanks. This compressed air rushes into the ballast tanks and pushes out the water, making the submarine lighter.

The rapidity and volume of displaced water is such that, in all but the most severe flooding casualty, the submarine will become positively buoyant and rise to the surface. As the submarine ascends toward the surface, the sea pressure on it is reduced, including the pressure in the ballast tanks. Against the reduced pressure, the air in the ballast tanks expands further. Therefore, more and more water is expelled and the submarine accelerates toward the surface. In other words, once started, the ascent cannot be stopped.

In a bona fide emergency, the submarine would conduct the blow without taking the time to confirm that the surface is clear, banking on the probability that there is no surface contact immediately above the submarine. There is a high probability that this would be true, as submarines routinely avoid operating near or under other ships. However, during demonstration blows, when no emergency exists, even this small risk is unjustified, and maritime law places the burden on the submarine to investigate the surface and ensure that there are no vessels present that might be hazarded by the submarine's ascent.

Final Preparations

While operating south of Pearl Harbor, the *Greeneville* had contact on only two or three surface ships—a very light workload for the operators. At 12:32, the *Greeneville* spotted a contact, which they estimated to be distant. It was the Japanese fishery high school ship *Ehime Maru*, then at a distance of 20 miles. The crew designated the *Ehime Maru* as "S-13." For the next 1 hour and 11 minutes, until the time of the collision, the *Greeneville* had nearly continuous sonar information on the *Ehime Maru*.

Modern submarines operate their sonar in "listen only" mode, called "passive sonar," rather than relying on active techniques to ascertain the distance of the ships they hear. Even though passive sonar provides direction, loudness, and sometimes frequency data, with time that data will yield an estimate of the distance, course, and speed of the ship. The longer a ship is listened to, the more accurate that estimate becomes. The vagaries of underwater sound conditions prevent sufficient certainty in a sound-only estimate to conduct the blow.

At 13:15, the captain of the *Greeneville* ordered various "angles and dangles," which are high-speed maneuvers performed while submerged, for the benefit of the 16 civilian guests. The decision to perform these maneuvers committed the submarine to being late, as there was insufficient time to do the angles and dangles maneuvers as well as the planned emergency blow maneuver and then to drive to the harbor entrance by 15:00, which was the scheduled entry time. Although the officer of the deck (OOD) technically gives the course, speed, and depth orders, in this case, the captain stood immediately behind the OOD and directed the maneuvers. This turned the OOD into a mouthpiece for the captain.

At 13:31, the *Greeneville* commenced its safety checks. First, a 360-degree listening search was conducted. This is done by holding the submarine steady in two different directions to listen in all directions, including behind the submarine. The policy is to maintain a leg of information with stable depth, speed, and course for three minutes. On board the *Greeneville*, the captain told the OOD he wanted him to get to periscope depth "in five minutes." This was impossible if standard policies were to be followed. The captain continued to direct the detailed actions of the OOD. During the investigation, the OOD reported, "I was a little surprised when [...] the captain directed me to change course. I felt that he [...] was kind of driving the ship at that point. [...] He had been kind of driving the ship before then, during the angles and dangles, when he gave me the courses and depths and speeds he wanted to drive."

The National Transportation Safety Board investigation reports the captain going from the control room to sonar, personally checking various equipment and directing the maneuvers of the submarine.

The second part of the safety check is to perform a 360-degree visual search with the periscope. This follows the listening search and happens with the submarine near the surface of the ocean. The submarine is below water, with only a foot or two of the periscope extending above the surface. This is the definitive confirmation that no ships are close.

At 13:38 and 30 seconds, the *Greeneville* arrived at periscope depth. The *Greeneville's* crew—with only passive information available—placed the *Ehime Maru* at less than 3000 yards. In reality, she was about 2100 yards, but this degree of uncertainty is not uncommon for passive contacts. While at periscope depth, the captain took over the periscope personally. He did not see the contact and ordered the ship deep at 13:40. The *Greeneville* had conducted the visual search for 90 seconds. But on this day, the sea was choppy and the sky hazy. Upon the report that the captain did not see the contact, the fire control operator adjusted the contact range to 9000 yards, about the limit of visibility for a contact of its estimated size. He did not report this action and no one noticed it.

The captain communicated a sense of urgency to the crew because he wanted to get back to port to drop off the visitors the submarine was carrying. He shortened the normal search and peremptorily directed the officer of the deck to go deep and conduct the emergency blow. His scan had been rushed, superficial, and blocked by waves on occasion. Neither the officer of the deck, during his safety sweeps, nor the captain, nor any crewmember monitoring the periscope video saw the *Ehime Maru*.

Operating the periscope takes some training. When operating the periscope, you are scanning a narrow portion of the horizon while rotating the scope. This results in the horizon "blurring" past to a degree. Several rapid sweeps are conducted, followed by slow sweeps to reduce the blurring. In addition, if the submarine is even a few inches deeper than normal, or the waves a little higher, the view will be blocked by wave action during portions of the circle. The operator needs to either mentally keep track of those blocked sections or pause the search when the wave hits and continue when it is clear.

On deployments and in wartime, submarine crews pride themselves on remaining stealthy and undetected. They drive with the periscope exactly at the waterline, avoiding exposure of even an inch of extra scope. This increases stealth and survivability but also puts a higher burden on the periscope operator. However, in peacetime, off the coast of Hawaii, and especially since the *Greeneville* would momentarily be on the surface anyway, the need to remain stealthy was obviated and the crew could have exposed more scope.

In the case of the *Greeneville*, this final maneuver ended tragically. At 13:43, the submarine smashed into the *Ehime Maru*. The *Ehime Maru* sank and nine lives were lost. The cost of the damage to the submarine was $1.44 million; the cost for the loss of the *Ehime Maru* was $8.8 million. Other costs included the recovery of the *Ehime Maru* ($560 million) and compensation ($2.67 million) to Ehime Prefecture for lost equipment and cargo, crew salaries, Japanese response efforts, mental healthcare for survivors, and memorial services for accident victims.

Based on the final report issued by the Navy Court of Inquiry, the *Greeneville*'s commanding officer (CO) was found guilty of committing two violations of the Uniform Code of Military Justice: Dereliction of duty and negligent hazarding of a vessel. He was "detached for cause" from his position as CO, which was documented in his navy officer record. He retired eight months after the collision, on October 1, 2001.

The Old Model: Pushing Information to Authority

The CO testified that he learned about two contacts around lunchtime but was told by the sonar supervisor that the contacts were distant, so he assumed they were more than 10,000 yards away. About 13:14, he told the OOD to perform the angles and dangles maneuvers but did not discuss the contacts. At 13:15, he ordered the *Greeneville's* speed to increase to 14 knots and positioned himself behind the OOD, where he ordered the specific course, speeds, and depths. The OOD merely repeated the orders to the driving officer and the helmsman. About 13:25, the CO demanded high-speed turns. According to the sonar supervisor, these exercises make it difficult to spot contacts. At 13:31, the CO requested a lower speed of 10 knots to prepare for periscope depth and demanded to be there in five minutes. The OOD later stated that he considered this unusual and that he worried about the time limit, since it made the required collection of all sonar reports, the development of a final picture, and the determination of the course impossible. He thought, "Here's a man with much more experience than I have, much more schooling than I have, [who] can much more rapidly assess and evaluate information [...]. I did not believe that he was putting the ship in an unsafe position, and [thought that ...] the contact picture allowed for safe periscope depth."

At 13:35, the CO was aware of two contacts and was convinced he had a "good feel for the contacts." Three minutes later, when the periscope broke the water surface, the CO took the periscope and began his own search routine. He later testified: "I panned to the right where I thought I would see the *Ehime Maru*. I looked over the remote repeater [own ship's data] and I saw the numbers and [thought] that looks right. That's where the guy is. Didn't see him. [...] I think the *Ehime Maru* was perhaps further to the right, and as I swept in low power [I] missed her."

Next, the CO called an "emergency deep as a training evolution. It was obvious that it took the control room party by surprise, which, for a training evolution of this type, I intended to do." Shortly afterward, there was a loud noise, and the submarine shuddered. The submarine had struck the *Ehime Maru*.

What we have here is the typical scenario of a culture in which hierarchy comes first. We have a leader who calls the shots and followers who believe in his superior knowledge and do what he demands, even if they worry about his orders. Pertinent information is delivered to the person higher up so that he can evaluate and decide. His actions are neither commented upon nor openly questioned. In the 30 minutes prior to the accident, the US National Transportation Safety Board investigation references the CO "directing" or "ordering" actions 10 times.

It is a hierarchical system that probably works as long as the leader is capable, has ample job experience, and there are no aggravating circumstances and stress factors such as time pressure (as in the case above), emergencies, or situations in which information is unclear, to name only some. These, however, are constellations in which a single person, left to their own devices, will make mistakes, as the tasks they are handling will have reached a level with so many complexities that one person alone is simply not capable of managing them all.

The New Model: Pushing Authority to Information

In a modern system, there is a constant exchange of work-related information among all parties involved about the way their information may be interpreted. The leader will give members of their crew leeway to think and manage on their own. They respect the expertise and competence of their crew members and refrain from interrupting the flow of work and work-related communication. For this type of leader, their hierarchical position means responsibility for the entire operating performance, be it a submarine, a company, or a project. They access information when necessary.

In this scenario, the CO of the *Greeneville* has been alerted with respect to the contacts (among them, the *Ehime Maru*). As is true of his crew, he is not sure where they are. Instead of deciding this with the help of the ship's data, he lets the various experts of his crew gather the necessary information and exchange their data to reach a conclusion. While they do this, he stands in the control room, drinks a cup of coffee, if he wishes, and remains quiet. When the OOD informs him that the contacts have reached the danger circle, he listens to the suggestion: to delay the emergency deep maneuver until the contacts are beyond 4000 yards, which will mean a 10-minute delay. The CO's answer could be: "Very well, officer of the deck. Inform me when you are ready to conduct the blow and prior to departing periscope depth." After that, he leaves the control room.

The submarine stays where it is and waits. On the surface, the *Ehime Maru* passes by, unaware of the submarine below.

Lessons for High-Reliability Organizations

The *Costa Concordia* grounding, which resulted in the loss of 32 lives, also reflects the pattern of the senior person in charge being responsible for the ensuing tragedy. In both cases, the reports read, "the captain ordered..." over and over again. Human tendency is to look at the incorrect decisions the captain has made as being the fundamental cause of the error. However, we are suggesting that an organizational structure in which the most senior person is directing operational movements is fundamentally fragile and susceptible to error propagation. A more resilient approach would be to restructure bridge crews so that captains do not have to give orders. Our phrase for this is "the person at the top can only say stop."

The challenge then is to build a sufficiently trained set of subordinates who do not require micromanagement. In the preferred case, the subordinates would operate with intent, understand the intent of the organization, and state their intentions back to the captain. The captain would act as a final safety monitor, perhaps asking questions, maybe even stopping the action, but resisting the pull to step in, give orders, and make things happen.

The principle is "push authority to information, not information to authority."

Note

1. Source for the *Greeneville–Ehime Maru* accident is the National Safety Transportation Board Marine Accident Brief DCA-01-MM-022.

17

The War on Error: A New and Different Approach to Human Performance

Tony Kern

For too long, human error has been accepted as an inescapable part of life that has to be managed after it occurs. It has resulted in unnecessary compromises. Recent research provides a body of knowledge that is capable of changing performance for the better. Applying it successfully demands a rigorous approach that results in known competencies and predictable performance.

Errors and their consequences are the products of internal and external conditions that can be seen and controlled in advance by people operating in real-time environments armed with the right body of knowledge, tools, and techniques. Everybody has a personal fingerprint of error and tends to make the same kinds of mistakes, be it when they drive, in their interactions with friends and family, or in the workplace. After they understand what their personal error pattern is, error control is a matter of learning new information and applying a set of tools.

These skills are not intuitive, and error control is not common sense. It is uncommon sense, yet well within reach if you take readily available information and apply it. The phrase "to err is human" should be replaced by "to improve is human, to grow is human, to learn is human."

T. Kern
Colorado Springs, USA

© The Author(s) 2018

273

J. U. Hagen (ed.), *How Could This Happen?*, https://doi.org/10.1007/978-3-319-76403-0_17

Why a "War on Error"?

On more than one occasion when speaking to civilian audiences, I have been told that I come across as "a bit too military." I always find that odd, as during my time in the military, my commanders frequently told me I was not military enough. Therefore, I think a short explanation for choosing a military model for combating human error is helpful. My battle against human error began—like so many battles do—with a tragedy. While serving as a B-1 Bomber instructor pilot in the US Air Force, two of my former students flew a perfectly functional aircraft into a mountain one night at more than 600 miles per hour. In 31 seconds, they went from operations normal to the end of their lives. The accident investigation cited "pilot error" as causal, which is not surprising, as nearly 80 percent of all accidents are caused by human error. From healthcare to cyber security, when systems fail, it is usually traceable to human causes.

As I searched for answers, I found that scores of academic models had been developed and fielded in an attempt to stem this tide of errors, but the percentage of human error incidents had remained relatively constant. I decided to try something different.

The "War on Error" effort began in earnest in late 2004. While working with the US Marines Corps aviation program, who were coming off a pretty gruesome safety year, a senior Marine asked me a simple question: "Tony, why do highly skilled, highly intelligent, and highly trained people continue to make dumb mistakes and kill themselves?"

This simple question would lead to five years of exhaustive research and development by a team of experts, resulting in the world's first systematic personal error-control program. Within one year of prototype testing, the results were so positive and promising that the Deputy Commandant of the Marine Corps for Aviation mandated the full War on Error program for every Marine aviator. Within 24 months, the US Coast Guard aviation program joined the effort, and the race was on to flesh out this new approach for the rest of the world.

But to understand how this research came to a different conclusion than previous error-management studies, let us go back to the war-planning model for a minute, where we will see, ironically, why this new approach is so effective for everyday people who know nothing about military doctrine.

War planners are tied to the principles of military science that have been proven through the thousands of years in the crucible of armed conflict. When confronted with the challenge of defeating human error, we asked a simple question: "If this were a human adversary, how and where would we attack it to have the maximum impact?" From there, we simply applied the standard planning processes, beginning with a threat assessment.

Threat Assessment

The initial threat assessment proved stunning in terms of sheer magnitude. Hundreds of thousands of people die unnecessarily each year around the world as a direct result of human error. In healthcare settings alone, it is estimated that well over 100,000 patients die per year due to iatrogenic (doctor/nurse-induced) causes. On our highways, every year, tens of thousands more drive fully functional cars into trees, bridges, and each other, resulting in completely avoidable deaths. In the United States, accidents are the leading cause of death for people under the age of 45.

In business, billions of dollars are lost each year as a direct result of human error, and not just from accidents, injuries, lawsuits, or increased insurance premiums. As evidence mounts about the causes of the global economic meltdown in the first decade of this century, it is becoming readily apparent that human error played a major role. Miscalculations and unchecked egos were principal components of the fiscal collapse of many organizations—add to this the number of senior executives and fast-rising managers who derailed themselves through completely avoidable human error. The list continues with error-induced product defects, inefficiencies, supply chain delays, and poor customer service, and it becomes obvious that human error puts the very engine of our profitability and economy at great risk.

But if all of these facts are known, why are we still making such little progress? Experts cite the randomness and wide variability of human error as the reason for these disappointing results. Some small successes are reported, but globally, human error is culpable in nearly 80 percent of mission failures with outcomes that include degraded productivity and recovery costs from preventable errors, accidents, and incidents.

Contrary to popular opinion, errors and their consequences are *not* predestined elements of fate. They are the product of internal and external conditions that can be seen and controlled in advance by people operating in real-time environments armed with the right body of knowledge, tools, and techniques. In the global industrial setting, the wild card of human error has cost hundreds of thousands of lives and billions of dollars across the globe. Traditional error-control approaches have been only marginally effective against this insidious threat.

If these losses had been intentionally inflicted by a human adversary, there would be an enormous public and political outcry, resulting in immediate mobilization of forces against the foe: One need only look as far as 9/11 for an example. Of course, the reason we have not responded aggressively to the challenge of human error as opposed to a human adversary is that we have grown accustomed to the presence of this enemy; it walks with us daily, so we do not recognize human error for what it is—namely, a leading cause of human tragedy and death.

One of the basic tenets of war planning is that preparation depends upon defending against an enemy's capability, not their intent. Intent is easily hidden through deception, distraction, or circumstance. Capability, on the other hand, can be determined by analysis. Forget for a moment that we are not talking about a thinking human enemy, although it often appears to be such.

The capability of error to harm is beyond question, and therefore deserves additional respect as an active and lethal adversary. Let us look at this threat in greater depth using a new model, in hopes that it may allow us to plan and take action in earnest.

Red Threat: Blue Threat

This initial step—the analysis of the enemy threat—is the first order of business that professional war planners and business strategists take in preparing to apply firepower against an adversary. This is a methodical and disciplined process that evaluates an adversary's strength and known tactics. The evaluation and synthesis of these factors, as they are related to external threats to success, are collectively known as the "red threat."

Following the completion of this external analysis, good strategists conduct the same analysis on their own capabilities to identify weaknesses, trends, and other information that might be used against them or result in self-defeating behaviors. These factors include a lack of disciplined execution, planning, or knowledge in key areas as well as poor leadership and failed teamwork—all of which often result in human error that is counterproductive to the mission.

Collectively, this group of factors is known as the "blue threat." The blue threat is the internal threat: the things we do to ourselves and each other that end up sabotaging our life, business goals, and missions. By far, the largest blue threat we face is our propensity for error. This line of thinking leads to a place where we must challenge conventional thinking if we are to make progress. Let us do a little myth busting with a short series of questions.

Aren't making mistakes just a part of being human? To some degree, they may be. But just saying "to err is human" is a cop-out for avoidable and correctable mistakes and gives up far too much ground. For too long, we have accepted human error as an inescapable part of our lives or tried to manage it after it occurs. It has resulted in unnecessary compromises. Recent research provides a body of knowledge that is capable of changing our performance, and our lives, for the better. Applying it successfully demands a rigorous approach that results in known competencies and predictable performance. But it is well worth it. Every year, on average, human error results in more unnecessary death and suffering than all of the wars in the world combined. Getting beyond safety statistics, industries suffer billions of dollars in lost revenue as a direct result of preventable human error, which results in job losses for thousands (and these numbers do not factor in the lost opportunities for progress and improvement).

How do you go about battling the blue threat? The key to victory over the randomness and variability of human error is first to realize that error is only random in a group setting. When you get down to a sample size of one—you—error is both predicable and preventable. We all have a personal fingerprint of error: We tend to make the same kinds of mistakes, whether it be when we drive, in our interactions with friends and family, or in the workplace. After we understand what our personal error pattern is, it is just a matter of learning some new information and applying a set of tools. Of course, first, you need to accept the fact that you are making avoidable errors and have the desire to change. Dietrich Dörner, in his excellent book *The Logic of Failure*, puts it this way: "Failure does not strike like a bolt from the blue; it develops gradually. We can learn, however. People court failure in predictable ways [...] we need only apply the ample power of our minds to understand and then break the logic of failure." The War on Error seizes on this statement and seeks to strengthen the "ample power of our minds" on an individual level.

Certainly, something this critical is already being taught in technical training or somewhere else inside most occupations, is it not? Oddly not, and I think I know a couple of reasons why. First, we have long assumed—incorrectly—that when we train someone to do something right, we are simultaneously training them not to do it wrong. This fundamental premise of our education and training programs is grossly in error and responsible for hundreds of thousands of lost lives and billions in lost revenue every year. The skill set for error prevention is unique—it is massively interdisciplinary—and currently not taught anywhere except in the few places where it was researched and developed over the past few years.

The second reason I believe we do not yet teach personal error control is because the world has gone brain dead on the issues of personal responsibility and accountability. No one wakes up in the morning wanting to make a mistake or thinking that they are going to. If we can provide them with the knowledge and tools to recognize and prevent their personal mistakes, most people who care about their performance will do so of their own accord.

How long does it take someone to get a handle on the blue threat? Some results are almost immediate; others will be refined over the course of a lifetime. It is important to realize from the start that error control is far less about training than it is about understanding. Self-awareness is a personal mastery skill that encompasses many complex variables, ranging from an accurate assessment of one's state of skill and knowledge to the physiological readiness to perceive, interpret, evaluate, plan, and act in a tightly coupled, error-intolerant environment. These skills are within our grasp, but they are not intuitive. They must be learned. Error control is not common sense, as many would have us believe. It is uncommon sense, yet well within our reach if we just take readily available information and apply it.

This is the reason the blue threat program was designed and developed. If I could leave you with one thing from reading this chapter, it would be this: Personal error control is a discipline, a way of life. Once you have mastered it, you will be amazed at the results and wonder why you waited so long to do something this simple and powerful.

The War on Error approach to personal performance is an interdisciplinary body of knowledge and a new way of viewing and interacting with the world around you. Once you learn to see the world through the lens of your individual behaviors and uniqueness (for better and worse), you achieve a level of self-awareness and self-assurance unreachable to those without your newly acquired skills. The time it takes you to develop this point of view will come back to you tenfold and more. You will make a new friend and mentor, namely the one that looks back at you in the mirror each day.

The iconic migrant worker organizer Cesar Chavez once said that "you can't uneducate someone who has learned to read." His point was that certain skill sets—such as reading—open doors to other skill sets. Learning to comprehend your error patterns and correct them is exactly the same thing. When you learn to avoid the self-sabotage of avoidable errors, a whole new world of performance stands before you.

This approach is not a cure-all for human failings. Thirty minutes of reading will not undo 30 years of life experience or 30,000 years of evolution, but it may give the new convert an edge, which is all that many of us need—an edge to leverage into an opportunity to shape a better future. One thing this chapter will definitely provide you is a place to start.

In addition, I hope that this personal accountability approach also proves effective for some to gain traction against personal performance barriers. It might be something as innocuous as procrastination or as serious as an anger management or substance abuse challenge. Whatever the challenge, if you are looking to tackle it head on, the words of French Field Marshall Ferdinand Foch during the World War I speak to one vital prerequisite: "The will to conquer is the first condition of victory."

Do not misunderstand—the War on Error does not replace the traditional leadership, team, or systems approaches that are already being used effectively in many industries. In point of fact, the personal accountability War on Error approach acts as a force multiplier for these proven approaches, making them far more effective. Results speak to this success better than mere words.

White Flags of Surrender

The most basic problem we face is that the battlefield upon which we must wage this struggle is strewn with millennia of status quo defeatism, centuries of apathy, and decades of techno-hubris—the belief that we can technically engineer our way out of human error. To some degree, many have already capitulated to the idea that "to err is human" and current losses are simply "the cost of doing business" until we can design the human out of the system altogether. That is certainly not the approach taken here. I believe that the human being is the strongest part of the safety and performance equation, although a lot of engineers and technology salesmen would tell you differently. However, even though technology, technical training, and organizational influence (culture) are important, you—as an individual mind operating in real time—are more so.

Not all believe this to be true. The following statements are all taken from current writings or talks given by respected professionals:

- People will always make mistakes—that is a given.
- Trying to stop human error is a fool's errand.
- It is easier to change situations than people.
- People make mistakes because of the design of the systems they operate in.
- Focusing on individual error is a blame-and-shame game.
- To err is human; it is easier to manage error than to prevent it.
- Human error mishaps are just the cost of doing business.

- We are forced to work with the crooked timber of human fallibility.
- Serious human factor experts moved beyond the individual error approach 20 years ago.
- The weakest link in the cockpit is wearing a headset.

Into the Fight with an Army of One

For the past four decades, the cure for the disease of human error has been approached indirectly (if at all) in most of the industrialized world through a variety of efforts that can be broadly lumped into the following five categories:

- blame and punish the individual;
- emphasize leadership (then blame and punish the leader for failures that occur under his or her supervision);
- teamwork strategies to capture or contain errors through better communication;
- systemic approaches that put multiple layers of protection in place to avoid or respond to errors; and most recently
- cultural approaches that focus on social factors such as trust and fairness to create a just culture.

Once again: The War on Error approach is not intended to denigrate or replace any of these, merely to supplement them.

Does the War on Error Produce Results?

After launching the War on Error inside the US Marine Corps aviation program in 2003–2004, their incident and accident rate dropped by nearly 60 percent from previous levels over the five-year duration of the program. Unfortunately, the program was never institutionalized, and after it was completed, the rates began to slowly climb back toward previous historic levels.

In 2009, FedEx Flight 80 suffered a tragic dual-fatality crash at Narita International Airport in Japan. This prompted FedEx Vice President Paul Cassel to reach out to ask about the War on Error initiative that had proved so successful inside the Marine Corps. The Narita crash was not the first hull loss for FedEx. In fact, for more than a decade, they had averaged one hull loss every 19 months—a level unheard of in the major airline world. A modified

War on Error program was put in place over a five-year contract and every FedEx pilot trained with it. The program was widely embraced by labor organizations (FedEx Air Line Pilots Association, International—ALPA), management, and line pilots. At the time of this writing, they have not experienced a hull loss in more than seven years.

As word spread about the successes of this innovative approach, the insurance industries became very interested. The United States Aircraft Insurance Group (USAIG) and Global Aerospace insurance company both adopted a means to provide key elements of the personal accountability program to their customers. In one case, a major aircraft manufacturer service center network was hemorrhaging red ink due to extreme levels of "technician-induced damage" to their clients' aircraft. The numbers were staggering, with more than $4 million in average annual claims occurring in this setting, reaching back more than a decade. Dave McKay, the president and CEO of USAIG, was aware of the success stories from FedEx and the Marines, and he recommended the War on Error approach in this new setting.

The aviation maintenance environment and audience required some reconfiguration of the approach, but the essence of building a culture of compliance from the line upward (as opposed to down through leadership) remained intact. The program identified the top six most costly maintenance errors committed worldwide—wrong part, wrong person, wrong fluid, improper movement, lost tool, and unsecured panels—which accounted for more than $10 billion in damages across the industry. We entitled these events Aviation Maintenance Never Events®, events that were totally preventable and should therefore never have happened.

Next, the program simply challenged the line personnel to prevent these from occurring on their next shift. The most critical part of the training was asking more than 1400 line maintenance engineers to respond to this question in writing on cards provided to them: "If one of these events did occur on your next shift, what factors in your local environment and organizational system would cause it?" The responses were overwhelming, with more than 12,000 unique data points culled from the responses through deep qualitative and quantitative methodologies. Local, supervisory, systemic, and training issues came into clear focus, and these data and a set of recommendations were sent to the host organization for action. Change resistance—typically the biggest challenge in any continuous improvement process—was eliminated by having the recommendations come directly from the line personnel as opposed to "another mandate from management."

The training and systemic changes were supplemented by a robust communications strategy, and the results were nothing short of stunning. An

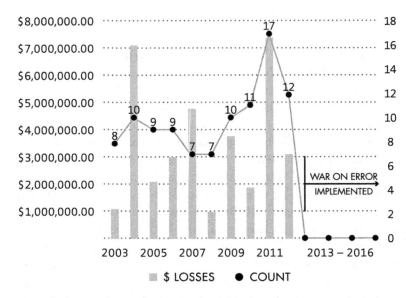

Fig. 17.1 Aviation service center insurance claims, pre– and post–war on error

organization that had struggled to maintain insurability and tried multiple approaches to stemming the tide of technician damage suddenly became a different organization. As Fig. 17.1 indicates, since the program was launched, there has not been a single event leading to an insurance claim from this customer. At the time of this writing, this represents more than $16 million when measured against the 10-year claims average.

This evolution of the War on Error into its third generation was critical, as it recognized other synergies not realized within most organizational improvement approaches.

Complexities in the Human Performance Challenge: A Combined Arms Approach

Not every human performance challenge has a training solution—training is seldom the sole solution for any human performance challenge. There are too many reasons to mention here. We have found that, in order to change behaviors (and therefore outcomes), organizations should supplement War on Error training with two vital force multipliers. The first is a robust communications strategy to reinforce the training and keep it top of mind. Visual reminders, talking points for key personnel, topics of the month, and written communications—all intentionally sequenced to reinforce the new information provided in the training. The second critical element is some type of quality assurance process that emphasizes the elements of the War on Error curriculum, such as formal evaluations and the enforcement of policy and procedures. This makes the new information need-to-know versus nice-to-know.

This combination of training, communications, and quality assurance follow-up has been highly effective across multiple disciplines. Unfortunately, many organizations fail to realize the critical nature of the combined arms approach and often attempt to either train a problem out of existence or enforce it out of existence, with predictably poor results.

Let us return for a moment to defining the enemy and its potential impact on your life, career, or organization.

A Thief and Murderer: Nothing Less

Human error is the thief of human happiness and the slayer of dreams, careers, potential, and all too frequently life itself. Viewing it as anything less hostile is to willfully expose your throat to the knife. These are harsh words, but they are intentionally so.

For hundreds of years, mankind has hidden behind Cicero's famous quote "To err is human." The cost is too great to continue on this apathetic and complacent path. So we are going to change the dialogue. To *improve* is human, to *grow* is human, to *learn* is human. But to persevere in avoidable error at great risk to our lives, family, friends, and career—that is inhuman.

The global cost of human error is almost incomprehensible, and very few will look at these costs without agreeing that something more should be done to prevent it. When viewed from a personal perspective inside our routine daily lives, the danger posed by our own errors appears remote. Like criminals who live among us in the shadows, error-producing conditions lie in wait, hidden, almost invisible. We ignore the threat because most errors are petty theft, annoying, occasionally resulting in the minor loss of productivity but certainly not life or career threatening.

Unintentional and avoidable errors end lives, poison relationships, squander wealth, feed addictions, and ruin careers. Error is a persistent and progressive thief who will continue to steal from you and your potential as a human being on an ever-greater scale until you make a conscious decision to stop being a passive victim.

Most of us do not recognize our own potential for error as a serious threat—to ourselves or our organizations. This is an often costly or lethal mistake, because errors that result in trivial outcomes of little consequence on one occasion can suddenly and without warning result in a life-changing or career-ending result on another.

It is important to recognize from the very start of any performance improvement that our decisions and actions are only one set of many variables that result in a positive or negative outcome. Sometimes our actions are the catalyst for success or failure. Other times external factors or the situation itself gets the final vote. That is why outcome-based assessment, that is, judging an action or decision by its end result, is a fool's errand when it comes to error control.

People are lulled into a false sense of security because a tragic outcome has not yet occurred. Our personal lives seem to support this laissez-faire approach.

Let us put human error lesson 1 on the table right now: *Things that have never happened before, happen all the time.* In the blink of an eye, the same petty thief you have grown accustomed to as a minor annoyance on the street corner becomes your worst nightmare. In hindsight, it becomes all too clear: You could have and should have seen it.

This leads us to human error lesson 2: *You have a choice to make.* If you choose to reject this empowerment approach, we ask only that you make it a conscious choice: If you choose to decline improvement, you are agreeing to endure the pain of regret, should your future avoidable errors lead to unwanted consequences or tragedy.

That choice is yours and yours alone, as are all choices and options presented in this chapter. The reason I want to force this decision is that in today's fast-paced world, far too many choices get made for us by our own indecision. But if you are not mindful of the dangers posed by avoidable errors and lost opportunities, you can reach a point where you have made unintentional but vitally important choices without thinking, without reflection, without planning, and with no way to reset the chessboard. You can end up not having the career you thought you would, the family you wanted, or living the life you meant to.

Or, you have the opportunity to choose a different approach. Life is not something that happens to you—you are something that shapes the present and future of your personal and professional life. You intentionally and mindfully create your future by:

- systematically structuring and learning from experience,
- mindfully living in the present,
- deflecting violation and error-producing conditions, and
- seeing and seizing new opportunities in real time.

A US Navy pilot once wrote: "In aviation you very rarely get your head bitten off by a tiger, you usually get nibbled to death by ducks." What he meant was that most error-caused accidents or incidents are the endgame of a series of interrelated events, interpretations, decisions, warnings, or actions that are allowed to progress without recognition or intervention. The final decision, which is action or inaction, may be relatively innocuous but sufficient in itself to remove a margin of safety or performance level previously eroded by other events. So it is in life, where we allow the detritus of poor performance to pile up, unaware that the next straw may well be the backbreaker.

The purpose of the War on Error approach is to take the battle away from being solely a vocational exercise and into the realm of a life skill that will follow the individual into the work environment. But there are many who have resisted this personal accountability approach and presented a false dichotomy while trying to force a decision between the "system model" and the "person model."

Political Incorrectness

Personal accountability and responsibility are not easy sells. This makes it difficult to see the value of putting in the time to learn a new discipline of thought and awareness. The softer, easier way is to blame something less personal. It seems to be okay if we continue in our error-prone ways, injure ourselves or others, and continue to put our careers and families at risk, but it is not okay to offend anyone's self-esteem. In many circles, accountability seems to be a four-letter word.

J. Reason, an expert on the topic of human error and a strong supporter of the system model, puts it plainly in *Human Error*: "Perhaps it is time we begin to inform those in high-risk industries about their own propensity for error[...]they do, after all, pose the most serious threat to the high-risk systems they work in." Whether it is in a high-risk industry or our day-to-day lives, this hits the nail on the head—and that is what the War on Error approach is all about.

Error has become a governmental, industrial, and societal opiate for explaining away serious performance and safety issues. But where the government, industry, and society have failed, the individual remains empowered. The science is there, the means and methods are available—all that is lacking is the transfer of knowledge and the individual will to proceed.

Index

© The Author(s) 2018
J. U. Hagen (ed.), *How Could This Happen?*, https://doi.org/10.1007/978-3-319-76403-0

Printed by Printforce, the Netherlands